*Also by Sibel*

The Fashion

My Perfect Wedding

### *About the author*

Sibel Hodge has dual British/Turkish Cypriot nationality and divides her time between Hertfordshire and North Cyprus. Her first romantic-comedy novel, *Fourteen Days Later*, was shortlisted for the *Harry Bowling Prize 2008* and received a Highly Commended by the *Yeovil Literary Prize 2009*.
Her second novel, *The Fashion Police*, is a hilarious comedy-mystery novel, the first in the series featuring feisty, larger-than-life, Amber Fox.

For more information, please visit www.sibelhodge.com

### *Praise for Fourteen Days Later*

"A very good read. Very enjoyable and fresh."
TRISHA ASHLEY

"A truly fun read. Very funny scenes."
LAURA LONGRIGG

"This story was impossible for me to put down."
COFFETIME ROMANCE & MORE

"You excel at physical comedy."
CORNERSTONES

"You have a taste for storytelling - a love of it. That's something that can't be taught or learned, and it's an essential part of being a writer."
ROMANTIC NOVELISTS' ASSOCIATION.

Fourteen Days Later

Copyright © Sibel Hodge 2010

# Fourteen Days Later

**Sibel Hodge**

*For all the underdogs out there…*

*"It always seems impossible until it's done"*

*NELSON MANDELA*

# Chapter 1

'Fourteen days,' said Ayshe. 'That's all it takes to change your life for the better.'

'You are joking, right?' I arched an eyebrow. 'Nobody can change their life in fourteen days.'

'That's not what it says in here.' Ayshe held up the magazine she'd been flicking through, her finger underlining one of the articles.

'"Orgasms or Chocolate? What do women really want?"' I read the headline aloud.

'What?' Ayshe looked at the magazine and adjusted her finger. 'Not that. This. "Turn Your Life Around. The Simple Fourteen Day Plan Anyone Can Do".'

'That's ridiculous.' Tucking my legs underneath me on the sofa, I picked at my frayed jogging bottoms.

'No, what's ridiculous is you still moping about over Justin. It's been six months since you split up with him. You need to move on with your life.' She rose from her chair and flounced down next to me, resting her arm on my knees.

I wriggled away from her. 'I'm having another iced coffee; want one?'

'It's too cold for iced coffee. It's the middle of November for God's sake,' she called out as I clattered around in the kitchen. 'Anyway, I thought you'd promised to cut down on your caffeine intake.'

When I returned, I sank down onto the sofa. 'I still haven't managed to get a plumber out to fix the dishwasher. Either they don't turn up when they say they will, or they won't come out for anything less than a total bathroom refurb.'

Ayshe watched me in silence.

I sat it out for a while, her steady gaze drilling into me. 'What?'

'Trying to change the subject isn't going to work. You can't avoid this much longer.'

'I'm not, it's true. You can never get hold of a plumber these–'

She clamped her hand over my mouth. 'You need to go out and do things – and don't give me that rubbish about you'll

1

never meet another man – he was the right one – he was the love of your life. I know four years together is a long time, but everybody always says that when they split up with people. You will get over him, but not if you keep refusing to move on with your life.' She pushed me on the leg.

I wasn't expecting the jolt and spilt my coffee all down my attractive jogging bottoms.

My thoughts drifted back to the time I'd discovered a size sixteen *Agent Provocateur* thong stuffed into the pocket of Justin's best work trousers during the usual laundry run. I was pretty sure his company hadn't suddenly changed their dress-code. I mean, smart trousers, shirt, and thong, wouldn't sound too good in the staff handbook. I was also sure he couldn't have picked it up innocently – as he'd told me – because he needed to dust the photocopier and thought it was a rag. And I knew it wasn't mine because I'd never really fancied a piece of dental floss chafing my bits and bobs.

She lifted her hand away from my mouth.

'So what else does it say then, this article?' I feigned interest, rubbing at the coffee stain with my hand.

'It's about trying to get more interests in your life if you're stuck in a rut. It was written by one of those new trendy life coaches who try and get you to organize your life better. Apparently, you have to set yourself challenges to have a brand new experience every day for fourteen days, to gain more confidence; something to do with re-evaluating things and re-balancing your yin and yang – or your Hong Kong Fuey – or whatever it is.'

I snorted. She ignored me and ploughed on regardless.

'The more things you do, the more confidence you gain, and you become a more focused and better person. You need to be more proactive with your life, and I think this is just what you need.'

I heaved a dramatic sigh.

'It's not just about meeting a man. It's about changing your perspective. Come on, what is there to lose? Worst case scenario, you might discover things that you never knew before, or find something new that you like doing. Best case scenario...' She shrugged. 'You might meet a "the one".'

I pretended to ignore her and fiddled with my hair.

'You never know if you don't try, and you need to take every

2

single opportunity you can to meet new people, instead of making the usual pathetic excuses you've been using for the last six months.' Sitting back on the sofa, she crossed her arms over her chest. The lecture was over.

'I don't know if I've got the time for a Hong Kong Fuey experience. I mean what with…work…and…' I tailed off, staring out of my flat window at the dreary, sludgy winter day outside. How much longer could I make excuses to keep my life on hold, waiting for Justin to come back?

'Helloooooooooo! Earth to Helen.' Ayshe poked me hard in the ribs. 'The most important thing is to keep busy and keep your mind open to new things. Look, I'll help you. We can even do some things together, but you need to get out of this flat and into the big wide world again and stop hibernating.'

I narrowed my eyes, deep in thought. 'You're marrying Atila in a few weeks. You'll be too busy to baby-sit me. And anyway, I'm not hibernating.'

But if I was honest, truly honest, I knew she was right. I'd spent so much time drowning in self-pity and pining for Justin that I'd lost myself. I needed to find out what I wanted for a change. A fourteen day challenge to myself might not be such a bad thing. Would it change my life? I was pretty doubtful. Would it get my yin and yang back? I felt a flicker of excitement at the thought of unknown possibilities.

'Actually…I haven't got any more wedding photos to do until yours,' I started with caution. No one wanted to get married in November anyway, so my diary wasn't exactly heaving. 'Maybe I could give it a try.'

'That's my girl. And you never know, come my wedding, you may have a new guy to bring, eh?'

I stood up, catching my reflection in the mirror. Anxious eyes like soggy limpets stared back at me. I must admit, I had let myself go a bit lately. My chestnut curly hair sprang out in all directions. I could do with a trim – maybe even a few highlights, and – aargh! – look at my eyebrows! Denis Healey eat your heart out. And as for my hairy legs and bikini-line – well, I was beginning to resemble a silverback gorilla. The only good thing to come out of it, I supposed, was that I had shifted a few pounds and was now a size twelve, although I wouldn't recommend The Getting-Dumped Diet to anyone.

Ayshe's cackling brought me back down to earth. 'You look

3

fine. Nothing a hair cut and a pair of tweezers won't fix.'

'So, if I do this challenge, what will be on the agenda for tomorrow? I might as well start as soon as possible before I change my mind.' I felt my mood lift slightly.

Relief spread across her face. 'I'll think about it and text you later. In the meantime, have a look through the local paper and the internet and get some ideas for new things to try. You won't regret it. I have a good feeling about this.' She looked at her watch. 'Aagh! Look at the time. Me and Atila are going to Mum and Dad's for dinner, which basically means Dad will be on the whisky again, cooking enough shish kebab to feed a small continent, and Mum will want to read everyone's Turkish coffee cup, predicting the same things she always sees: babies, rings, and marriage!' She leapt up from the sofa, grabbing her bag and coat.

'I love Yasmin and Deniz's Turkish Cypriot cooking.'

'So do I. It's just that fifty-two Sundays a year of shish kebab gets a bit too much. You can come, as well, if you want. You know they think of you as their surrogate daughter.' Her oval, dark eyes implored me.

'No, I'm fine. I'll just have a think about my new life-changing challenge. I'll do some work on the computer and have an early night.' I pulled the door open for her.

'OK then, text you later.' She kissed me on both cheeks, Turkish style. Her long, sleek black hair fanned out over her shoulders as she dashed up the corridor.

'Bye – and by the way, it's feng shui, not Hong Kong Fuey!' But she'd already disappeared up the stairs to her flat on the floor above.

Just as I was shouting this enlightening piece of information, Charlie, who lived in the flat next to mine, opened his door to collect the paper from outside. I stared at the incredible sight of him wearing nothing but a pair of pink, spandex hot-pants.

'Helloooo, dahling. What's feng shui?' He paused, deep in thought, ignoring my startled expression. 'Is it a restaurant?' Without waiting for an answer he peered at the big coffee stain down the front of my saggy jogging bottoms. 'Is that a new look?'

'No,' I said, trying not to look at what must have been a sock shoved down the front of his hot-pants. What a cheek, I thought, as I scrutinized his own rather unique attire. 'Are you on

4

something?'

'I'm just high on life.'

I retreated back inside as I heard him calling out, 'We must do drinkies soon!'

Sitting at my computer desk, I grabbed the paper from the floor where I'd deposited it the night before and read it with renewed interest. If I didn't find something to do for my challenge, I was sure Ayshe would have a brain wave. An hour later, I'd worked my way through the adverts, the classifieds, and another coffee, but nothing inspirational had pinged out at me.

I switched on the computer and waited for it to bleep and spring into life. I had some photos to enhance and mess around with so I could finish a proof book for the Ponsonby-Smythe's – a rather eccentric couple whose pictures I'd taken last weekend.

I called up their photos, staring at the happiness which radiated from their faces and a twinge of jealousy tugged at my insides. One of the hardest things since splitting up with Justin had been smiling to all the ecstatically happy brides and grooms who were embarking on a whole new exciting life together, while I was carrying a dull ache around inside.

Fiddling around with the programme, I made all her teeth black. Then I decided to squash the picture down and turn her from a nice size ten into a short, dumpy Sumo wrestler, but this only made me feel slightly better.

After an hour of messing around, I was startled by the sound of my phone meowing, signalling a text message. I leapt up and retrieved it from my bag, which was sitting on the wooden floor, spilling out its contents.

The message read: 'Your mission, should you choose to accept it, is to volunteer to walk dogs in Hartham Park. Report to the Canine Animal Rescue Centre at 09.00 hours. Do not pass "Go". This message will self-destruct in ten seconds.'

And that was how this whole crazy thing began.

I relaxed with relief because that didn't sound too bad. I'd even been toying with the idea of getting a pet to keep me company. Not that I'd had much to do with dogs since I'd made my mum's dog a birthday cake when I was about four-years-old, and it had exploded in the oven – the cake that is, not the dog. The funny thing was that Rover did die rather suddenly afterwards from some kind of strange gastric complication. But

5

anyway, it didn't seem too crazy for my first challenge, and nothing as outrageous could happen again.

As I got undressed for bed that night, I took off my attractive jogging bottoms and threw them into the bin. In a moment of madness, I also decided I could do with a whole drawer-full of new knickers and grabbed a handful of oversized ones, which didn't fit my new svelte figure – well, OK then, my almost svelte figure – and threw those into the bin also. Now I had a plan to force myself into action, I decided I needed to be firm with myself and do something to freshen up my appearance. Gazing at my legs, I promised I'd have a grand splurge of de-fuzzing tomorrow.

My eyes wandered down to my neglected toenails. Rummaging around in my bedside drawer, I took out a bottle of quick drying, chip resistant varnish in Pillar Box Red, which still looked useable and commenced toenail-painting duties. After waiting the designated drying time, I crept under the sheets and drifted off to la-la land.

What would tomorrow bring?

## Chapter 2
## Monday, day 1 – I Shouldn't Get a Pet

I rolled out of bed the next morning at seven-thirty and realized two things. One: it was the first night in six months that I hadn't dreamed about Justin, and two: something pretty freaky must've happened last night.

My heart skipped a beat as I flipped back the covers to discover bright red stains everywhere. It looked like a blood-bath, something out of a scene from *The Godfather*. I checked the rest of the bed to make sure no one had mysteriously deposited a horse's head in my bed overnight, and then found the culprit. My toes, and also half my feet, were encrusted in bright red smudged nail varnish.

Quick-drying, my arse! Oh well, I would have to deal with that later. I didn't have time to take it off again now, otherwise I would be late for my challenge of the day, and last night, in the depths of my sleep, I'd resolved to take it all seriously.

I padded barefoot into the kitchen and switched on the kettle. While waiting for my coffee to brew, I put a slice of bread in the toaster and turned on the radio. Bob Marley's soulful voice was singing, 'No woman, no cry, no woman no cry.' I sang along enthusiastically until someone in the next flat banged on the wall and told me to go away and do something to myself that probably wasn't even humanly possible.

After I'd taken a bite of toast, I realized I wasn't at all hungry, so I wrapped it in tin foil and shoved it into my bag, thinking I would eat it later if I got a bit peckish after my walk.

Complete with my morning caffeine rush, I retraced my steps back to the bedroom and opened the window, peering out to check the temperature. For once it wasn't raining or hailing, or anything else that involved vast amounts of water. I thought that was a good sign until I glanced down to the car park just as Clive, my lecherous neighbour, emerged from the entrance to the flats below my window, wearing a ripped T-shirt and paint splattered jeans. His unkempt shoulder-length hair looked like it hadn't seen a dose of shampoo since the sixties.

He looked up and waved. 'All right, gorrrgeous.' Then he pointed to his mouth and proceeded with his nasty little party trick of removing his denture plate with his tongue and wiggling it around, giving me a bird's eye view of the single false tooth attached to it. 'Ha-ha.' He sauntered off with his jeans so low on his hips, I could see his builder's bum winking at me.

'Ew.' I wrinkled up my nose and hurried away from the window, wondering what to wear for a spot of dog walking.

I pulled on a skirt and jumper and stuffed my feet into knee-length boots. Slinging on my coat, I grabbed my bag and headed off in the direction of the Canine Rescue Centre.

The day was crisp but bright with just a smattering of cloud, and the sunshine gave me an unexpected boost, which I'd lost since my break-up with Justin.

I arrived at the centre, red-faced and out of breath. The reception desk was empty, but an elderly man leaned on the front of the counter, waiting for someone to appear. Boxes were strewn around the floor half opened, as if in the middle of being unpacked.

'Morning, love.' He doffed his flat cap at me.

'Morning,' I replied.

'Nice day for it, eh?'

For what? I wondered. Climbing Everest? World peace? Mass suicide?

'Mmm,' I mumbled, catching my breath back.

'Done it before, have you, love?'

'What's that?'

'You know, walk the doggies. I've been doing it every day since my wife died.'

'Oh, how nice.' God, that sounded terrible. 'I mean, not your wife dying, of course.'

'He never misses a day, do you, Eric?'

I turned to see a middle-aged woman walk behind the desk. She gazed up at him, patting his hand.

Maybe there was more to this dog-walking lark than met the eye. There certainly seemed to be a bit of romance blossoming here!

'This lady is here for walking the doggies.' Eric smiled at the receptionist.

'Sorry about the mess. We've just extended the office, and we're still unpacking. It's much better now, though, there wasn't room to swing a cat in the old one. Now, have you got a doggy-bag, dear?'

'Oh, sorry, I didn't realize you had to bring some food for them.' Then I remembered the half-eaten breakfast in my bag. 'I've got some toast. Will that do?'

'I meant bags for the poop!' She gave me a warm smile and handful of plastic bags. 'Well, you're both in luck. There are two dogs left for walking today.'

'Who's left then, pet?' Eric asked her.

'We've got Fang and Pussy. Which one would you like, dear?' she asked me.

A sudden vision of a rabid Rottweiler versus a small, cute little puppy came to mind. Was it a trick question? I mean, come on, who was going to choose a dog called Fang over a cute little pooch named Pussy? Stranger still, though, was why anyone would want to call their dog Pussy?

Eric peered at me, awaiting my decision, while the receptionist stared at me.

'Er...I think I'll have...Pussy, then, if you don't mind.' An uneasy feeling crept over me.

'Okey-dokey, then, dear.' She nodded, trotting off to collect the dogs.

A few minutes later, she returned with a black Labrador, flecked with grey around her temples, and a German Shepherd, the size of a small horse. Thank God I'd gone for Pussy, I thought, as the horse-dog licked his lips and eyed me up like an industrial size tin of Pedigree Chum.

'Here you go, Eric.' She handed him the German Shepherd. He gave her a wave as he disappeared out of the door. 'It's OK.' She passed me the lead for the Labrador. 'She probably won't want to walk too far, she's very arthritic.'

'Come on, then. Nice Pussy.' I opened the door, not believing that I'd actually uttered the words, 'nice pussy' in public.

The dog was very slow on her feet and trotted beside me, stopping every two minutes to sniff the ground.

Trot, trot, trot. Sniff, sniff, sniff. At this rate, the ten minute walk to the park would take an hour. I gazed at the 1920s-style houses on either side of the road as Pussy took her time waddling along, smelling the doggy telegraph messages. I studied the manicured gardens and the bay windows and porches and wondered whether I would ever live in this kind of house with my future husband – if I ever found one before I turned into a Zimmer frame-wielding, pension-collecting spinster, of course.

9

A few metres ahead of me a nice-looking guy emerged from his front door. Wearing a well-cut, charcoal business suit and carrying a black briefcase, he strode along his path, sweeping a hand through his immaculate hair. When he neared the kerb, he clicked his car keys and a beeping sound emanated from a silver Porsche 911 in front of the house. At the same time, Pussy decided to sniff around the wheel of his car with heightened interest. As I waited for her to finish, I sneaked a look at him sliding into the driver's seat and straightened myself up, trying to appear casual as I checked him out. Mmm, not bad. This was definitely a good idea of Ayshe's. He placed his briefcase on the passenger seat just as Pussy decided to arch her back and squat on the pavement. I tugged on the lead slightly, but she gave me a look as if to say 'I ain't moving lady!'

I whispered to myself please let it be a wee, please let it be a wee, groaning inside at the thought that I might have to clear up something larger and smellier in front of Mr. Porsche-driver.

'Pussy!' I tried to drag her away.

The driver's window slid down, and I was sure he was about to say something. Instead, he looked on in horror as Pussy deposited a massive, steaming plop on the pavement, inches away from his car.

'For Christ's sake get that bloody animal away from my car!'

Pussy had now finished her business and turned around to sniff it with delight.

'Oh, God!' I exclaimed, blushing an interesting shade of vermillion.

I fished a plastic bag out of my pocket to pick up the Mr. Whippy style plop which was now deposited on the pavement in all its glory. Pulling a disgusted face, I put the bag over my hand like a glove and retrieved the offending dollop, turning the bag inside out when I'd finished.

'Dirty old bitch!' he yelled in our direction as his tyres screeched and the car flew off up the road.

I wondered how he knew Pussy was a girl, then realized he was talking about me. How insulting! I'm not that bloody old.

'Oi!' I shouted after him, sticking up my fingers and waving them in a frantic up and down motion.

A crowd of rubbernecks had gathered, gawping at me open-mouthed and sniggering. Not wanting to lose face, I pretended everything was hunky-dory and, with a flick of my hair, I dragged Pussy along the path, nonchalantly swinging my bag of plop and plonking it into the nearest bin.

Pussy's bowel movement must've had the same effect as a weekend at a canine spa snorting Sanatogen, because as soon as we reached the park she had a complete personality change. She zigzagged through the fallen Autumnal leaves, kicking them in the air and chasing them around. After twenty minutes of re-energized action, she insisted on bounding round the park with me struggling to keep up.

When I found myself back on the path leading out of the park, Pussy spied something in the distance and sprinted off like Linford Christie from the starting blocks, managing to pull the lead out of my hand as she shot off. I ran at warp speed factor one, shouting after her, but she was intent on her mission.

She seemed to be running towards a man who was strolling along with a pram, unaware of the danger ahead. With a sudden leap, she jumped into the pram. I had a quick flash of terror as I imagined the headlines: 'Wild dog savages baby in sleepy suburb!' The man was screaming and shouting at Pussy, trying to get her out of the pram. Huffing and puffing, I finally caught up with them.

'Agh!' My eyes darted into the pram expecting to see blood and gore.

Instead, to my surprise, Pussy was sitting on top of the baby, wagging her tail with fervour. She'd squeezed her whole body into the tiny pram and was licking the baby's chubby little face like there was no tomorrow. The baby – thank God – looked like it was quite enjoying the experience and giggled with delight, its eyes about to pop out on stalks in excitement.

'What were you thinking?' the man snapped as he managed to half-lift, half-tip Pussy out of the pram.

'I'm so sorry, she's not my dog. I think she's a bit over-excited.'

'That is certainly not the word for it!' He threw me a filthy look as he wiped the dog drool off the baby's face. 'Be more careful next time,' he said, marching off.

I warned Pussy about her behaviour, but she took no notice and looked around with wild eyes, trying to find some other mischief to get into. Then she decided to change her naughty thoughts and sat down with tail wagging and eyes full of apology.

'Come on.' I tugged the lead, desperately wanting to get her back to the centre before any more mishaps occurred, but she wouldn't budge.

Trying to coax her in my best Barbara Woodhouse voice, she just crinkled up her eyebrows and stared at me with huge, doleful eyes. I crouched down to stroke her soft black fur and that's when I realized it was all an act. She was just lulling me into a false sense of security and, before I could yell 'No!' she was off again.

She'd caught sight of a squirrel munching on an acorn under a vast oak tree, and she dragged me off towards the nearby woods. This time, however, I was determined to hang on for dear life. As I tried to get up in a hurry, I stumbled and was teetering out of control as she pulled me towards the trees. My feet crunched on the leaves as I staggered to right myself and my arms flailed in the air. Suddenly, the ground dipped beneath me, and I lost my footing. I went over on my ankle, and then before I could regain my balance again, she dragged me down a bank. I fell to the ground with all the grace of a rhino on roller-skates and landed on my back in a patch of slimy mud as little white stars exploded behind my eyeballs.

An involuntary sound escaped from my lips as the air flew out of my lungs. I lay there, winded for a few minutes, dazed and confused. As I tried to sit up, I was pushed gently back down again by a tall, bald man, in a black cashmere sweater.

'It's all right, I saw everything. You've had a fall.' He peered down at me. 'Don't worry, I'm a doctor. You might have concussion.' He produced a slim-line torch from his pocket which he shone into my eyes.

'Where's my...Pussy,' I slurred.

'Hmm.' He looked puzzled, glancing over his shoulder at the crowd beginning to form. 'Confusion and slurred speech, possibly a case of concussion,' he volunteered to the others, then turned back to me. 'I need to check you out. Does anything hurt?' He clicked the torch off and put it in his pocket.

I tried to sit up again, but he instructed me in a firm voice, 'No, I need to have a look at you before you get up.' He put his hands under my neck and gently palpated. 'Does it hurt here?' He worked his way along both arms and then up my legs, feeling through the soft suede of my boots.

'Only my ankle.' I forced a smile, struggling to regain my

composure as I ventured a look at his shiny head, which was Bic-razored to death.

'Good job I was having a sneaky cigarette in between patients and saw what happened. OK, everything seems fine, but I think you might have sprained your ankle. My surgery is over there.' He motioned to a row of Georgian houses on one side of the park. 'Can you make it if I help you?'

By then my breathing had returned to normal. 'I think so.' I nodded and instantly wished I hadn't – my head still felt a bit woozy.

He led me, bedraggled and groggy, the short distance to his surgery. I hobbled along beside him, holding on to steady myself as he steered me up the front steps which were  lined with wrought-iron railings. We entered a shiny black door with a semi-circular fanlight above it. Once inside, the pristine whiteness hurt my eyes, and I squinted as he led me past a wooden reception desk and along a corridor. We reached a door with a name-plate that read: DR SAVAGE.

'Right, let's get these boots off and have a look, shall we?' He lowered me onto a very firm grey couch.

As he started unzipping them, I studied him with interest. He was in his early forties with olive skin and the palest green eyes I'd ever seen. He really was rather tasty. I gazed at him for a few moments, then my eyes widened with foreboding as I suddenly remembered my woolly mammoth legs. Why hadn't I shaved them last night when I'd had the chance? A warm glow crawled up my neck.

He removed my socks and stepped back in amazement. 'For a minute I thought you were bleeding.' He picked up my heel in the palm of his hand, scrutinizing it.

I lifted my head from the comfort of the couch, realizing he was talking about my rather unique pedicure. I felt myself growing hot and clammy, crackling with shame.

His eyes wandered up my leg, taking in the bristling, dark hairs, a centimetre long. I clawed at the neck of my jumper.

'Alrighty, then.' I cleared my throat, swinging my legs off the couch and onto the floor.

'Wait a minute.' He perched on the edge of his desk. 'I have to take some details. Procedure, you know, in case I get sued!' He waved his hand, as if the very thought of suing him was absolutely unbelievable. 'Name?'

13

'Helen Grey.'

'Address and contact number please?'

I rattled off my details quickly, willing him to get a move on so I could get out of there.

'Well, it's as I suspected, just a sprain. You'll need to take it easy for a few days. Put your foot up and rest. You can put a bag of ice on it, or frozen peas, and take some of these if the pain is too bad.' He handed me a prescription.

'Thanks very much.' I flashed a quick smile, stood up and hobbled out of the surgery as fast as my gammy foot would allow.

Once outside, I sat down on the steps and phoned Ayshe to beg her for a lift to my flat. I leaned back. And then I had a ghastly thought.

Where the hell was Pussy?

# Chapter 3

'Oh, Goddy God!' I groaned.

I was expecting Ayshe, but instead her brother Kalem rolled up in his battered old Land Rover. Actually, I could hear it coughing and spluttering up the road before I even clapped eyes on it. At some point it must have been white, but after years of off-roading, it was a kind of a murky-brown colour with just a hint of the original paintwork left. Even Dulux would have had trouble describing this particular shade – 'crusty chocolate' perhaps or 'rancid coconut'?

I'd known Kalem since the day I started primary school, when he'd taken great delight in yanking my ponytail and chasing me round the playground, inciting all his mates to jump on top of me. Ayshe, who'd spotted it, came running over and proceeded to punch him on the arm, shouting something in Turkish to him. And that had been the start of my wonderful friendship with her. Because I'd known him for so long, we had a brother-sister type of relationship. He would argue lipstick was eyeliner if he knew it would wind me up, which he did, at any possible opportunity. But it was our love of Ayshe that kept us from killing each other.

I heaved myself into the passenger seat.

'H.' He acknowledged me with a nickname he'd used since we were kids and which still grated on me and gave me an irresistible urge to punch his lights out.

'Kalem! What a nice surprise,' I said through clenched teeth. He was the last person I wanted to know about my recent predicament. 'Why aren't you at work? Haven't you got any ice sculpture classes to teach?'

'It's half-term. Anyway, I teach woodcarving and sculpture, not ice sculpture.'

'Oh. Where's Ayshe?' I asked, observing his usual attire of a faded green Land Rover sweatshirt – which had more holes in it than a packet of Hula Hoops – and some even more faded army issue trousers. His cropped dark hair needed a trim, but then, who was I to talk lately? He'd boasted once that his mates often joked that he looked like David Beckham, only more swarthy and exotic looking. I mean, it was a pretty accurate description, and there was no denying it – he was heart-clutchingly gorgeous.

15

But when I'd heard this, I'd erupted in fits of laughter, which seriously annoyed him. He never mentioned it again – I can't think why not.

'She's stuck in some marketing meeting and can't get away, so she called me instead.'

'Um…I've got a bit of a problem.'

'What? You mean apart from the obvious.'

'Ha-ha. I've lost the dog I was supposed to be walking, and I need to find it before it does any more damage.'

'Well, it's your lucky day. Ayshe filled me in on your little trail of destruction. I've already been up to the Canine Centre to talk to them. They weren't too impressed – 'care in the community reject' – I think were the words they used to describe you.' His eyes shone with humour. 'Saddam Hussein would have paid a fortune to have had you working for him. You're a one-woman weapon of mass destruction.' A huge cackle of laughter escaped from his lips.

My cheeks glowed. 'We need to check the park. I've got to get that poor dog back as soon as possible!' My voice cracked, the morning was beginning to take its toll on me.

'And just how are you going to hobble around the park in that state?' He glared at me with intense brown eyes, pointing to my ankle.

'Look, don't worry. I'll do it myself.' I eased the door open and started to manoeuvre myself out.

He leaned across me and tried to close the door again, giving me a waft of some rather yummy aftershave.

'What are you doing?' I yelled, panicking as he pulled the door shut, banging my ankle in the process. 'Owch!'

'The dog's OK,' he yelled back at me. 'If you'd just let me finish!'

I sank back in the seat and waited. 'Well?'

He took a deep breath. 'I've got better things to do than baby-sit a thirty-year-old, you know.' He narrowed his eyes at me like a cat weighing something up with cool detachment before pouncing.

'How on earth do your students put up with you?' I glared back.

'They love me.'

'Where's Pussy?'

'Pussy?' he guffawed.

16

'Oh, shut up!'

'Pussy...' He laughed, dragging out the conversation.

I waited.

'Pussy...' he started again.

This time I slapped him on the arm.

'Pussy ran back to the Centre and said, 'please don't let that nutty woman take me out for a walk again!' he reeled off in a garbled rush.

My eyes cleared with relief. Now I knew Pussy was safe, I didn't want to be in the car with him a minute longer.

'Right, can you take me home now then, please?'

'With pleasure.' He released the handbrake, driving off.

It was so uncomfortable in the Land Rover that the slightest bump in the road made me wince in pain. I stared out of the window rather than making conversation with him, but he wasn't letting me off that easily.

'Don't they ask for any references before they let you take out dangerous dogs?'

'It was a Labrador!'

'Ah.' He nodded. 'I forgot. It's you that's dangerous.' He paused. 'I think you need to lay off the caffeine, it's making you too hyper.'

I couldn't be bothered to think of the perfect retort, so we drove the rest of the way in silence.

'Ha! What's that on your back?' Kalem snorted when I heaved myself out of the Land Rover.

I twisted round to discover a patch of crusty brown mud all over my bum – looked like I'd had an incontinent attack actually.

'Arse,' I muttered.

'Couldn't have put it better myself.' He grinned at me. 'Are you going to be OK?'

'Yes, I'm fine.'

He raised an eyebrow, shifted the Land Rover into first and trundled up the road.

I limped up the stairs to the flat, hanging on to the banister for support. Once inside, I curled up on the comfy, brown leather sofa that I so adored – even though the raised stitching on its arms made it look like a sun-baked elephant's foreskin – and moulded a bag of frozen peas onto my ankle. God, that was a bit cold! The answer phone was blinking at me. Reaching over from

17

my foetal position, I hit the play button.

'Just to let you know that you haven't paid me for the last shipment. If you don't deliver in the next two days I won't be responsible for my actions. Know what I mean, eh?' That was it. No name, no number, nothing. And his tone – well, it was just a teensy bit creepy.

Wrong number, I decided, and instantly forgot about it as my eyes wandered round the room. God, the place was an absolute tip, and I really must tidy it up soon.

I flicked on the television, trying to break the oppressive silence. The choice was disappointing: either a talk show with some sort of a fight going on between the guests or a boring antiques programme with a sun-tanned-to-death presenter.

With only Jerry Springer and a cold-pack for company, boredom got the better of me and I fell into a depressed sleep.

A pounding on the door woke me from my slumber. Rubbing my eyes, I swung the door open to see Ayshe looking at me rather concerned.

'Who goes there?' bellowed Charlie next door.

'Put a sock in it!' Ayshe shouted.

I wasn't the only person who'd witnessed his sock-stuffing antics before.

'Ooooh, tetchy!' he yelled back.

'How are you feeling?' she asked, wandering in with a Tupperware bowl, which she put on the black granite kitchen worktop.

I sniffed the wonderful aroma of freshly-cooked Turkish food. 'I feel a bit ridiculous, if you must know.'

She rubbed my arm. 'Well, at least you tried something. You can't be knocked for that.' Pointing to the dish she added, 'Atila's made you some mousaka. He didn't think you'd feel like cooking as usual and you'll need to keep your strength up for your challenges.'

Ayshe busied herself in the kitchen, putting the mousaka in the microwave and arranging a knife and fork on a tray, as if I were an invalid.

'So...any thoughts as to what tomorrow's challenge is going to be? I mean, I actually feel like giving the whole thing up after today. I don't know if I can carry on with this.' I flopped my head down into my hands, tugging at my roots.

18

'Oh no,' she wagged her finger at me, 'that's not going to happen. You've only just started.'

I lifted my head as the microwave chimed.

Taking the tray out to the diningroom table, she jabbed a finger at one of the chairs. 'Sit and eat,' she ordered. Sitting down with one leg beneath her, she made me eat half of it before she let me in on her little secret. 'Speed-dating: that's what is on the agenda for tomorrow. And you have to go. It is the law,' she insisted in a very bad Inspector Clouseau accent.

'A bunch of saddos trying to talk to as many other saddos until a clock buzzes. That sounds like fun! I'd rather poke forks in my eyes.'

'Anyone doing a fourteen day change-your-life-challenge has to go. Those are the rules according to Ayshe – and Inspector Clouseau. And anyway, you might meet someone nice. Sometimes it's the one you least expect that makes you happy.'

'Great.' I rubbed my forehead.

'Listen, I've got to go; Atila's a bit annoyed. He took a chicken out of the freezer this morning to defrost and the cat's eaten it. He's not a happy bunny. If I said "foul" and "mood", in the same sentence you'd know exactly what I mean! I've got to nip out and get a take-away before he starts to erupt into a full-blown volcanic explosion. I'll pick you up after the dating thingy. Text me when you're finished, and I'll come and get you,' she gushed and breezed out the door.

After I'd cleared up the remnants of my gastronomic experience, the phone rang. I debated whether to ignore it, but I had a sudden intuitive flash that it could be Justin, calling to tell me how wrong he'd been, begging for forgiveness because a spot of rumpy-pumpy with the boss over the office equipment just wasn't as thrilling any more, or the late night dick-tation was getting out of hand. I'd always wanted to believe in the idea that everything happens for a reason, but no matter how hard you analyze and dissect things, sometimes you just can't figure out what that reason is. Is that fate's way of giving you what you deserve, or is it trying to teach you a valuable lesson that you're just not ready to decipher yet?

I dived for the phone. 'Hello.'

'Hello, is that the home-owner?'

For God's sake! I'd been plagued by a spate of annoying telesales people at all hours for the last month.

'I don't want double glazing, or a holiday, or anything else you're selling,' I said.

'Why not? You don't know what it is yet,' a Pakistani voice told me on the other end.

Why not? Because if I wanted double glazing, I'd almost certainly go and order some myself. And if I wanted to listen to a two-hour spiel about vacuum cleaners just to get a holiday, then I'd effing well do that!

'Because I'm having sex with my husband, and you've just interrupted me,' I replied.

There was a few seconds silence on the other end. 'Pardon? I didn't quite hear you, madam.'

'I said; I'm making love to my husband.'

'Oh, I am sorry. I'll call you back later.' He hung up without waiting for my response.

No sooner had I put the phone down than the bloody thing was off again.

'Hello.' I snatched it from its cradle.

'Hello, Ms Grey? Can I offer you a cheap gas and electricity supply? We guarantee to beat the price of your current supplier.' Same voice again.

'You just called me a minute ago! I'm still having sex with my husband. Why are you phoning me again?'

'I thought you would have finished, madam.'

'What, in two minutes?'

'Well, when would be convenient? Five minutes?'

'More like forty-five minutes. You've completely messed up my rhythm now.' I threw the phone down in anger.

Two minutes later, it rang again.

'I'm still having SEX!' I shouted, slightly more shrill than I anticipated.

The sound of heavy breathing greeted me on the other end of the line. Urgh, how disgusting! He was actually getting excited.

'Hello, Helen, it's Annabel Ponsonby-Smythe here.'

Oops.

I gulped. 'Sorry Annabel…' I quickly debated what sounded worse: I'm not really having sex, and I'm talking utter drivel, or I was having sex, but I've finished now. Probably best to say neither. 'I thought you were someone else.'

'Don't worry dear, I know all about this telephonic intercourse

20

that's all the rage now with you youngsters. If I was twenty years younger, I'd be at it myself, it must be considerably less messy. I won't keep you–'

'No, don't go. What can I do for you?' I squeaked, trying to put my professional head on.

'I was just wondering if you'd finished the proofs for my photo book yet, only we're off on our honeymoon tomorrow. Dahling Jeremy has finally got a window in his busy work schedule, and I was hoping to have a little peek before I left.'

'Of course, what time are you off tomorrow? Hopefully I can get it finished and drop it off to you before you leave.'

'We're leaving for the airport at two o'clock dahling, so if you could come for coffee and petits fours at say eleven-thirty?'

That would give me plenty of time, no problem.

'Yes, that will be perfect. I'll see you tomorrow.'

'Righty-ho, then, I'll let you get back to your sex now. Enjoy!'

# Chapter 4
## Tuesday, day 2 – Single Men Are Freaks

The following morning I'd reneged again on my promise to cut down on my coffee intake. Instead, I'd drunk the caffeine equivalent of almost a whole box of Pro-Plus tablets and was pretty much buzzing on the stuff. I doggedly got down to some serious work on the computer, organizing my files, sending a few emails, and finally finishing off the proofs for Mrs. Ponsonby-Smythe.

The pain in my ankle had subsided to a dull throb, although maybe that was something to do with the cocktail of caffeine mixed with several strong painkillers. I checked my watch. Quarter past eleven: plenty of time. Annabel's plush mews house was only a short distance away. I grabbed the book, darting out the front door as fast as my throbbing ankle would allow.

I banged on the brass lion's head door-knocker with minutes to spare, but there was no reply. I tried to peep in the window at the side of the house without looking like a prospective cat burglar, but heavy drapes blocked my view. Strange, I'm sure she said eleven-thirty. After waiting several minutes, I knocked again. I was about to turn and leave when a tall hippy-looking man, covered from head to foot in paint, opened the door.

'Hi.' I peered up at him.

'Hi, you must be Helen.' He reached his hand out to shake mine.

'Yes, that's right. I was supposed to be meeting Annabel at eleven-thirty. Is she here?' I asked as he gave me a wet-lettuce handshake.

'There was a change of plan. The airline rearranged the flight times, and they had to dash off to Heathrow early.' He gestured inside the house. 'Come in, come in. I'm Adrian Ponsonby by the way, Annabel's brother. I'm house-sitting for her while she's living it up in the sunny Indian Ocean. It's all right for some! I was just about to have an early lunch. Do you want a cup of tea while you're here? I'm making one for myself anyway, so it's no trouble.'

Ayshe's advice that I needed to take every opportunity to meet new people resounded in my head. I mean, he wasn't my type at all, but what the hell, why not?

'Well...OK, thanks.'

He led me past the drawing room, where I'd discussed Annabel's wedding requirements at our original consultation, into the well-lit breakfast room, just off the muted eggshell Shaker-style kitchen. A painting stood on an easel by the window and paints were strewn on top of the table next to it. The painting was an explosion of vibrant yellows and reds with several orange blobby-looking things in the centre of it. It was surrounded by a few larger black and brown swirly things smudged in along the edges, with what appeared to be a little black stick-man nestling in the corner. It looked like an explosion in the Chocolate Orange factory.

He caught me looking at it. 'It's very abstract, don't you think?'

'Absolutely.' I leaned forward, scrutinizing it. It was the worst painting I'd ever seen in my life, but I didn't want to hurt his feelings. 'It's very good.'

'If you look really hard there's a surprising feature within the picture. Can you see it?' He indicated that I should get closer.

'No...I'm not getting anything.' I studied the picture hard.

'Don't worry, you'll see it eventually. I get more of the stuff on me than on the painting, I think.' He pulled up the bottom of his shirt and gazed down at the paint splattered everywhere.

'I'm having trouble trying to think of a title for this particular piece. Any ideas?' He turned to me with an enquiring look.

Revenge of the Chocolate Orange perhaps, I mused. Or Nuclear Reactor Strikes Back? 'How about Total Oblivion?'

He threw me a very peculiar look, changing the subject. 'Please, sit.' He pulled out a breakfast bar chair for me, and I duly plonked myself down.

'Annabel's only left green tea in the cupboards, I'm afraid. Will that do?'

After all the coffee I'd consumed that morning it was probably a good thing anyway, and I was sure I'd heard somewhere that green tea was the new wonder substance for detoxifying. I thought I needed a hefty dose of that right now.

'Um, fine.'

He handed me a cup of steaming green liquid that looked like iguana piss. I stared at it, then gave it a quick sniff. It smelled revolting. I tried hard not to heave, and quickly placed it back on the breakfast bar out of sniffing range.

'So,' he ran his fingers through his long flowing locks, as he reclined on his chair, 'you're the wedding photographer. I missed Annabel's wedding, I'm afraid; I was laid up with food poisoning.' He nodded to himself. 'Campylobacter: it was awful.'

'Oh, how terrible. You're OK now, though?'

'Oh yes, fine. Had to try and get better a bit sharpish. I've got an exhibition and auction of my work tomorrow night, and I've still got a few pieces to finish.' He pointed to the painting which had taken centre-stage in the room.

'That's great.'

'Hey, you must come. Yes, you absolutely must. I've got an invitation upstairs somewhere. Hang on, I'll get you one.'

He sloped out of the room and left me studying the paintings with disbelief. It was Picasso meets Damien Hirst. One of them even looked like an exploding brain, hardly the sort of thing you'd want on your living room wall, unless you were a serial killer.

'Here you go.' He snuck back in the room without a sound and handed me the invitation. 'I see you're admiring my brain.'

He must've mistaken the expression on my face for admiration, instead of slight queasiness. 'Yes, it's very...vivid.'

'Wait 'till you see what's on show tomorrow. There's a lot more where that came from. I bet I could even get you to buy a piece.'

'Maybe,' I murmured with a vagueness that meant not a hope in hell. Still, I was supposed to be trying new things, and this was certainly new, in a Hannibal Lechter kind of way. 'Can you give this to Annabel for me?' I pulled the proofs from my bag and handed them over.

'Sure, no problem. Thanks for popping round.' He led me back to the door. 'Don't forget, I'll be looking for you on Wednesday.'

'See you tomorrow.' I waved my invitation at him and scurried out the door.

# Chapter 5

I completely splurged out on my beauty preparations for that night's challenge. Soaking in the bath with a scrummy-smelling lavender bath-bomb, I spent a frantic half-hour tackling the hairs on my ever-increasing bikini-line and legs. When I finished my skin was raw and tingling. Next, I plucked my eyebrows until bright red lumps appeared. Great! Just what I needed!

Peering into the wardrobe, I wondered what to wear. What look should I go for? I hadn't done this for so long. Understated, sexy, trendy? How about a pair of jeans? I couldn't possibly go wrong with those. I went for the subtle look with my make-up, applying a thin line of black liquid eyeliner and then got totally carried away with lashings of mascara. My eyebrows still looked a tad on the red side, so I patted them with face powder, which reduced them to just a soft glow. A muted beige lipstick finished the look. I tousled my long hair with my hands whilst posing in the mirror. Mmm, not bad, I thought.

I caught a cab to the hotel which was hosting the speed-dating. The taxi driver gave a knowing smirk when we arrived at the venue. Fumbling around for some money, I handed it to him, then dithered a while, psyching myself up.

'In your own time, love,' the driver said over his shoulder in a bored voice.

Taking a deep breath, I summoned all my confidence and got out of the cab, striding up to the reception before I could change my mind. A girl who looked no more than sixteen stood behind the desk.

I leaned over so as not to be overheard. 'Hi, I'm here for the speed-dating,' I whispered to her.

'Pardon?'

'The speed-dating, where is it?' I repeated, slightly louder this time.

'I'm sorry, what?' Her lips curled into a superficial smile.

'Where's the speed-dating?' Even louder.

'Sorry, madam, I'm not quite getting you.'

'Speed-dating! Where is it?' I finally shouted, looking round to see if anyone had heard me.

An elderly man, reclining in a sofa by the desk reading the

Financial Times, looked up at me with interest. He shook his head to himself and went back to the paper.

She pretended to cough, but I could hear the snigger underneath it as she smiled at me.

'Over there, in the conference room.' She poked her finger towards a set of double doors next to the bar area with a sign which said in big bold letters, SPEED-DATING.

Deciding I needed a hefty dose of Dutch courage, I meandered over to the bar, my heels clicking on the slippery marble floor, as I tried hard not to slip over. A couple of men were already propping up the bar ordering some drinks, so I waited patiently for them to finish, resting my elbow on the mahogany surface.

They were having a ridiculous conversation about the benefits of lager versus real ale. I snuck a surreptitious glance at them, whilst they waited for their drinks. I thought I recognized one of them, but I wasn't certain, and I couldn't really place him, so I looked harder. Then it came to me in a flash of recognition. Bugger, I thought. One of them was none other than Mr. Porsche from yesterday. If that was the calibre of available single men, I'd never meet Mr.. Right in a squillion years.

'Well, ultimately it doesn't really matter what you drink, as long as it gets you absolutely bladdered. That's what really counts!' laughed Mr. Porsche's mate, who was the size of an overstuffed hippo, with insipid piggy eyes, orangey-coloured freckles and bright ginger hair.

'Yeah, last night I crashed out on my mate's couch after a skinful and fell asleep. By the next morning, I'd spilt a whole can of lager on it.' Mr. Porsche paused for effect. 'Only trouble was, I'd drunk it first.' He erupted in guffaws of laughter, slapping Hippo on the back.

They collected their drinks and wandered off into the conference room.

I ordered a red wine and soda with ice.

'No one's ever asked for that before,' the barmaid shot me a strange look, as if I'd ordered something completely bizarre like a Marmite cocktail.

I took a couple of sips, debating to myself about whether the night could get any worse. I knew Ayshe would kill me if I didn't do it, so I took myself and my wine off to the conference room.

I stepped inside to find three rows of individual tables with women sitting on one side and an empty chair on the other. A group of men huddled on the other side, trying their best to look cool. Suddenly, I spotted a Miss Whiplash impersonator, with jet-black straight hair pulled back into a long ponytail. She wore a spray-on black pencil skirt, teetering on the highest stilettos in the whole universe. God, how could she walk in them without getting a hip displacement or, for that matter, bunions?

'OK, yes please, Miss!' She banged a gong and pointed at me while everyone else in the room turned to gawp.

Oh God, what have I done now?

'Please take a seat at that table.' She pointed to a table with a spare chair. 'Please fill in your contact details on this sheet, so we can pass it on to any prospective datees. I'll also need to take a twenty pound registration fee.'

I felt like I was at school again and almost said 'Yes, Miss', but I bit my tongue and sat down, sweeping the room with my eyes, checking it all out. It was pretty damn full! I filled out the form and she collected it along with the money.

'OK. The rules are this…everyone has to write their name on a label and stick it on themselves – the women have got some labels on their tables along with some plain sheets of paper – the men can get their labels and paper from me before they sit down.' She waved a stack of labels in her hand. 'When I give the word, all these gorgeous men must go and sit at a table and talk to the beautiful woman opposite for exactly three minutes.' She paused, surveying her audience. 'Then, after three minutes, I will sound a gong and the men have to move in a clockwise direction to the next table and talk with the next lovely young lady, and so on and so on. Ladies, you do not move at all.'

God forbid we did something wrong, this place was running to a clockwork formula.

'When all the men have been round all the ladies once, you must all make a note on the sheet of paper of any people you are interested in swapping details with and hand it to me. If the same parties want to swap details, then I will pass on their information to you. So, is that clear? Are there any questions before we start?'

No one dared.

'Right then chaps and chapesses, we're off!' She banged her gong frantically.

**** 

27

A tall gangly man who looked like a weasel sat down at my table and began rubbing the end of his nose with his index finger, not once but four times in quick succession.

'I'm Sean.' He did it again.

'Helen.' I held out my hand to shake his, taking in his stuck-in-the-70s, wide-collared shirt – first four buttons undone – stick-on-chest wig and gold medallion.

'I don't do hands,' he said.

'Alrighty, then…so, what do you do for a living?'

'I'm a property developer. Sold millions.' He rubbed his nose again. 'I've just done up a sweet little number of flats in Docklands. Sold 'em all for four hundred and fifty grand a piece.'

Did he think I had idiot tattooed on my forehead?

'And, do you know what? The punters are so stupid. They only cost a fraction of that to do up. The fixtures and fittings I put in are the cheapest going. I make a mint, an absolute mint.'

'So, what brings you here, then? I would have thought you'd have the girls flocking round you!'

'I'm a bit fussy. I've been on so many dates lately. The birds can't get enough of me.' Rub, rub, rub, rub.

'Right. Why do you think you haven't met the perfect woman yet, then, with all that choice?'

'Well, I don't do commitment.' He shrugged 'And that's the thing about women, always whingeing about getting a ring on their finger. Am I right or am I right?' He droned on without waiting for an answer. 'I don't think they like competing with me either. I'm tall, good-looking, extremely rich. Let's face it, I'm a bloody good catch. And they just get jealous of all the attention I get from other women.' Rub. Rub. Rub. Rub.

I took a sip of wine, and almost choked on it.

'Well, what do you do?' he asked me.

Ha! I thought. I can tell a few little porky pies too, if you want to play that game.

'I'm a professional pole-dancer.'

'Wa-hey!' He went into finger-rubbing overdrive.

Bong! I was saved by the bell.

The next one to sit down hadn't made any effort at all. He wore a pair of ripped jeans and had long greasy hair, complete with bushy sideburns, which nearly took up his whole face.

He leaned forward to me. 'Don't believe a word that guy says.

28

He's a complete liar, I can tell by his body language. All that finger-rubbing – it's a classic example. He does it every time he tells a lie.' He leaned back in the chair. 'I'm a psychology student, I know about these things.'

Now this would be interesting!

'I think you could be right there.'

'Anyway, I've prepared a list of word association questions to see if we're compatible.' He took a piece of paper out of his pocket. 'I'm going to call out a word and then you give me the first answer that comes into your head. Are you ready?' He unfolded the paper and began to read from it.

'I guess so.' I ran my fingers through my hair, wondering what that signified in body language. Complete boredom, perhaps? Beam me up Scotty?

'Christmas?'

'Ooh...turkey.'

'Bunny rabbits?' he went on.

'Chocolate,' I said. Was he for real?

He made a note on his paper. 'Interesting.'

Was that a good or bad answer?

'Holes?' He tapped his mouth with the end of his pen.

'Doughnuts.'

'Dinosaurs?' An intense look crept over his face.

'Eggs,' I laughed.

'Grass?'

I narrowed my eyes, head on one side for a moment. 'Sheep.'

'I hear what you're saying!' He nodded, scribbling something on his notes. 'OK, let's try another. The sea?'

'Turnips.'

He looked up at me. 'Wow! That's very interesting. How did that question make you feel?'

'Bananas.'

'Hang on a minute. I haven't done another word association.'

'Oh, sorry.' I crossed my hands in my lap and waited for more.

'OK, here's a tricky one for you. Butter beans?'

'A massive amount of wind.'

'Are you taking this seriously?' He squinted at me.

'Absolutely.' How could he doubt me?

'Bananas?'

'We've already had that,' I said.

'No, that was an answer, not a question. I can say it again if it wasn't a question the first time.' He let out a dramatic sigh. 'Bananas?'

'Food.'

He suddenly leapt out of his chair. 'I knew it, I knew it!'

I frowned. What was he on?

'I knew it would all come down to food. You see it's simple when you know what's going on. I've been working on a new theory for my thesis.' He leaned forward as if he was going to let me in on a huge secret. 'It all comes down to food, you know. All the problems in the world – all the trouble – all the wars – are actually about food. Take Iraq for example, that war was totally about food.' He nodded manically.

'So it had absolutely nothing to do with oil, political aspirations, or…crazy dictators, then?'

'No, absolutely not. It's all about food.'

Two words: complete nutter.

BONG!

Thank God.

As I saw the next one approach, I couldn't believe it. He was the spitting image of Gary Newman, complete with leather trousers covered in strategically placed zips – only a bit older and more wrinkly than when I'd last seen him belting out 'Cars' in the 80s. It was so uncanny, I was convinced it was him.

'Hi.' He sat in front of me.

I perched on the edge of my chair, studying him. 'Has anyone ever told you that you are the absolute double of Gary Newman?'

'Oh, for God's sake!' He shot up, tipping his chair back and stormed off out of the door in a hissy-fit.

All eyes turned to look at me for a moment and the room went deadly silent. I turned the colour of a beetroot and doodled on my piece of paper. Then, after what seemed like an eternity, everyone resumed their conversations, while I sat there alone in stunned silence. I was quickly losing the will to live.

I heard the door to the conference room swing open again and my gaze slid to the door, expecting to see the return of Gary Newman. Instead, a dark head popped through the opening and quickly scanned the crowd. My eyes sprang open in surprise. It was Kalem. What was he doing here? Had he come for the speed-dating? No, surely not. Speed-dating wouldn't be his thing at all, and anyway, he already had a girlfriend. His eyes locked with mine for a few seconds, a confused expression on his face, before he wandered over to me and slipped onto the now empty chair opposite.

'What are you doing here?' he asked.

'Speed-dating,' I whispered, bowing my head in shame.

Kalem looked round the room. 'How come you're the only one not talking to anyone? Have you managed to upset everyone already?'

'Look, it's bad enough that I'm actually here, without you rubbing it in, as well. Anyway, what are you doing here?'

'OK, come on then, ask me some questions while I'm here.' He leaned back in the chair, folded his arms across his chest and flashed me an amused smile.

I mimicked his calm and rather annoying posture. 'How is it that you always manage to turn up at my most embarrassing moments?'

'Well, Helen—'

BONG!

'Damn, there goes the bell. I'll let you get back to your non-speed-dating, then.' He grinned as the Hippo appeared. Kalem examined him for a moment and whispered in his ear, 'Definitely a lesbian.' And he casually slipped out of the room.

The Hippo heaved his hefty buttocks down and the chair groaned in protest.

'You got rid of that other bloke pretty sharpish, didn't you?'

'I told him he looked like Gary Newman. He wasn't too impressed, though. Did you think he looked like him?'

'Who the fuck is Gary Newman?' His eyes formed into two small slits.

Here we go again!

I suppressed a sigh. 'Oh, never mind.'

'What do you think of real ale?'

'Not a lot.' I glanced at him, willing him to go away, feeling severe boredom and rigor mortis creeping in.

'What about lager, then?'

'Even less, actually.' My eyes wandered round the room.

'Less than what? Guinness or Newcastle Brown Ale?' His piggy eyes bore into me.

I stared back in silence, clenching my jaw.

'Come on...get with the programme,' he sneered.

'What programme?' I said.

31

'What?'

'You just said, get with the programme. What are you talking about?' I folded my elbows across my chest, blinking at him.

'No I didn't!'

'Yes, you did.'

'No, I didn't!'

'Yes, you did!' I hissed.

'Christ, you're a bit of hard work, aren't you, missy. No wonder the last one left.'

When was this night going to end?

'Are you a complete moron?' I gave him my sweetest smile.

'Are you a complete moron?' he repeated in a whiney, high-pitched voice.

God, how juvenile! I rolled my eyes, gazing off in another direction. He was the most infuriating excuse for a man I'd ever met.

'I won't be putting you on my list, that's for sure,' he said.

As if I would even want to be on his list!

'Good.' I carried on looking elsewhere; if I ignored him for long enough maybe he would just go away.

'You know what your problem is?'

I tried to ignore him.

'You're a lesbian.' He scratched his armpit and the whole of his flabby arm wobbled.

'No, I'm not!' I swallowed hard as a shiver of revulsion rippled up my spine.

'Yes, you are.' He waved his piece of paper rather rudely at me.

'I think I'd know if I was a lesbian!

BONG!

Hallelujah.

Before Hippo left he leaned over and whispered 'Lesbo' in my ear.

'Ew!'

I drank the rest of my wine, wishing I'd bought a whole bottle and wondering if it was possible to commit hara-kiri with it.

A run-of-the-mill looking man was the next to appear. He wasn't great-looking, but he wasn't bad. He had golden-brown hair, and a closely trimmed goatee beard. Our eyes locked and I couldn't tear myself away. They were the most startling topaz colour, framed by long, luxurious eyelashes. Any woman in her right mind would have been completely jealous of them, and with good reason. I was hypnotized into their depths.

'Hi, I'm Nick.' He smiled, fluttering his eyelashes.

'Helen.' I returned the smile.

'I've never done this before. It's a bit strange.'

'It's totally weird. This is my first time too.' At last! A normal guy! I felt myself beginning to loosen up for the first time all evening.

'It's just that it's really hard to meet people when you get to our age. All my mates are married so it's not as if you're likely to meet people clubbing and stuff, like you can when you're in your twenties. You have to resort to some pretty strange things,' he said.

'I agree. It definitely gets harder as you get older. All my friends are attached, which just leaves single old me.' I nodded, gazing into his eyes.

'So what do you do?'

'I'm a wedding photographer. It's good, I enjoy it.' I played with my hair.

'Wow! That's interesting. I'm just a boring old plumber.' He shrugged, returning my intense stare.

'But everybody needs a plumber – in fact, I need one now. I've been trying to get one to fix my dishwasher for weeks but they keep letting me down.' He could tackle my creaky pipes and washers any day.

'Yeah, I am pretty flat-out, but I could definitely take a look at it for you.' He grinned at me and his whole face lit up. 'If you put my name on your sheet of paper, I'll gladly come out. It's probably only a five minute job.'

'Well...that sounds good.'

'No problem. So what do you like to do, Helen?'

'Oh, you know, the usual sort of stuff...swimming, yoga, romantic walks, the cinema, eating out, cosy nights in...um, usually anything that involves quite a lot of alcohol...' I trailed off, tilting my head. I didn't want to come across as some kind of alcoholic, so I added, 'Ha-ha.'

Who was I kidding anyway? I hated exercise of any variety and I did love the old vino.

He nodded. 'Great! Same things as me. Do you like boxing?'

'It's great, I absolutely love it!' I lied, silently willing him not to ask me any hard questions about it because I didn't have a

33

clue.

'I've got some really good tickets to the next David Haye fight. Should be pretty awesome. Maybe you'd like to go?'

'Maybe I would.'

BONG!

Just when it was starting to get interesting!

A coloured guy with dreadlocks, who I hadn't spotted before, swaggered over to my table. He lifted my hand and kissed it.

'Dat big fat ginger man......he a pig, mon,' he drawled in a strong Jamaican lilt. 'Dat not dem way to speak to no lady.'

He didn't introduce himself and his name label was stuck on upside-down. I manoeuvred my head to the side, trying to read it. 'Kingston' was scrawled in tiny letters.

'He said I was a lesbian. I'm definitely not a lesbian,' I said, with a brisk shake of my head, catching a waft of his overpowering aftershave, Cannabis Pour Homme.

'Hey lady, I know dat. You's not one of dem big fat mamas.' He made a curious sucking sound with his immaculate white teeth.

'I tink I might be a lesbian, dough, because I lurrrve de women.'

'Where are you from?' I regarded him with interest. He was a charmer in a funny sort of way.

'Me from Brixton, mon.' He slouched down in the chair and rested his feet on the table. Miss Whiplash glowered at him so he sat back up again, making another sucking noise.

'No, I meant originally.' I put my elbow on the table, resting my chin on my hand.

'Me is from Jamaica, mon. Where else would me be from?'

'I've always wanted to get married there!' I had a sudden flashback of Justin promising to take me there for a wedding in paradise.

'Irie.' He bobbed his head up and down, looking around the room to see if anyone else was checking him out.

I was suddenly daydreaming of Justin and me on a white sandy beach against a backdrop of palm trees, the turquoise sea kissing our bare feet. I had flowers in my hair, and a long floaty, white wedding dress – which showed off my bronzed-to-oblivion tan – and he was wearing a black tuxedo with the trousers rolled up.

I came back to reality with a start.

'So, what do you think of Bob Marley?' I blurted out.

34

'He verrrry overrated.'

'What kind of music do you like?'

'S Club 7, Boyzone.' He broke into his own version of 'S Club Party', swinging his shoulders from side to side and singing in a deep, husky voice.

'You don't strike me as an S Club 7 kind of guy.'

He coughed and puffed out his chest. 'Well, me favourite singer dough be Bounty Killer.'

'Who?' I'd never heard of him, but I was feeling a bit peckish. I could have killed for a Bounty myself.

'He cool, mon.' He nodded, sucking his teeth. 'I tek you der one day. You and me, we av babies together.'

Where? To see Bounty Boy?

'That would be...lovely.'

BONG!

He swaggered off, all thoughts of babies with me and Bounties forgotten.

Then it was the turn of Mr. Porsche, and I was not looking forward to this!

'Hello, I'm Wayne, nice to meet you. I love your outfit.' He held his hand out to shake mine.

'Hello, Wayne.' I smiled sweetly. 'We've met before, haven't we?'

'Have we?' He sat down, trying to place me.

'Yes, I'm the "dirty bitch" from yesterday.'

He narrowed his eyes at me. 'You! Do you always go round shitting on pavements?'

'Do you always call people rude names?'

'Only when there's a complete and utter need for it.'

'Anyway, it wasn't me, it was the dog.'

'Same difference, dogs shouldn't be allowed on the path.' He shrugged.

'How do you propose they get to the park, then? Helicopter? Anyway, I cleared it up!'

'Well, I should bloody well hope so,' he said.

'So Wayne, what do you do, when you're not being so self-righteous?'

'I'm a stockbroker, a pretty dammed good one too. And what do you do when you're not running round shitting all over the place?'

'It wasn't even my dog.'

35

'Oh, well, that's all right, then!'

'Have you got a phobia about dogs or something?'

'Only their shit, which carries hundreds of bacteria.' He steepled his fingers and reclined on the chair.

'Well, you don't have to eat it.'

'Did you know that dogs not only carry E.coli, but also giarda, parasites, salmonella and faecal coliform bacteria?'

'Strangely...no.' I leaned in closer to him. 'Do you eat chicken?'

'Yes, what's that got to do with anything?'

'Did you know that chicken is the only known carrier of spongicefalitis?'

'No.'

'Well, it is. And do you know what that does to you?' I didn't know what the hell it did to you either. I'd only just made it up that second.

He looked puzzled. 'No.'

'Well, it's the same kind of virus as ebola. The symptoms are vomiting, diarrhoea, internal bleeding, an excruciating amount of pain, and then finally organ failure and death.' I sat back with a smug smile on my face. He was just about to ask a question when Miss Whiplash bonged again. He walked off deep in thought.

'Right, everyone, please write a list of the people you would like to swap details with and then hand it to me,' Miss Whiplash ordered.

Everyone started writing energetically and I scanned the room. I knew there was only going to be one person on my list. Nick.

We handed in the sheets, milled around and waited expectantly. Hippo waddled up to Mr. Porsche, bragging about how many dates he'd get.

'OK, then,' she said when she'd finished. 'If you queue up here I'll hand out your papers and then the rest – as they say – is up to you.'

When it came to my turn, I grabbed mine and hot-footed it out to the loos, hoping that by the time I left everyone else would be gone. I texted Ayshe to come and pick me up, then scanned the form with interest.

The men who wanted to swap details with me were: Sean, Wayne, Nick and Kingston, although I thought Kingston would have swapped details with anybody that had a pulse and Mr.

Porsche just wanted to find out how to avoid spongicefalitis. As the only person I wanted to meet again was Nick, his were the only contact details on the sheet.

I leaned back against the wall and thought of Nick. A smile crept up to the corners of my mouth.

# Chapter 6

I cranked open the loo door an inch and peered out. Only a couple of stragglers remained so I propelled my way to the entrance where I discovered Kalem waiting for me in the Land Rover.

Oh God, he was still here. I knew he would thoroughly enjoy taking me to pieces, bit by agonizing bit.

'What are you doing here?' I looked around to see if anyone had seen me.

'Oh, that's nice isn't it?'

I climbed in.

'Come on, spill the beans. Why were you at the speed-dating?'

'I thought it was the B.O.G meeting tonight. We usually have one a month here, but I must've got the date wrong.' He tried to shift the Land Rover into gear, but it made a loud crunching sound as he jammed the gear-stick backwards and forwards until it hit the right spot.

I giggled. 'What's a B.O.G meeting? Sounds a bit dirty to me. Do you roll around in manure, or have mud wrestling competitions?'

He glanced over at me. 'No, it's the Biodegradable Organic Group. We're co-coordinating a local action group to raise awareness about local organic produce and environmental issues.'

'Sounds like heaps of fun.'

'It is.' He turned his head back to the road. 'Let's take you, for example–'

'What about me?'

'Well, when you buy your milk, do you have any idea the process it takes to make it, or where it comes from?'

'Tesco?' I said, studying his profile.

He tutted. 'What about…chickens. Where do you think they come from?'

I turned my head back, gazing at the open road. 'Tesco, and sometimes Sainsburys.'

He shook his head slowly. 'Do you know the difference between organic chickens and battery chickens?'

'No.'

'Well you should. If you knew the conditions that battery chickens were kept in, anyone with an ounce of human decency wouldn't buy it.' He paused. 'Did you know that there are hundreds and hundreds of chickens crushed together twenty-four hours a day in tiny little pens, covered with their own urine and faeces? Or that they often suffer from broken legs and wings with no medical treatment, and sometimes have to share their pen with the bodies of their fellow chickens that've died a painful death?'

I screwed my face up. 'Urgh.'

'And not only that: they have no exercise; they get no fresh air or see the light of day in their short, miserable lives.' His eyes glanced in my direction and then back to the road.

'How depressing.'

'Well, if you think it's depressing, think how the poor chickens feel.' His voice wavered. 'You have to buy organic. It's the only animal friendly thing to buy.'

'Can't we talk about something else? I gazed out of the window.

'Like what?'

'Why do you drive this old heap? Why don't you trade it in for a new Range Rover or something a bit sporty?' My eyes wandered round the rusty interior, taking in the spider's webs.

He shrugged. 'I just like the simple things in life.'

'Well this certainly fits the description.'

He glanced in the rear-view mirror and jerked the car to a halt, looking at me in silence.

'What?' I asked.

'Would you prefer to walk home?' His eyes challenged me.

'Um…' I tilted my head for a second. 'No.' I matched his gaze.

'Well, shut up, then!' He hit the accelerator and drove off again. 'Did you know seventy per cent of all Land Rovers are still on the road today?

He was such an anorak.

'I can honestly say I didn't know that, and…to be honest I don't really care.'

'Well they are.'

'Thanks for that piece of useless information. I'm sure I'll sleep better at night now, knowing that.'

'Anyway, how would I get to my B.O.G meetings in the

country if I was driving a Jaguar or a Porsche?'

'Walk?'

'I see you dressed up for the occasion.' He gave me the once-over.

'I don't think you're one to talk.' I glanced at his desert camouflage army trousers; they had a gaping hole big enough to fit a small pterodactyl through.

'I've been working on the Land Rover.'

'Oh.' I stared out of the window.

We drove quietly for a while, lost in our thoughts – his were probably something that involved dirty, smelly engines. Mine involved plumbers in sexy-looking boiler suits – unbuttoned at the chest – waving a spanner in one hand and a bag of tap washers seductively in the other.

He broke the silence, shouting over the spluttering of the engine. 'So, have you seen Justin lately?'

'No.'

'You must have really loved him, eh?' His voice softened.

'Yes…yes, I did.'

After a pause: 'He didn't love you, though, did he?' His sarcasm sliced through the air.

'Oh, shut up.' I punched him on the arm.

'And now he's shagging his boss, best sex he's ever had apparently.' He turned to look at me with a straight face.

I gazed at him, then we both smiled and burst out laughing. 'Anyway, I've got a date!'

'Have you now? Not with that big fat bloke, is it?'

'Oh God, he was a pig. No; someone else. He's going to take me to a boxing match.' I thought of Nick and felt a slight glow.

'But you hate boxing!'

'I know, but I quite liked the guy who asked me, so I thought I'd give it a try.'

'Hang on a minute. Wasn't it you who described boxing as a bunch of thuggy-looking blokes punching the crap out of each other for money?'

'I might have said something like that.' I turned my head to avoid him.

'You did. I distinctly remember it,' he said, pulling up outside my flat.

I scrambled out, then leaned back into the car. 'I'm sure it'll be more interesting than a B.O.G meeting.' I grinned.

# Chapter 7
## Wednesday, day 3 – I Hate Modern Art

The next morning I awoke to the sound of the phone ringing with annoying persistence in my ear. I'd fallen into an exhausted slumber after my mishaps of the previous forty-eight hours.

'Did I wake you up? It's after nine,' Ayshe's voice gurgled down the phone.

'No, I had to get up to answer the phone anyway.' I rubbed my eyes.

'You've got to give me all the gossip on last night.'

I sat up, yawning. 'You wouldn't believe it. It was positively hellish.'

'I've thrown a sicky today. Got some boring board meeting – they should be called "bored" meetings – I don't need to be there anyway. Do you want to come up for breakfast?'

'I'd love to. Give me ten minutes and I'll be up. Get the bacon butties on.'

'Only if you don't tell Mum and Dad.'

'What?'

'You know; Muslims consider pigs to be unclean. Even though my parents have lived in the UK for fifty years, and they're not religious, they've still got a thing about not eating pork. Me and Kalem haven't had the heart to tell them we love bacon.'

I leapt out of bed, caught my foot in the corner of the duvet and fell into a heap on the floor. Picking myself up, I scrambled around for something to wear and then marched up the stairs to Ayshe's.

'Morning.' I breezed in to the sound of bacon sizzling under the grill. Atila was making sandwiches in the kitchen and Kalem was sprawled out on the sofa, having devoured half of his already.

Ayshe's black and white cat, Felix, inched his way over towards Kalem, sniffing the air with anticipation.

After a hearty breakfast, I filled Ayshe in on the details of last night. We huddled together in the kitchen so that the boys couldn't overhear us.

'So I've got a date...maybe. I guess I'll just have to see if he

41

calls me.'

'See, I knew this challenge thing would work!'

'So, does a date count as a challenge, then?' I asked.

She furrowed her brow for a minute, deep in thought. 'Yes.'

'Well, tonight I've been invited to an art exhibition, and that can count as one of my challenges. I've never done that before, but I've got no one to go with. Please say you'll come.'

'Oh, no! I can't tonight. We've got to go and see the manager of the Priory. There's been some kind of misunderstanding about the colour scheme for our wedding reception. We ordered lilac and cream for the ribbons and table decorations, but the ones which have come in are puce. I haven't got a clue what sort of colour puce is – although it sounds utterly revolting – so we've got go over and see if they'll do.' She pulled a disgusted face.

'Oh.' I sighed. I could hardly go on my own.

'What about Kalem? He's into arty things. There might be a spot of woodcarving to get him excited.'

'No, it's OK, don't worry. I'll have to think of something else for today's challenge,' I said.

Kalem chose that moment to saunter into the kitchen and deposit his plate in the sink. 'You girls talking about me again?'

'Helen needs someone to go with her to an art exhibition tonight, and we've got to see this woman about our puce decorations.'

He shrugged. 'Yeah, I'll go.'

'What about Emine, won't she mind?' I glanced at him.

Emine was Kalem's rich, Turkish Cypriot girlfriend who was always dragging him off to dinner parties with her horsey friends and trying to get him to eat nouvelle cuisine. She carried around a whole chemist's supply of Esteé Lauder-this and Láncome-that, all stuffed into a massive handbag, and refused to leave the house without full make-up on and far too much dark lip-liner, which gave her an odd-looking trout-pout. Not that I'm being bitchy, of course.

'No,' he replied.

'I think they've had a row,' Ayshe whispered to me.

'Whatever,' he muttered, wandering back to the lounge.

'Right, that's settled. Oh, and I've thought up a challenge for tomorrow too,' Ayshe said.

Great. 'Oh, excellent' When she didn't enlighten me, I gazed at her. 'Well?'

'I'll tell you tomorrow.' She smiled.

'Now breakfast is out the way, I'm going to start on one of my new chocolate recipes. I've realized that the only way to be taken seriously as a chef is to write a book,' Atila said, jumping to his feet and busying himself in the kitchen. At six foot two he had difficulty leaning over the beech kitchen worktop and had to jack-knife over it. His floppy hairdo kept falling into his eyes. He pushed it away, totally engrossed in his task.

'Goody, I love chocolate,' I said.

'I've been thinking of a title for it. You know how sex sells everything these days? All this Naked Chef stuff and Nigella Lawson sexing it up in the kitchen. I've been thinking about calling it Foreplay in the Kitchen, Sex in the Diningroom. What do you think?' He beamed at us.

'Your mum won't like it,' Ayshe said. 'She even turns the TV off if they mention the word "sex".'

'Why not? We're the second generation Turkish Cypriots with a London influence: an infusion of both cultures. Times are changing and we have to keep up with them.'

'I'd buy it,' I replied.

Ayshe planted a kiss on Atila's lips and gazed up at him. I felt a burst of envy and looked away. They were so well suited – both bubbly, happy people. They'd met at the opening night of his new restaurant. Ayshe hadn't been impressed when we'd had to wait two hours for our dinner to arrive, and even less impressed when she'd noticed a dirty finger mark on the edge of her plate. Unfortunately, the inexperienced waitress repeated Atila's response to Ayshe's complaint word-for-word, which was something like: 'You can tell the fussy cow that it doesn't come out of an effing tin. She can bloody well inspect the kitchen for herself if she wants to.' Which Ayshe did, storming off into the kitchen to confront the rude little man. After she'd been suitably impressed by his culinary skills and his art of persuasion, a quick courtship followed. They got engaged and moved in together shortly afterwards. He was normally very calm and chilled out, although I had witnessed him in the restaurant, barking orders and swearing constantly. It was all very like Gordon Ramsey. Strange how all these chefs turned into Jekyll and Hyde characters the minute they stepped foot into a kitchen.

An hour later, my stomach was grumbling as a luscious aroma

43

wafted from the huge Range which took up most of the tightly-packed kitchen.

'Da-dah!' Atila presented us with a round, chocolatey, doughnut-looking thing on a plate. It had a slightly hard shell and a manicured dollop of cream was gently melting on the side.

'Looks great.' I sniffed it.

'Wait until you cut into it.' He eyed us.

I stuck my spoon in and a rich dark chocolate sauce oozed out.

'Ooh, that's gorge...' Ayshe said.

'Mmm...' I took a bite. 'Awww...' Then another. 'That is fab.' I licked the spoon dry, savouring the experience.

Kalem ate his in two minutes flat. 'What's all the fuss about? It's just chocolate.'

'You can't get in the way of a woman and her chocolate, though.' Ayshe gulped down another mouthful.

Atila sat on the arm of the sofa, his eyes twinkling with glee. 'What should I call it, then?' He looked around the room, waiting for suggestions.

'Well, if it was mine, I think I'd have to call it "a chocolate orgasm",' I said, breaking into a post-orgasm type of grin, polishing off every last morsel on my plate and then looking to see if I could nick some of Ayshe's. 'Now that is what women really want.'

'Yes!' Atila slammed the palm of his hand on his knee. 'That's it, that's it. Perfect for a sexy cookbook.' He grabbed my face and planted a kiss on my cheek. 'Anyone for another?'

'I don't know. Are we talking about real ones or chocolate ones?' I asked.

The warmth of the art gallery hit me as we walked in from the crisp night air. Low conversation hummed as people wandered about, drinks in hand, looking at various paintings. Surprisingly, Kalem had ditched his usual scruffy clothes and had instead opted for a smart casual look. He actually scrubbed up pretty well when he made the effort.

'Drink?' A waitress offered us a tray of glasses and winked at Kalem.

'Did she just wink at you?' I hissed.

'I get it all the time,' he muttered, wandering over to a humongous piece of artwork, which was drawing a lot of attention.

I tutted. If anyone was likely to be chatted up tonight it was going to be him!

The painting was set on a white background, covered with multi-coloured splashes of paint. It looked like a five-year-old had splattered paint across the canvas in a tantrum. In fact, I distinctly remembered doing the same thing at nursery school.

'That is fabulous,' an elderly man standing next to us said to his wife.

'The expression in it is so…captivating,' his wife said.

I craned my neck, looking for the title of this particular piece. *Colourful Ejaculation*, it read. The price tag next to it was four hundred pounds. I sipped my wine and almost gagged.

'It's absolute crap. A two-year-old could have done that, and he wants four hundred for it. I could make that at home for about a fiver,' Kalem whispered.

I glanced round to see if anyone had heard him. 'Shush! Don't embarrass me.'

Adrian chose that particular moment to creep up behind us.

'Helen! What do you think?' He swept his arm round the room, drawing our attention to all his paintings.

'Well, we've only just arrived, but it's great,' I fibbed.

'Come with me. I've got to show you this.' Adrian completely ignored Kalem and led me by the arm to a much smaller piece which was a series of black and grey slashes of paint with a huge eyeball in the centre.

Did people actually buy this stuff?

Adrian peered at me. 'Well? What are you getting from it?'

'Grey and black with quite a lot of red?' I blurted out.

Kalem cracked up with laughter.

I narrowed my eyes at him.

'You're not getting subtlety and representationalism?' Adrian asked.

What the hell was that? 'Yes…a bit of that too.' I nodded.

Kalem rolled his eyes to the ceiling.

Adrian waved at someone in the distance. 'Oh sorry, I must mingle. Please, enjoy!'

'I need another glass of wine.' My eyes sought out the waitress who was over in the corner chatting up a man old enough to be her father.

'Get me one while you're there.' Kalem handed me his empty glass.

I returned with some refills. 'Come and look at this one.' I led him over to the picture I'd seen at Annabel's house.

I studied it hard. 'If you look closely, there's something hidden in it.'

He leaned over to get a better look. 'What? All I can see is a little stick-like man and some blobby things.'

'Ah, I don't know. I couldn't see it either, but it's very expressionalistic.' Was there even such a word?

He muttered something under his breath.

'What?'

He sighed. 'Nothing.'

'I think this stuff is great. I might even buy something.'

'Are you crazy? Actually, I think you are.' He turned to face me. 'What is it with you and these weird challenges you keep doing?'

'What's wrong with it? It's about time I got out and had some fun.'

'But you're pretending to be something you're not, just to try and get a bloke. It's never going to work.' He grabbed my arm, looking deep into my eyes.

I shook him off and my glass of red wine erupted like a volcano down the front of my dazzling white shirt. I gazed down aghast.

'I'm really sorry,' he said, looking sheepish.

As people turned round to gawk, I pushed past him in search of the loos. How embarrassing! And who was he to tell me what I should and shouldn't do? I'd bloody well show him. I dabbed at the stain with a paper towel and some water, but it just smeared into an even bigger mess. Maybe no one would notice as it now blended right in with the collection of art hanging on the walls.

When I made my way back, Kalem had got fresh glasses for us both. I took one and glared at him.

'I'm sorry,' he whispered.

'It's OK. Don't think this is going to come out, though.' I looked down at my shirt. 'You'll have to fork out for another one.'

'Of course.' He looked away, shame-faced.

'I'm going to buy that colourful ejaculation,' I said, and stalked off in search of Adrian.

'You'll regret it.' Kalem trailed behind me.

Adrian was deep in thoughtful conversation with a couple who had their backs to me.

'Ah, Adrian,' I butted in.

'Oh, it's Helen, isn't it?' The woman turned to me.

'Clarissa! How are you?' I was surprised to see her. I hadn't clapped eyes on her since my college days when she'd been a stunner and always had loads of hot dates. I couldn't believe how much she'd changed. I'd been taking photography and Clarissa was doing a beauty therapy course, but looking at her now, you'd never have guessed.

'I'm absolutely wonderful. This is Charles.' She took hold of her husband's arm. 'Oh! What happened to your top?'

'Slight accident.' I gritted my teeth. 'Nice to meet you, Charles. This is Kalem.' I jerked my head in Kalem's direction.

'Oh, it's so fabby so see you! It's been...God, ten years or something.'

I studied her with interest. She was the same age as me but looked much older and more frumpy. She had a 1980s perm and wore huge glasses. She'd put on quite a few pounds since the last time I'd seen her. In fact, she was positively chunky. I quickly checked her husband out. He was a chunk, too, with very lank, greasy-looking hair, which looked as though he'd dipped his head in their chip-pan.

'We're very close friends with Adrian. What do you think of his art?' She leaned towards me, smiling.

Kalem coughed, muttering something under his breath.

'It's brilliant.' I glowered at him. 'Actually, Adrian, I wanted to buy a piece.'

'Oh, which one? We've got our eye on a few pieces too,' Charles piped up.

'First sale of the night.' Adrian rubbed his hands together with glee.

'The ejaculation thingy.' I grinned at Kalem.

'But that's the biggest piece here!' Charles said.

I nodded. 'I know. It's great, isn't it?'

'We've got a number of Adrian's works. The most expensive was two thousand pounds. Can you believe it? And that was with a discount,' Clarissa said.

'Unfortunately there are a number of other people interested in it too,' Adrian said.

'We'll be bidding, won't we Clarissa?' Charles smiled at his wife.

'Of course.' She gave a vigorous nod of her head.

'You must excuse me. I'm going off to organize the bidding war.' Adrian sloped off.

'I'm so glad you've finally settled down.' Clarissa looked between Kalem and me.

'Oh...um...he's not–' I started.

'I always used to say you'd never find a man,' she cut in. 'It's so nice that you've finally found someone. You must come to dinner. Mustn't they Charles?' She glanced at her husband.

'Absolutely,' Charles agreed.

'Oh...well Kalem's not actually my–'

'Yes, how about Saturday? We can have a little dinner party. Just the four of us,' Clarissa insisted.

I looked at Kalem for some help, but he just raised his eyebrows.

'How about it?' Charles asked.

'How about it?' I turned to Kalem, willing him to get me out of this misunderstanding.

Instead he replied, 'Why not? We're not doing anything on Saturday, are we darling?'

'Er...no,' I muttered.

'Come to us at seven-thirty for eight. Do you know where we are?' She paused, then carried on without waiting for an answer. 'We're in Hampstead. We live in a lovely town house – very georgianesque.'

'Good, that's settled,' Charles said.

'Oh,' Clarissa shrieked, 'they're starting the auction. Quick, Charles, we must get a frontal position.' She dragged Charles off.

I cringed as a picture of Clarissa in the frontal position sprang to mind.

'Why didn't you say anything? She thinks we're a couple!' I hissed at Kalem.

'I know you think that's a crazy idea, but it was worth it to see you squirm.' He laughed. 'Come on, you wouldn't want to miss the auction, would you?'

A crowd of people had gathered around Adrian, jostling for a good position. Clarissa and Charles pushed their way to the front and waited eagerly for the auction to begin.

'Right, I'm starting the bidding for this at four hundred

pounds.' Adrian scanned the room. 'Thank you, sir.' He tipped his head to the elderly couple we had seen earlier.

Clarissa bobbed her head up and down like a rabbit in heat, scanning for potential bidders.

'Yes, madam, four hundred and twenty-five.' Adrian smiled at her and looked around.

My hand shot up.

'Thank you, four hundred and fifty.' He nodded at me.

Clarissa turned to see who else was bidding, and I looked away.

'Thank you sir, four hundred and seventy-five pounds.' The old couple had bid again.

'Five hundred!' Clarissa shouted.

'Thank you, madam! Any advance on five hundred?' Adrian asked.

I shot my hand up again. 'Five hundred and fifty!' I blurted out. All reason was gone now; it had vanished in a puff of smoke. I'd show them all!

Clarissa looked at me, whispering something to Charles, who shook his head. She then sighed loud enough to be heard in China.

Kalem elbowed me in the ribs. 'What are you doing?'

'Shush.' I elbowed him back.

'Are you nuts?'

'Any more offers?' Adrian went on. 'No?' He searched furiously for a reply. 'In that case; sold to the lady in the white and red shirt.' He pointed at me. Everyone stared, apart from Clarissa and Charles, who stuck their noses in the air.

I scribbled out a cheque and handed it to Adrian together with my address and telephone number. If I completed the transaction as quickly as possible, maybe I could ignore the fact I'd just spent so much bloody money on the worst painting I'd ever seen, just to annoy Kalem. I decided to make a hasty exit and dragged Kalem out of the door before I did anything else I would regret in the morning.

As I walked with Kalem back to the Land Rover, he didn't say a word, which was even more annoying than if he'd called me a nutcase. I gazed up at the stars, glinting like cat's eyes, cursing myself for being so stupid. An owl did a graceful fly-by, but instead of the usual twit-twoo, I was convinced it sounded more like, idiot too. Even the wildlife was laughing at me. I shook my

49

head – it couldn't possibly be saying that!

We rumbled along through the darkness in silence.

'What's up?' I asked when we pulled up outside the flats.

'It's your money, but you don't even like it.'

'How do you know I don't?'

'I just know.'

I leaned back, folding my arms. 'Saturday will be a fun night, then.' I changed the subject.

'Mmm.'

'You don't have to come.'

'Yes, but I want to see what other ridiculous situations you get yourself into. It's actually quite fun,' he replied, winking at me, which suddenly gave me a curious, fluttering sensation in the pit of my stomach.

# Chapter 8
## Thursday, day 4 – I Want a Baby

Oh, craparama, I thought, waking up to the reality of what I'd done last night. How could I be such an idiot? I put it down to being premenstrual and slightly not-quite-right in the head.

My mobile rang, cutting into my thoughts of self-doubt and loathing.

'Hello?' I answered, sitting up in bed.

'Helen, it's Angie.'

'Hi, how are you?' I smiled. I hadn't seen Angie in ages.

'Great. Listen, I was just wondering if you've organized a stripper for Ayshe's hen night yet – only Barry said he'd do the honours if you haven't.'

Her husband, Barry, was not my idea of a sexy strip-a-gram with his puny shoulders and a miniature pot belly – and he had bandy legs – what was she thinking?

I almost had to ram my fist in my mouth to stifle the urge to giggle. 'No, it's all sorted. You don't have to worry.' I imagined Barry getting down and dirty on Ayshe's knee and shivered.

'OK, never mind, then. Think he was getting a bit excited about it. Ooh, and guess what? He's put me in for this week's *Reader's Wives'* in the *Porno Monthly Magazine.*'

I couldn't contain myself and had to put my hand over the phone, so she wouldn't hear me laughing. 'Excellent news, I'm sure your parents will be thrilled to bits.'

'Anyway, gotta go. Lauren's just puked up all over my riding crop.'

'How did a one year old get hold of a riding crop? Anyway, you don't go riding!' I said.

'You just wait until you're married. You'll need to do a few things to spice it up in the bedroom too. Or maybe I'll just swap Barry for a new vibrator and a bar of chocolate!' She giggled. 'Alright then, see you next week. No! Don't touch the Rabbit!' she shrieked to Lauren as she hung up.

As soon as I'd snapped my mobile shut, it meowed at me. I flipped it open. It was a text from Ayshe: 'Your mission of the day – hospital-visiting. Report to the children's ward at Queen Elizabeth Hospital at two o'clock. Be there or be square! And I heard what you did last night – are you mental?'

Well, that wasn't so bad. I loved kids. In fact, I wanted a whole brood of them. The only trouble was finding the right person to have them with and by the time that happened my eggs might have shrivelled up like sun-dried tomatoes.

So I strolled up to the hospital and presented myself to the Ward Sister promptly at two, complete with a handful of KitKats and a collection of Barbie magazines.

'I'm so glad you've come,' Sister said. 'Poor little mites, they get so bored in here. It's nice to see young people taking the time and trouble to do some visiting.'

She led me down the corridor to an alcove with four beds in it and a large window to one side. A play-pen containing games, toys, and books took up most of one corner. One of the beds was empty, but the other three were occupied. The one nearest the window was home to a geeky-looking blond boy with an enormous forehead, who was busy reading a book on astrology. On the bed next to him was an older boy, who was asleep and snoring with his mouth open, surrounded by various electronic hand held games. The first bed I came to housed a small and rather cute boy of about five with a very long fringe like a pair of curtains, which almost covered his eyes.

'Here we are. If you can take this part of the ward, we've got some other visitors doing the rest. This is Timmy.' She pointed to the cute one. 'And then we have Hugo in the corner.' This was the one with the big forehead. 'And John.' She nodded at sleepy.

'Hello.' Hugo looked at me. 'Are you our volunteer for the day?'

'Yes, I'm Helen.'

'I've had my tonsils out,' Hugo said, then instantly changed the subject. 'I think you should see Timmy first, he's a bit down.' He gave me a wise nod.

'OK.' I sat down on the plastic chair next to Timmy's bed. 'What are you in for?' I looked at him.

'I've had my dicks cut out,' Timmy whispered.

'Sorry?' I sat back, surprised.

'It was hurting and they had to cut it out.' He looked down at the sheet, fiddling with the edges.

'Oh, my God, that's awful.' I took his little hand in mine. 'Did you have two of them, then?'

'No, only one I think.'

'How do you go to the loo?' I asked.

'With my tinky.' He squinted up at me.

'Didn't you just say they had cut if off, darling?'

Hugo jumped in. 'They didn't cut his dick off. They took his appendix out.'

'Oh, I see!' I nodded with relief.

'I think sharks are nasty and ugly and have big teeth, just like Billy Gibson. He's not my friend no more.' Timmy turned on his side, looking at me with miserable brown eyes.

I stifled a giggle.

'How do mermaids get pregnant?' he asked.

'Er...' I quickly changed the subject. 'Do you want a KitKat?' I whipped open my handbag, dived in and pulled one out.

'He's not allowed any sweets at the moment,' Hugo interjected. 'Nurse says so.'

I put it in the locker beside his bed. 'I'll leave it in here, and you can eat it when nurse says so. OK?'

'OK,' he replied, eyeing the KitKat with interest. 'Can you get me a book, please?'

I wandered over to the corner of the ward, rummaging around in the books. 'Any particular one?' I looked over my shoulder at him.

'The one about the dolphin and the radiogator.' Timmy smiled for the first time.

'The what?'

'He means the dolphin and the alligator,' Hugo said.

I grabbed the book and took it over to him. 'Here you go.' I ruffled his hair. 'Are you OK now?'

'Mmm. Did you know that dolphins breathe out of a bum on the top of their heads?' he replied, then became engrossed in the story.

'Come and talk to me.' Hugo put down his book.

I picked up my bag and sat next to him. By this time John had started waking up and glared at me.

'Who's that thing?' John asked Hugo, pointing at me.

'Hi, John, I'm Helen, your visitor for the day. Did you have a nice sleep?'

He replied with a blank look.

'I'll come over and see you in a minute.' I smiled at him.

'Just ignore him.' Hugo leaned in towards me. 'He's really

53

rude!'

I picked up Hugo's book, examining it. 'So you like astrology?'

'It's very interesting.' Hugo nodded at me. 'I bet I can guess what star sign you are.'

'OK, go on, then.' I wriggled in my seat.

He put his fingertips to his temples and concentrated. 'Gemini. Am I right?'

'Wow, are you psychic?'

'Ah, so I am right. The sign of the twins.' He paused. 'Do you have a split personality?' He scratched his head.

'Well, half of me thinks so, the other half's not so sure. What sign are you?'

'Leo. We're very compatible, then.' He gave me a cute smile. 'Why are you visiting us?'

You know how every now and then, you meet someone that you have some kind of spooky connection with, like you've known them for years? That's how it was with Hugo. He had this reassuring air about him that made me want to unburden myself. I told him all about Justin and the fourteen day challenge, and it actually felt therapeutic to talk about it with a complete stranger, even if he was only a little boy. He didn't even think I was a fruit loop, which was a bonus.

'I think you're very brave, trying all these new things. Most people are scared of change, you know – hey, I've got a good idea. Have you ever had your Tarot cards read before?'

'No.'

'Shall I give you a reading? You might be able to find out how this challenge is going to end.' He reached over to a pack of cards resting on his bedside table.

'Oh, yeah.'

He handed me the pack. 'OK, you have to shuffle them really, really well and then take one out and lay it face up here.' He pointed to the bed cover in front of him.

I shuffled for a few minutes, then turned one over and placed it down. 'Death.' I pulled a slightly disturbed face. 'That doesn't sound very good.' I glanced at him, bubbling with anxiety.

'It's quite a good one actually. It means changes are going to happen. You're entering a growing phase, and you have to get rid of old and unhelpful habits.' He read out from a little booklet.

'Interesting.' I picked another card.

'Ah, the Empress.' He flicked through his book. 'This is a good one. You may be pregnant or have impending news of a wedding or of children arriving.' He tapped the card.

I thought about Ayshe's wedding. Maybe Hugo really was psychic and did have the gift for reading these things. 'Right, this one is the High Priestess.' I laid it down in front of him.

'Another good one. It means you have to act more on feelings than facts, and trust your intuition.'

'Oh, good.' I laid down another. 'The Magician.'

Hugo had a quick shufti at the book again. 'Now is the time to stretch yourself to new limits. You have to be daring and adventurous.'

'Why are you talking to the swat?' John butted in, wiping his snotty nose on his arm.

I smiled at John and then turned my attention back to Hugo.

'I'm going to boarding school soon,' Hugo said.

'Wow, how old are you?' I asked.

John threw an Action Man, and it hit me on the leg. I rubbed my leg and tried to ignore him.

Hugo leaned past me, frowning at John 'I'm ten. But I'm much more intelligent than my age.'

I had a sneaking suspicion he was right. 'Won't you miss your mum and dad?'

'No, I don't see them much, they're too busy working. I have a nanny,' Hugo replied.

'That's coz they don't like you,' John said.

'Shut up!' Hugo flushed. 'Tell him to shut up.' He looked at me.

'John, I'll come and see you in a minute. Why don't you let me talk to Hugo?' I asked.

John glared at me, huffing in a loud voice. He started cramming sweets into his mouth and throwing the wrappers on the floor.

'Nurse will tell you off.' Hugo pointed at the wrappers.

'Nurse will tell you off,' John mimicked and carried on regardless.

'Why don't you put those in the bin?' I nodded at the wrappers, looking at John.

'Why don't you make me?' John scoffed.

'You could always play with your computer games until I get to you,' I said to John.

He stared at me for a while and then picked one up, fiddling with the controls.

I turned back to Hugo. 'Have you got any brothers and sisters?'

'No, I'm an only child.'

'Well, never mind. I'm sure when you go to boarding school you'll make lots and lots of friends.'

'No he won't,' John snapped.

'Yes I will!' Hugo shouted.

John sat up in bed and pulled a face at us.

After half an hour of John's annoying banter, Hugo had finally had enough.

'Shut up!' Hugo shouted.

I looked at Timmy, who was reading and stuffing the illegal KitKat into his mouth.

'You shut up.' John turned his nose up at Hugo.

I swivelled in my chair, rested my elbows on the back of it, looking at John. 'Do you know what doctors do to little boys who are naughty?'

'What?' He stuck his chin in the air, defiant but curious.

'They take away all their toys and give them to children who are being good,' I said.

'Oh, yeah! They can't do that.'

'They can and they do,' I informed him.

John's eyes darted between Hugo and me. Apprehension slowly registered on his face as he tried to decide whether all his toys would be carted off. 'How do you know?' He was wary, just in case I was actually telling the truth, but I didn't think he was convinced.

'Oh.' I raked my hand through my hair. 'It's well known, isn't it Hugo?'

Hugo took my cue and nodded. 'Oh yes, it's definitely true.'

That seemed to shut John up for a while, so I carried on with Hugo. 'Would you like a chocolate bar and a magazine? Sorry, but I've only got a girls' magazine. It's Barbie.'

'That's OK. It's good to learn about the opposite sex. Justin probably should've read Barbie.'

'Ha! You're reading a girl's one. Hugo's gay, Hugo's gay.' John stood up on his bed and started jumping up and down on it.

'Get down,' I hissed at him

'Make me, make me!' He jumped harder.

He certainly wouldn't be getting a Barbie magazine, I thought. And this week there was a special feature on beauty tips and the latest gossip about Barbie and Ken.

'You can't take away my toys.' John pointed his finger at me. 'My mum will beat the shit out of you!'

'That's no way to speak to a lady,' Hugo warned.

I shifted in my chair and faced John. 'Why will your mum beat me up?'

'She just will. She beats everyone up. I'm going to tell my mum, she's going to beat you up,' He chanted.

'John, get back under the covers and be quiet!' Sister came in and tucked him in bed so tight that he couldn't move. 'He's trouble, that one,' she said to me, then hurried off.

I thought about suggesting to her that perhaps an enema might shut John up, but she'd already gone.

I gathered up my bag and handed Hugo the rest of the KitKats. 'Here, you can have these, you're such a sweetie.' I gave him a kiss on the head.

'I wish you were my mum.' Hugo gave me a solemn smile.

I swallowed back a lump in my throat the size of a boiled egg because at that moment, I wished for the same thing. 'Somehow, I think you'll be just fine as you are.'

'So will you.' He waved the Tarot cards at me.

As I hurried out of the alcove, I passed a big, butch woman stomping up the corridor. Her sleeves were rolled up, revealing arms covered in tattoos from elbows to knuckles. She gave me a dirty look as I walked off. In the distance, John was telling her I'd been horrible to him, and he thought that she should give me a good kicking. I didn't really want my face rearranged, so I rushed down the corridor like the Energizer Bunny with new batteries.

As I turned the corner, I bumped into somebody and my bag went flying, spewing its contents all over the polished floor.

'Uf,' I exclaimed, as I eyed – among various other things – my shimmering lipstick and Tampax rolling along the floor.

'Helen Grey!'

I glanced up to see Dr Savage. 'Hi.' I scrabbled around on the floor, picking things up and stuffing them back into my bag.

'Are these yours?' He picked up a pair of red, furry handcuffs I'd recently bought to give to Ayshe on her hen night.

'Um…yes, but, they're not really mine.'

'That's what they all say.'

'Do you normally pick up furry handcuffs that have jumped out of people's bags? Is it an occupational hazard?' I laughed.

He smiled at me, looking confused. 'Well, actually no. How's that ankle of yours?' He bent down and felt it. 'Looks OK.'

I shot a dismissive hand through the air. 'Oh, it's fine.'

'Are you visiting someone?'

'I've been visiting the children's ward.'

'How sweet of you. Listen, I tried to call you to check on your ankle, but I think I must've written your number down wrong. I've been looking out for you in the park, but haven't seen you walking your dog.'

'Well, it wasn't actually my dog.' I didn't really want to admit that I'd borrowed it for the occasion in case I sounded like a loser with a capital L.

He put his hand on my elbow, steering me towards the main entrance. 'Ah, that explains it. Listen, I wonder if you fancy going out for a meal with me sometime?'

'I'd love to!' Wow, this challenge thing was really hotting up.

'Great. How about tomorrow night?'

'Um...' I tilted my head, giving the impression of trying to recall what my enormous social diary held for me. I tapped my forefinger on my cheek for a few seconds. 'Yes, that's fine.'

'Well, I have your address, so I'll pick you up at seven-thirty?'

'Yes, OK. I'll see you tomorrow.' I watched him wander back into the hospital and sneaked a quick shufti at his backside.

I was still admiring the view when I heard a familiar voice call my name from behind me. My jaw dropped. It couldn't be. No, I was hearing things.

I heard it again.

I panicked. Breathe. My mouth drained of saliva as I spun round and came face to face with Justin.

'Helen! I thought it was you.' The corners of his blue eyes creased as he dazzled me with his icy-white teeth.

I swallowed hard, trying to bring some moisture back to my parched throat.

'J...Justin. What a surprise. What are you doing here?' Needles danced a beat on my scalp.

'I've come to visit a friend – actually a friend of a friend.'

'I'm sorry to hear that. Is it anyone I know?'

'No one you know.' The words sounded forced.

'Oh…good.' I paused, wondering what to say to him. 'Which ward are they in?' I thought I'd try and make polite conversation.

'Er…the…' he coughed loudly into his hand, masking his words. I could've sworn he said maternity ward, though. 'How are you anyway? You look great.' His eyes wandered over my body, lingering on my breasts.

'I'm dry – I mean…fine.' My hand shot to my throat and fiddled with my necklace.

'You certainly look fine.'

'Well so do you.' I glanced at his expensive suit and immaculate hair.

'Have you got time for a coffee?' He reached out and put his hand under my elbow, steering me inside towards the cafeteria.

I was powerless to say no. Somehow I managed to put one foot in front of the other even though inside I'd turned to gravy.

He stood next to me in the queue as if this was the most natural thing in the world, as if we'd never been apart. I sniffed the air next to me, breathing in his familiar spicy aftershave.

'Why don't we sit by the window?' He headed off towards a table.

I sat down, resting my coffee in front of me. My throat ached for moisture, but I couldn't drink it. The way I felt now, I'd probably end up pouring it all over myself.

He grabbed my hand, taking me by surprise. 'Helen, I've missed you so much. I'm so glad I ran into you. I've been trying to pluck up the courage to phone you for weeks.'

I felt his soft, perfectly manicured hand resting in mine, his thumb gently stoking my fingers. The effect was explosive. And scary.

'Have you?' I managed finally.

'I've been thinking a lot lately, and…I want to try again.' His thumb worked its way underneath my palm. Light, feathery touches designed to make me cave in.

'Oh!' This was the last thing I expected to hear.

He took a sip of coffee, his eyes wandering over my face, drinking me in. 'I know I've made a mistake, but I really want you back.'

I leaned back against the chair. 'Well…this is a big surprise Justin. I'm…I wasn't expecting this at all.' I slipped my hand from his. My head was spinning. Did I want this? Did I want him back? I'd spent the last six months trying to get over him.

'Are you seeing someone else?' Justin asked.

I shook my head as a nervous laugh escaped from my lips. 'No…It's just that this is a big shock.'

He ran a hand through his spiky hair. It wobbled slightly, then fell back into place. 'I can understand that and–' his gaze travelled to his Rolex. 'Damn!'

'What's the matter?'

'I'm sorry, but I've got a meeting in five minutes on the other side of town.' He rose from the chair. 'Look, here's what we'll do; I'll let you think about things for a while and give you a ring next week to see how you feel. I've been a very bad boy, I know that. But I know we belong together. You're the only woman for me, Helen. We can talk next week and try to sort things out. I won't pressure you, I promise.'

He looked so sincere I almost jumped into his arms, but my brain was screaming a warning at me.

'Remember, I'll call you.' He took hold of my hand again and lifted it to his lips. Softly, he kissed the back of my hand and strode away.

When he'd gone, I pinched myself to see if it was real. As quickly as he'd swept back into my life, he'd gone again. I'd dreamed of this moment for so long and yet when it happened, somehow it felt wrong. I'd imagined more apologies, more promises that things would change, but there was none of that. I thought the conversation would be longer, deeper, more heartfelt. Did he really want me back, or did he just want someone?

Later that evening, I was on wedding-preparation duty. I sat cross-legged on Ayshe's floor, helping her wrap almond biscuits in shiny silver paper – well, I tried to help, but neatness was never one of my virtues – she had to undo most of mine and was busy rewrapping them.

'How did you get on at the hospital?' Ayshe asked.

'You'll never guess what happened. Go on, guess.'

'You won the hospital lottery?' she murmured, engrossed in her task.

'No.'

'They mistook you for a mental patient and sectioned you?'

I couldn't wait any longer and blurted out what had happened with Doctor Savage and Justin.

'It's weird, but since this whole change-your-life thing started, I haven't really thought about Justin at all. And then today, he turns up out of the blue wanting me back.' I stopped wrapping the biscuits and turned towards her.

'Surely you're not even considering going back to him.'

I sighed. 'I just don't know what to do. I've been racking my brain all afternoon, trying to think. I'm so confused. Just when I've started to get my life back on track, he turns up again.' I took a breath. 'Since this whole challenge thing started, I'm starting to really question what I want. I'm not sure that Justin is it anymore. And the one thing that really hit home today is just how desperately I want children. I want to settle down and have my own family, instead of borrowing yours all the time.'

So, here's the thing I haven't told you yet: officially, my nan is my only living relative. Unofficially, of course, there's Ayshe's family. My parents died in a car crash when I was five, and I'd gone to live with my nan, who'd brought me up. We'd always enjoyed a close relationship, and she was a constant source of inspiration to me. Sadly, she was now suffering from Alzheimer's and was completely cuckoo. But the reason I hate to mention it is because you'd probably be thinking of that well known phrase 'time heals,' when, in fact, all it does is fade the past into a kind of sepia blur, like a hazy, out of focus photo. And I'm not proud of this, but no matter how hard I try now to remember my parents, I really can't. Instead, all the memories I have are of Ayshe's family taking me under their wing at the worst time of my childhood. Birthday parties they had for me, making me feel the centre of attention, as if I was special, trying to let me forget that it should've been my parents baking me the cake and playing pin the tail on the donkey. The family gatherings they always included me in, giving me a sense of belonging, despite the fact that my parents couldn't. Knowing that I could always go to them with a problem, and they would drop everything to be there for me. Don't get me wrong, my nan had always been great, and I loved her to death, it's just that for the longest part of my life, I felt like I'd been stealing my best friend's life. And the thing that only really hit me today was that maybe I just wanted my own family and sense of belonging so much, that I'd pinned all my hopes on Justin, even though perhaps he wasn't the right one.

'I think deep down that you know what the right choice is.

61

You just have to have more faith in yourself to make it. Maybe the answer will come if you stop thinking about it.' She put her arm round my shoulder and paused for a while. 'You have to come shopping with me on Saturday. I need a new outfit for my hen night, and you need to get out of those old clothes. There's nothing like a bit of retail therapy to boost your confidence.' She looked me up and down. 'Oh – and Charlie has sort of invited himself to the hen night.'

'Charlie! But he's a man. He can't come on your hen night.'

'Yeah, but he's gay so it doesn't count. Anyway, you know what he's like. I'm sure he'll liven up the night.' She giggled. 'Atila told me today that he's booked a surprise for you and me the day after the hen night. He won't tell me what it is yet, but he thinks we'll love it, and it can count as part of your daily challenge as well – I can't wait, it sounds so exciting. And from next Wednesday onwards I've got three whole weeks off work, yippee!'

'Mmm, wedding next Sunday and then off on your glorious honeymoon. Oh, you're so lucky to be getting married.' I poked her in the leg. I was slightly green with envy. Well I was only human.

'It will happen to you, too, I know it will. Stop worrying about your life so much and chill.'

I stuffed one of the biscuits we were wrapping in my mouth. 'These are really good, where did you get them?' I mumbled, spilling crumbs down my front.

'Mum got them from the Turkish deli – oh, and speaking of her, she's organized a family dinner next Monday night. She wanted to do a traditional Turkish henna night for me before the wedding, and you have got to come.'

I reached for another biscuit and dunked it into my mug of cold coffee. 'Ooh, sounds like fun.'

'You know what Mum's like. It'll probably be completely over the top and Dad will be pissed again.'

She slapped my hand away as I reached for another biscuit.

I uncrossed my legs, picking up a letter from the coffee table. 'Do you want me to post this? I'm going into town tomorrow. Thought I might get Marco to try and do something with my hair.' I studied the writing on the envelope.

'Mmm, it's about time.' She looked up at my hair.

'I didn't know you donated to the Animal Defence League.' I

62

waved it about.

'Thanks, but it's not mine. It's Kalem's. He's sent them money for years – hey, you know what; I think the right guy for you is someone who's like Kalem.'

'Huh?'

'Trouble is,' she mused, 'you always go for the wrong type. What you need is someone more basic.'

'Basic?' I frowned. 'You mean boring?'

'No. I mean someone more down-to-earth, who's stable, sensitive and more family-orientated instead of the usual materialistic arses you normally go for who take longer to do their hair in the mornings than you do. The problem is that you're obsessed with perfection, but you've got a distorted view about what perfection really is. You think the perfect man comes in the perfect little package: flawless good looks, perfect job, rich, expensive car. It's easy to get swept up by all that. But that's just surface stuff. It's what's on the inside that counts.

I ran a hand through my unruly curls, deep in thought until Ayshe sprang up, collecting a pile of the neat little packages – well, hers were neat, mine looked a bit shite. 'Come on, get your feet out. I'm going to give you a proper pedicure. I saw that mess you made last time you tried. What if the doctor gets to see your feet again?'

# Chapter 9
## Friday, day 5 – Stilton Sauce Stains

I scurried into town the next morning at the crack of dawn, hoping to book in with Marco before the busy weekend rush started. He was a bit of a bully, but he really did work wonders with my hair – apart from the time he'd given me a crispy perm which was so tight I looked like Shirley Temple and had to walk around with conditioner on my hair for two days, trying to get it to relax.

I pushed the door open to find Charlie sitting alone in the shop, highlighting cap on and Clingfilm wrapped round his head. Marco was Charlie's on-off boyfriend. Today it must have been on.

Marco danced over towards me. 'Helen! Where have you been?' he sang in a camp accent, picking up sections of my hair, studying it with intense interest. 'Urgh!' He jumped back, discovering the split ends. 'You are sooo freaky!'

'Can you do anything with it?' I asked.

'He's doing me now,' Charlie butted in.

'Now, now, I can do both. I am the great Marco.' He flounced, very prima donna-ish, clapping his hands loudly to call Susie, his long-suffering assistant. 'Sooz! Get the lovely Helen gowned up and put her there.' He pointed to the empty leather chair next to Charlie.

'How are you, then, Charlie?' I sat down, staring at the ridiculous sight of him crammed into black leather trousers, which were so tight they must have been shrink-wrapped onto him, and a shrieking pink, shiny top. His belly was contorted into rolls of flab beneath it, which looked severely uncomfortable, and I was sure he'd been stuffing socks down his trousers again.

'I'm fabby, darling.'

'Why aren't you working?' I eyed his sock with suspicion.

'Waiting for inspiration.' Charlie glanced over and caught me looking.

Charlie was an IT boffin who worked from home, mostly late at night, banging around like a crazed insomniac.

He picked up a pair of reading glasses and slid them on. 'Who would you most like to look like?' He waved an *OK! Magazine* at me.

'Out of who and who?' I glanced over at him as Marco shoved his beaky nose in the colour charts.

Charlie looked baffled. 'Who?'

'You said who would I most like to look like. Is there a choice between certain people, or is it out of any of the six million billion people in the whole world?'

'Oh, I see what you mean.' Charlie nodded in thought.

'Oh, don't be ridiculous,' Marco snapped at Charlie.

Marco pushed a colour chart under my nose. 'You must have some streaks put in. I was thinking...soft copper and caramel. Hmm? Oh, my God, I think I can see a grey hair!' He blinked at my head about five million times. I moved closer to the mirror and studied my hair.

No, he must be mistaken, I couldn't see anything – wait a minute, though – oh, God! There was one. It was standing up on end and opera singing to the whole world its existence. I tried to pull it out but Marco slapped my hand away.

'Ha!' Charlie scoffed. 'I knew you couldn't go a whole day without being a bitch.'

'Oh, shut up! I know what I'm talking about.' Marco glared at Charlie.

'Oooh, grumpy knickers.' Charlie flicked through the magazine.

'Whatever you think, Marco,' I said.

'Sooz!' Marco bellowed in my ear and his giant Elvis quiff wobbled like a jelly about to collapse.

Susie ambled over with a disinterested look on her face. Her hair colour changed every time I went in there. This week it was pink and white.

'Mix up these colours and then get Helen a latte,' he barked at her.

Charlie held up a picture to me. 'OK, out of David Beckham and Posh?'

'What?' I asked.

'Who would you most like to look like?' He rolled his eyes.

'Oh, we're back to that, are we?' I studied the picture.

Marco tutted at him and began sectioning off my hair; he applied lowlights and then wrapped them carefully in foil.

'Neither,' I said.

'No.' Charlie insisted. 'You have to pick one.'

'Why would I want to look like David Beckham?' I asked.

Charlie crossed his legs, squashing his sock. 'Well, I would.'

'But you're a man, sort of.' Marco pointed the end of his comb at him.

I took a sip of my coffee and splurted it out, laughing.

'What have you done to your eyebrows? I'm soo jealous, I love them.' Marco scrutinized my eyebrows.

'She finally started plucking them again,' Charlie said.

'Ah. I've started up my salsa and merengue classes again.' Marco looked up at me in the mirror. 'Had to stop for summer, no one wants to be gyrating around in the heat, do they? You should come. From what I hear, you've been moping around in your flat ever since you threw that shagger out.'

'Who told you that?' I shrieked, glancing over at Charlie, who looked sheepish.

Marco cocked his head at Charlie. 'He did.'

I sighed. 'Well, it seems that the Justin wants me back.'

'Agh!' Charlie gasped. 'What are you going to do? You can't go back to him!'

I gulped. 'I'm not sure.'

Marco wagged a bony finger at me. 'Mark my words: once a shagger, always a shagger!'

Four lattes and five *OK! Magazines* later, my hair was tousled and teased to perfection. Marco described the new look as, super-freaking-sexy. On the outside I looked like a new woman, but inside, I wrestled with emotional turmoil. I spent most of the afternoon trying to figure out what to do about Justin. One minute I'd made up my mind to give it another try and the next, I'd decided it would never work. Thoughts buzzed round in my brain about Justin and how happy we'd been in the beginning. He'd always been a big charmer: full of sweet talk and showering compliments, until the day he started his new job and everything began to change. It was just little things at first, like admiring himself in the mirror constantly, strutting round the flat like a peacock on Viagra and using more beauty products in a day than I used in a whole year. He'd go to work reeking of aftershave and come home smelling like the women's perfume counter in Boots. And then gradually he became more and more distant, getting back later every night. But of course the crunch had come when I'd discovered the offending underwear. Or had it?

It suddenly dawned on me that I must've known what was going on all along. Maybe not on the surface, but on some deep, intuitive level. You know how you look back after the fact and start to piece together all the little strands of information and events, finally discovering that they don't fit together like they should? I'm sure that most of us have been lied to and betrayed at one time or another, but for all these months I'd refused to admit to myself that I knew and chose to ignore it. Because what would that make me? A desperate idiot for putting up with it for so long? Or a straitjacket candidate? Perhaps naïve was a better description. In fact, I was beginning to question whether I'd even been in love with him at all. Had it just been some kind of insane infatuation? Or was I so consumed with the longing to have my own family that I'd denied the obvious for so long, clinging onto something that wasn't even really there in the first place?

I massaged the jumbled pile of muscles in my neck, hoping to ease the tension which felt like an avalanche had fallen on my head. I couldn't stand it anymore and decided to take my mind off things by surfing the net with the intention of buying Ayshe and Atila's wedding pressie. I'd never actually bought anything online before, but Ayshe assured me she'd done it hundreds of times and nothing could possibly go wrong. I was always worried about those horror stories you hear where people steal your credit card details and your identity – though I wasn't quite sure why anyone would want my identity – or my credit card, for that matter. It was almost maxed-up to the limit. But I'd promised Ayshe I would get her a much fawned after cappuccino-maker, and she'd given me the web address of an exclusive little coffee outlet called The Coffee Bean. I selected the model the happy couple wanted and added it to my shopping basket. One hundred and nine pounds and ninety-eight pence. I hummed away to myself, entered my credit card and delivery details and clicked the send button. Don't know what I was worried about, really, it all seemed quite simple.

And then the computer got stuck, mid-send.

I waited for about five minutes. Nothing happening. I clicked on the back key and was transported through cyberspace back to the credit card and delivery details again. So I repeated the exercise, filled in the details and clicked the send key. It got stuck again.

'Bugger,' I muttered, going through the whole process again. And again. And again. This time I was getting seriously annoyed. I gave up after another five goes and wandered, frustrated, into the kitchen to make some coffee. I'd just have to do the normal thing and pop into Argos or John Lewis – or anywhere, in fact, that your order wasn't going to get lost in a jumble of computers in cyberspace.

I slurped from my mug and sat down to check my emails. Ten of them had just appeared in my inbox. Clicking on the inbox file, I paused, mid-slurp. The colour drained from my face. They were all from The Coffee Bean confirming my order for ten cappuccino makers!

'For God's sake!' I put my chin in my hands and stared at the screen in disbelief. 'Shit, shit, shit. I don't want ten! I only wanted to spend a hundred and ten quid, not eleven hundred. They'll never have to buy a cappuccino maker again for the rest of their lives.'

I went back to the website and scanned it frantically for a contact number. Grabbing my mobile, I paced up and down listening to the ringing tone echoing in my ear.

'Come on, come on.'

I glanced at the clock. Six o'clock. Damn, I bet they've all gone home. I stamped my foot as a recorded message informed me they were now closed for the weekend; no one would be there until Monday morning. I bit my fingernail. There wasn't any other option, I'd just have to phone them on Monday and hopefully cancel nine of the bloody cappuccino makers.

I took great care getting ready that night for my date with Dr Savage. God, I realized I didn't even know his first name! I decided to go for the casual, sexy look and pulled on a pair of bootleg jeans and a low-cut, clingy, black top. Squashing my boobs into a new M&S push-up bra, I admired the effect in the mirror. My pièce de résistance was a pair of black, sparkly, pointed toe high-heel boots. Ayshe had picked them out in Asda, where she assured me they were the spitting image of the new Jimmy Choo winter collection, only about five hundred pounds less.

I'd just downed a glass of wine and soda – purely for medicinal reasons, of course – and was busy putting the finishing touches to some dark brown eye make-up and a vibrant orange lipstick when the door bell rang. My eyes flew to my watch. It was only seven. He wasn't due for another half an hour. Blimey, he was keen! I rushed to the door, then hung back behind it, giving my hair a quick scrunch up before casually opening it.

'Oh,' I exclaimed when I saw Justin standing on the doorstep.

'Hi, Helen.'

I expected my heart to melt at the sight of him, but strangely it didn't. 'Justin, what are you doing here? I thought you were going to give me time to think about things.'

'What's there to think about? You know you want me back.'

'I just need some time to sort things out in my head.'

'You look a bit tarted up. Got a date, have you?'

'Yes, actually.'

'Can I come in? ' He sauntered past me without waiting for an invitation, wafting Wild Stallion aftershave all over the place. His spiky hair had been gelled with enough hair products to keep Nicky Clarke in business single-handedly. I glared at his head. It looked like he'd poured a whole bottle of Sun-in over it.

I cocked my head to one side. 'Well?'

'I thought we went over this yesterday. I realized I've made a mistake.' He sat down, stretching his arm along the back of the sofa, making himself at home. 'I really miss you, Helen,' he said through his plump lips, which looked a bit peculiar, as if he'd been at them with collagen injections.

I sank down next to him.

He leaned over and took my hand in his. 'I know I've made a big mistake. Why don't you just forgive me, and we can move on?'

I gazed into his little wishy-washy pale blue eyes and wondered, for the first time, what the hell had I actually ever seen in him? And how had I never noticed how permanently fake-tanned he looked? I pulled my hand away and walked over to the window.

'What, you suddenly turn up again in my life and just expect me to pretend nothing happened?' I regarded him with wild-eyed suspicion. For the last six months, I'd dreamed of this happening. But now I realized, for the first time in a long time, that I was much more confident and assertive. I was actually feeling happy again. The challenge I'd thought was such a stupid idea at first was having a really positive effect on me.

'Can I have a glass of wine, for old times' sake?' He tried his best heart-stopping smile that I used to love.

I stomped into the kitchen and sloshed wine into a glass. With all the stealth of a cat stalking its prey, he snuck up behind me and wrapped his arms around my waist.

'Mmm, you smell gorgeous.' He sniffed my hair. 'I'd forgotten how beautiful you are.'

I pulled away and handed him the glass 'And what about Miss Photocopier?'

He hesitated and averted his eyes. 'Sandra? That was over weeks ago. It won't happen again.'

And that's when I knew he was lying.

I swilled the wine in my glass. 'And that's supposed to make it all right again, is it?'

'Well…yes. Come on…you know you want me back. We can just pick up where we left off. No harm done.'

He must have developed selective amnesia.

I listened to him, hearing but not really believing my ears, his words slicing through me.

And then everything clicked in to place. He hadn't changed.

I had.

'It was just a little indiscretion. Helen…I was good for you, wasn't I?

My glass froze en route to my mouth. '"Indiscretion?!"' I shook with pent-up resentment. 'You call shagging someone else behind my back for a whole year "Indiscretion?" The trouble with you is that you just can't seem to keep it in your own pants.' My eyes flew to his crutch, just so that he was completely clear what I was talking about.

He flinched. 'You know I don't like the word "shagging".'

'Ah, what word would you prefer, then? Rogering, bonking, nookying-to-death, humping, or any of the above?' I stormed back into the lounge.

Justin followed closed behind me. 'Well, it was never serious with her, it was just a physical thing. Not like with you and me. Come on, you must know that. I've only ever cared about you.' He held his arms out to me, full of self-indulgence, completely ignoring what I'd just said.

'You can't just come in here and expect everything to be back to business as usual.' I took a bigger gulp of wine and contemplated throwing the rest of it over him, but I really didn't want to make a mess on my lovely oak floor.

'Why not?'

I followed that with an eye roll. 'Because it doesn't work like that in the real world, where you're hurting real people's feelings, but then you wouldn't realize that because you only live in the Justin world.' I gave him an icy stare.

'But I've just had a massive pay rise and bought a new BMW!'

'What's that got to do with anything?' I shot him an incredulous look. 'Money's not the most important thing in life.'

'What else is there?' Surprise registered on his face.

I narrowed my eyes at him. 'Hmm…let's see. How about happiness, love, and trust? Caring about your partner and not just yourself? Or being a genuine, kind person on the inside? How about being faithful?'

He stood up, chucking the rest of his wine down his throat. 'Well, I think you'll change your mind when you realize what you're missing.' He sniffed, clearly annoyed at my unexpected display of animosity.

I grabbed the door knob and flung it open, giving a big enough hint that I wanted him to go. Dr Savage suddenly appeared as Justin and I were having a glaring competition. He was just about to knock when he saw that the door was already open.

'Hello.' Dr Savage smiled. His smooth, bald head looked like he'd had a session with the polish and a feather duster. 'Not interrupting anything, am I?'

'No, Justin was just leaving,' I hissed through clenched teeth.

'You'll regret it.' Justin stormed past me, puffing out his chest. 'I'd watch out if I were you. She's trouble,' he snarled at Dr Savage, a rivulet of threat running through his voice.

'Look, I don't want to get in the middle of anything.' Dr Savage's eyes darted between Justin and me.

Justin stepped closer to Dr Savage, his fists coiled, stopping inches away from his face.

Dr Savage took a step back. And then another.

'You're not. Good. Bye. Justin,' I forced the words out. The atmosphere was oppressive. I held my breath.

Justin glowered at Dr Savage. A minute passed. Then slowly, he unclenched his fists and stormed down the hall.

My eyes followed his back as he disappeared, and I allowed myself to exhale.

'What was all that about?' Dr Savage reached into his pocket, pulled out a crisp, white handkerchief and mopped his brow.

'He's my ex-boyfriend. It's nothing, I'm sure he won't be causing any more trouble.' I felt the anxiety slip away. I'd made the right decision.

'You're sure? You're sure you're OK?'

'I'm certain.' I flung on my black leather jacket and scooped up my bag, shutting the door behind us.

'Well, in that case. Shall we go? You look lovely, by the way.'

'Thanks, but I have to ask you, what's your first name?'

'Oh, I'm sorry. I didn't say, did I? It's Heathcliff.'

'Heathcliff?'

'Yes, my mother was really into Wuthering Heights.'

We wandered down the stairs and bumped into Kalem, Yasmin and Deniz coming up.

'Merhaba canim.' Hello darling, Yasmin said, in Turkish, kissing me on both cheeks and drawing me into her cuddly warm body, just as she'd always done ever since I was a kid.

'Hello,' boomed Deniz in his usual loud voice. He looked half-cut again. 'Wow!' He peered at Heathcliff's bald head. 'Have you tried rubbing goat shit on it?' Deniz pointed to his own bushy head of curly, black hair and thick moustache. 'It's what we used to do in our village in Cyprus. It's a wonder-cure for baldness, you know.'

'Strangely, no,' Heathcliff muttered, looking bewildered.

Kalem creased up with laughter and looked at me. 'You've been to the hairdresser too, haven't you? It looks good.'

'What are you two doing tonight? Yasmin asked.

'We're going for a meal, and I thought we might go to a nightclub after,' Heathcliff said.

'Agh!' Yasmin and Deniz said in unison. Yasmin's hands flew to her face as her eyes widened with shock. Deniz glared at Heathcliff.

Heathcliff looked uneasy. 'What's wrong with a nightclub?

'In Cyprus, a nightclub is actually a brothel.' Kalem grinned and sauntered off.

I was dead impressed when we arrived at the newly opened trendy bistro, Le Jardin. Apparently, there was a waiting list a mile long to get a table here. How had Heathcliff managed it in just one day?

The maitre d' led us past the glossy chrome bar, with cream Italian leather bar stools, and into a corner table, which nestled between several equally glossy potted palms and a very impressive water feature of a mermaid and a dolphin. I didn't know what sort of a look they were trying to achieve, but it looked rather like the mermaid was humping the dolphin.

A very young-looking waiter handed us a menu as we sat down on the uncomfortable chairs. I balked as I slowly read it, realizing that, really, you could have fed a family of four for a week for the price of one meal alone! An army of waiters hovered around like lawyers round an accident victim, waiting to land the second someone finished their meals, so they could jump-start the plate-whipping-away frenzy.

I looked over at Heathcliff, who was trying to get comfortable, and then observed him with interest as he rearranged the already perfectly-presented table. There were two wine glasses, one large and one small. He swapped them round, then fiddled with the cutlery, straightening his knife and fork again and again. Next, he tackled the napkin, which had been very cleverly moulded into the shape of a swan. He carefully unfolded it, refolded it, and unfolded it again.

'Can I get you something to drink?' the waiter asked.

Heathcliff studied the wine list. 'How about a bottle of Chateauneuf-du-Pape?' He looked up at me.

'That sounds fine.' What did I know about wine? Justin always used to buy the most expensive bottle with the longest name, but I usually just went for the cheapest, as long as it tasted nice and didn't give me a humongous hangover. 'And some soda and ice please.' I leaned back in the chair and tucked my hair behind my ear. 'How did you get a table here?'

'Ah, I have a little confession to make. I was supposed to be having a business meeting here tonight, but they cancelled yesterday morning, that's why I was able to take you out. I'm usually so busy it would have taken weeks to fit you in otherwise.' He picked his knife up, gave it a quick blow and buffed it up to a shine which rivaled his gleaming bald head. He then carefully placed it back into a perfectly straight position.

'So what are you having?' I tried to find the cheapest dish on the menu.

'I think I'm going to go for the foie gras, followed by fillet steak with a stilton sauce.' He closed the menu, picked up his napkin and folded it into a neat little square.

'I'll have the prawns in garlic butter to start and then steak,' I decided.

The waiter returned with our drinks on a silver tray and attempted to pour the wine. I handed him the bigger of the two glasses and told him that I was going to mix mine with soda and ice.

'You can't do that! You can't mix the glasses up. You have to use the smaller one,' Heathcliff said.

The waiter looked to me for further instructions on his wine pouring etiquette.

'No, that's fine. Please pour it in here.' I wiggled the big glass in the air.

Heathcliff raised his eyebrows at me. 'How odd.'

'So, what's it like being a doctor?' I swirled my wine in my big fat glass.

'Well, I am a workaholic, I'm afraid. I usually work around eighty hours a week.' He unfolded and refolded his napkin.

'How do you find any time for a social life?'

'That's the sacrifice you make, I'm afraid. My wife and three children were never too impressed with it.' He shook his head. 'Ex-wife, that is.'

'Gosh.' I downed half of my glass fast and then saw the waiter almost running across the quarry tiled floor to try and refill it before I could lift it to my lips again.

'Did you know sixty per cent of all backaches could be avoided by adopting the correct seating position when sitting and driving?' He shifted uncomfortably in his chair.

'I totally didn't know that.' I sat back, fiddled with my fork and realized, with some surprise, that he had me doing it now.

'Oh, yes, absolutely.' He seized his wine glass, wiping it with his napkin and then looked in horror at a drop of red wine that had splashed onto it. 'I don't think these chairs are in the best position for spines, really.' He folded the napkin and hid the stain.

'Interesting,' I mumbled as the waiter laid the starters in front of us.

I sniffed the wonderful aroma of melted garlic butter and poked my fork in a sumptuous king prawn.

He gaped at me. 'Do you know what prawns do?' He took a bite of his paté.

I had a vague recollection of someone telling me they ate the poop of other fishes, but I didn't particularly care because they

74

tasted so scrumptious. 'What do they do?'

'They are the Hoovers of the ocean and frequently eat the faeces of other marine animals.' He pulled a disgusted face.

I gathered up another little poop-guzzler and popped it into my mouth. 'And do you know how they make foie gras?' I remembered that Kalem had told me about it once.

'No.' He dabbed the corner of his mouth with his napkin, then refolded it so that no one could see the dark smear of paté caked on it.

'They force-feed the geese to horrendous proportions and then whip out their gigantic over-sized livers to make it. Yuck, isn't it?'

He put his paté down and stared at it. 'Wow! I don't think I fancy that now.' He pushed his plate to the centre of the table and back again. Then he spent five minutes intricately examining his cutlery for spillages.

I tried to spear my last prawn with my fork, but it slipped in the melted butter sauce and somersaulted under the table. 'Oops.'

'Where's it gone?' Heathcliff lifted up the tablecloth and scanned beneath it with a worried look on his face.

'So, how old are your children?'

'Seven, five, and three.' He patted down the tablecloth. 'I only get to see them once a month as I'm so busy working.'

He finished his drink and I poured him another before the waiter could even glance in our direction.

'Oh, that's a shame.'

'Did you know four thousand people a year die from accidents in the home?'

'No,' I said, as the waiter removed our plates and brought us our main courses. God, the service was a bit quick! Actually, it was a bit too quick for my liking. It was as though they were trying to hurry us along so they could throw us out of the door and cram in yet another sitting – hardly a relaxing culinary adventure.

When the super-fast waiter leaned over Heathcliff, he managed to spill a minute drop of stilton sauce on his trousers.

Heathcliff shot out of his chair, staring at the stain. 'Oh, my God. Oh, my God!' He went completely over the top.

'It's OK, I'm sure it will wash out.' I stared at him in amazement as the waiter apologized and scurried back into the kitchen before he could get a bollocking.

'No, it won't do. It just won't do. Please excuse me. I'm going to have to wash this off.' He rushed to the loos.

I waited several minutes for him to return. When he didn't, I thought the only decent thing to do was to start polishing off my dinner before it got cold. After I'd scraped my plate clean of every last delicious morsel, he reappeared sporting a big greasy stain down his leg and groin area.

'How terrible.' He sat down, his face red and clammy.

'It's all right. Looks like you got it out.' Why was he getting so stressed about a bit of dirt on his trousers?

'I feel soiled and violated.'

I stifled a laugh. 'Don't worry. Let's forget all about it and talk about something else.' I waved my hand as if it was no problem while secretly worrying I think this guy has a cleanliness obsession!

The evening went pretty much downhill from there. Over coffee and brandy, he recounted the national statistics on deaths from MRSA, the benefits of water births versus caesareans, the average life of a red blood cell, and numerous other medical facts known to man and Heathcliff. As we drove back to my place I politely invited him in for coffee, but was slightly concerned about the reaction I would get from him when he saw my less-than-squeaky-clean abode.

As I flicked the light on in the kitchen, he gazed around the room, then gaped open-mouthed at my mug tree from which hung red, blue, and yellow mugs arranged in a rather haphazard fashion.

'What's all this?' He pointed at it.

'A mug tree.'

I sprang towards the kettle, slightly perturbed. As I made the coffee, he started re-arranging them in patterns, so that the two red ones were opposite each other, ditto for the two blues and the same again for the two yellows mugs; all facing in a clockwise direction.

'You can't have the same colours next to each other. It has to be colour-coordinated. They must be opposite each other.' He downed his coffee with a few swift gulps, staring at the mug tree, as if it was going to rear up and batter him to death. 'I've got an early start at the surgery tomorrow. I must dash.' He gave me a chaste kiss on the cheek and wiped his mouth with a handkerchief.

After his hasty exit, I flung the mugs willy-nilly into the sink. The Matching Pairs Police would have to arrest me for this little misdemeanour.

The answer phone was twinkling at me, so I listened to the message as I cleaned my teeth. It was the same creepy guy again from the other day. I dithered mid-brush.

'Me again. I think you've forgotten something, haven't you? I still haven't got the readies off ya. Don't forget my money this time, otherwise you'll be sorry.' It was all very ominous and scary. I seriously hoped he had got the wrong number because I didn't have a clue what he was on about.

# Chapter 10
## Saturday, day 6 – Mussels Are Wicked

I lay in bed next morning, staring at the ceiling, deliberating whether it was actually possible to meet a normal guy once you reached the age of thirty. Was it so hard to find a man without baggage or strange obsessive compulsive disorders about cleanliness?

Yes, I did have a few quirks, but I certainly wasn't a raving nutter like Heathcliff. The fact that he had three kids he hardly ever saw didn't really bode well for my perfect picture of settling down to a happy family life with someone either. Let's face it: most single men the same age as me either seemed to be mentally challenged, divorced, or had a commitment phobia the size of outer space.

In spite of my present predicament, I now knew for certain that I didn't want someone unfaithful like Justin, even if it meant being on my own for the rest of my lonely life.

It also struck me, as I stared at a spider trundling along the coving that I'd only been doing this life-changing challenge for six days, and yet I already felt like a different person. I was regaining myself and finding out what I wanted for a change. My yin and yang were finally on their way back home. Yee-ha!

At eleven o'clock I was strolling down Oxford Street with Ayshe on the promised shopping-fest. After all my day-dreaming, I hadn't had time for breakfast and, for the first time in ages, I felt an overwhelming hunger. So I dragged Ayshe into Starbucks for a super-skinny mocha latte – instantly cancelling it out with a super-fattening, double-chocolate muffin.

'So the date was a bit weird, huh?' She shrugged her coat off onto the back of the chair.

I bit into my muffin. 'He had an obsessive compulsive disorder! He kept cleaning his cutlery and arranging it just so. Then he totally flipped when he got some stilton sauce down his front and ended up with a cheesy crutch. And he was a workaholic, so it's not likely I'd actually get to spend any time with him either.' I picked up some crumbs on the end of my finger.

'So you won't be seeing him again, then?'

'Definitely not.' I shook my head.

'And what about Justin?' She leaned closer to me, resting her chin on her elbows

I filled her in on his visit the night before. 'I've decided not to get back with him. He's still lying to me, and what hope is there for our relationship if I can't trust him?' I took a sip of coffee. 'I think I was looking for Mr. Right in all the wrong places. Maybe I've been so obsessed with what I thought was the perfect man because I wanted to try and have this picture-perfect little family life with someone at any cost, but now I'm even more determined that things will be completely different next time I get involved with someone. I'm fed up with being a doormat and being the only caring person in my relationships. I want to be cared about too.' I hesitated. 'So, it looks like I've proved you wrong. I can be proactive with my life.' I gave her a smug smile.

'I'm glad to hear it.' She wagged her finger at me.

'I know, I know. You were right as usual. In fact, I'm going to ring Nick right now.' I reached into my bag, pulled out my mobile and dialed his number before I had the chance to change my mind. Even if nothing happens between us, at least I might get my dishwasher fixed.'

Ayshe watched me, amusement dancing over her face.

His phone rang several times until the voicemail kicked in.

I took a deep breath. 'Hi Nick, it's Helen here. We met at the er…speed-dating the other night. I was just wondering if you'd be able to come round and have a look at my dishwasher for me. Anyway, you've got my number so…hopefully I'll speak to you soon. Bye.' I realized I hadn't taken a breath and exhaled deeply.

'Well, even if he doesn't ring, you know what they always say?' Ayshe spooned out the remnants of froth from her mug.

'What's that, O wise one?'

'You always meet someone when you least expect it. And there's always something better round the corner.' She wagged her finger at me.

'Trouble is; I've been out of the dating game for so long, I don't really know what to expect any more. And from what I've seen so far, it seems like most of the single guys out there are a bunch of complete freaks.' I gave a heavy sigh and stood up.

'So are you looking forward to the dinner party challenge tonight?' Ayshe faked a posh accent as we trundled out of the door and walked on down the road.

'Yes, I am actually. It will be nice to catch up with Clarissa.'

'I have to say, though; I don't think that a dinner party is exactly a difficult challenge.'

'Well that's where you're wrong. Clarissa thinks that me and Kalem are a couple, and that's going to take some pretty Oscar-winning acting.'

'Why don't you just tell her the truth, then?'

'Because I don't want her thinking I'm some kind of sad, old, stuck-on-the-shelf spinster.'

'Well Kalem says he can't wait for tonight!'

'Why? I thought he'd be trying to get out of it.'

She linked arms with me. 'He says it's hilarious watching you make a total prat of yourself.'

'Great. That's all I need.'

We spent three hours traipsing round the shops. I bought two new pairs of jeans, a couple of tops and ten pairs of sexy new knickers from *La Lingerie*, complete with multi-coloured scented beads thrown in the paper bag with them. Ayshe still hadn't found an outfit for her hen night yet, so we searched frantically to find something before the shops closed. The pre-Christmas rush was in full swing, and in some shops the boisterous crowds were spilling out the doors. We even witnessed people fighting over a pair of the latest JLo jeans in a size four. A size four? How did anyone get to be a size four anyway? That was so not normal – and thinking about it, how did JLo squeeze her voluptuous backside into a size four?

We threaded our way across the busy road to the other side, heading for a large and trendy shop that had a glittering display of dresses in the window.

'What about this?' I held up a sexy black dress.

'Too short.' She dismissed it, rummaging around in the trouser section.

I followed her and then pulled out a pair of tight trousers. 'These?' If Ayshe didn't want them, I was going to try them on.

'Too sparkly.'

'I like them.'

She pulled out a slinky, knee-length, black dress. 'This is nice. I can wear it with my long boots. What do you think?' She held it up in front of her.

'Try it on.'

We waited in the large queue for the changing rooms. It was stiflingly hot with an unpleasant odour of sweaty bodies wafting under our noses.

'God, it stinks in here,' I whispered, fanning the air around me with my hand.

She sniffed. 'We can squeeze into one changing room – it'll save time.'

We fidgeted in line until it was our turn.

'Do you think my bum looks big in this?' I asked, pouring myself into the trousers. 'Do I need to buy some of those big scaffolding knickers that come up to your chin to hold it in?'

'No, it looks positively pert.'

The security tag was strategically placed right in the crutch to cause maximum discomfort. 'Ooh bugger, that hurts.'

'My turn, hurry up. I can't stand the smell in here.' Ayshe kicked off her shoes and jeans.

'That looks great,' I said when she'd got it on.

We squeezed through the horde of irate shoppers and stood in the long queue at the till in front of the harassed and grumpy shop assistants. After handing over our hard-earned cash, we pushed our way out of the door – and just then a loud ringing noise erupted.

'Come on.' I dragged her off down the road. 'These security things are always going off for no reason.'

Suddenly, I felt an almighty bang on my shoulder as someone grabbed me from behind, and I thought I was being mugged.

'Aaarghhh!' I screamed, turning round to see a couple of beefy looking security guards frowning at us.

'Right, come on miss. You're coming with me,' Beefy Number One grunted, very a la Grant Mitchell style.

'What's going on?' Ayshe gasped as Beefy Number Two tried to pull her back into the shop.

'Security. You match the description of a couple of shoplifters in the area and the alarm's gone off,' Beefy Number One said.

'But we've paid for these!' I tried to look in my bag for the receipt but Beefy Number One attempted to pull it off me.

'Oi, get off!' Ayshe yelled as Beefy Number Two yanked her bag off her shoulder. 'You just touched my boob!'

'No, I didn't!' Beefy Number Two looked astonished.

'Yes you did. Help, help, he just touched my boob,' Ayshe

told everyone milling around in the street who were all staring.

'I didn't,' he protested to the onlookers.

'Hey, did he just molest you?' a fat American woman called out. She looked like a Greenham Common, ban-the-bomb type, wearing a giant flowery poncho.

'Yes!' Ayshe yelled as the Beefies started getting agitated.

'That's sexual harassment,' Fat Woman cried. One of her eyes was slightly skew-whiff, so it wasn't clear which one of the Beefies she was actually looking at. 'Little Hitlers. Think you can do whatever you want.' She kicked Beefy Number Two in the leg.

I was having a frantic tug of war as I tried to grab my shopping bag from Beefy Number One's pudgy little hands. 'I've got a receipt!'

Beefy Number One tugged it back. 'You'll have to show us that inside.' And then he cried out in pain, 'Ow!' as Fat Woman punched him in the back.

'I know your sort – any excuse to start touching up women,' Fat Woman growled.

'I didn't do anything, I'm married!' Beefy Number Two said.

'Who'd marry you? You're nothing but a woman-hater, you big brute,' Fat Woman exclaimed in a loud voice.

A few of the Japanese tourists started doing a David Bailey impression: snapping away with their cameras, eyes bright, jabbering away in Japanese. This was probably the best thing they'd seen all day.

'If you don't come quietly, we're going to do a citizen's arrest,' Beefy Number Two growled at us. 'We've done it before and it wasn't a pretty sight.'

I could well believe it.

'He's done it again: get off my boob!' Ayshe gave Beefy Number Two an angry glare.

'It wasn't me.' He lifted his hands off her. 'Look, no hands.' He held his hands up, turning round to show the crowd. This initiated loud gasps from the Japanese tourists who went into Nikon overdrive.

'Pervert!' I growled at him.

'Animal!' Fat woman shouted.

'Boob-molester!' Ayshe yelled.

'How do we know you're a real security guard and not just a woman toucher-upper who's rented a security guard outfit?' Fat woman said to the Beefies.

'Yeah,' Ayshe agreed.

'Let me see your ID,' I shouted.

The crowd looked at us all with bewilderment as the Beefies pulled out their work identification cards with much reluctance.

Beefy Number One flashed me his card.

'Eunace.' I read. 'Is that your real name?'

'Yeah, what's wrong with that?' he grunted.

'More like Eunuch!' Fat Woman scoffed.

'Let's have a look at yours,' Ayshe asked Beefy Number Two who pulled his card out and showed it to us.

'Satisfied?'

'Come on,' they said in unison, as they dragged us off kicking and screaming to the security office.

Did they rehearse their lines beforehand? I wondered.

Eunace grabbed our bags and deposited them on a desk while Beefy Number Two pushed us roughly into some wooden chairs and then stood guard in front of the door with legs akimbo and arms folded, just in case we made a quick getaway.

'Right, then, let's have a look in here.' Eunace tipped the contents of my handbag out and onto the desk in front of him. 'Half-eaten packet of extra strong mints, a purse with sundry items – what's this?' He peered at the Tampax and read the wrapper with interest. 'One big, fat Tampax, a mobile phone, lipstick and...a prawn.' He turned the bag upside down, giving it a vigorous shake.

He frowned as a little white tablet plopped onto the desk. 'And what's this?

I glanced at it impatiently. It was a painkiller which had fallen out of its blister pack and had wormed its way to the bottom of my bag.

'Neurofen tablet.' I curled my lip, simmering away with frustration.

He held it up to Beefy Number Two. 'Do you think it's drugs?'

'Oh, don't be ridiculous!' I'd reached boiling point now.

'Shall we call the Drugs Squad?' Beefy Number Two looked at Eunace.

'It's a bloody painkiller,' Ayshe snapped.

'Have you ladies been in trouble before?' Eunace grabbed Ayshe's bag and started on hers.

83

'No! And this is an invasion of privacy. Haven't you ever heard of the Human Rights Act?' she asked.

'Empty crisp packet; two mobiles, wallet in the name of Atila But, three and a half toothpicks, and an empty sandwich wrapper.' He picked up the phones and wallet and glared at her. 'Did you steal these?'

Ayshe rolled her eyes. 'No, they're my fiancée's.'

My phone, which was now resting on the table, burst into a telephone version of Donna Summer's Bad Girls. I lunged for it, but Eunace was deceptively quick for a Mr. Blobby look-a-like and got it first.

'Hello,' he said in a gruff voice, and then paused, listening to the voice on the other end. 'Who were you trying to ring? I'm trying to ascertain if this mobile is stolen.' He nodded. 'Mmm, hmm.' He handed it to me. 'Someone called Nick.'

'Hi, how are you?' I stood up, walking to the corner of the room for a bit of privacy.

'I'm good, thanks. Who was that?' Nick asked. 'Are you OK? You're not in trouble, are you?

'No, it's no one.' I let out a nervous giggle. 'Just a little misunderstanding.'

'Oh, right. I got your message. I've been a bit flat-out with the plumbing, otherwise I would have called you before. How are you?'

'I'm pretty good.' I shot Eunace an angry look.

'I'm just phoning to say that I can get round to look at your dishwasher tomorrow, about eleven if that's OK?'

I smiled to myself, then caught Eunace looking at me, so I glared at him. 'Yeah, that sounds great.'

'Oh, I'm glad you said that. Where do you live?'

I gave him my address.

'Great. I'll see you tomorrow, then.'

'OK.' I hung up.

I slumped back down into the chair, rested my mobile on the desk and looked at Eunace with cool detachment. He glared back until my phone went again, and he grabbed it at rocket-launching speed before I could even jump out of my seat.

'Hello.' He puffed up his chest, full of self-importance. 'Oh, the Fraud Department, is it?' He threw me an I-knew-you-were-a-thief kind of a glare. I held back the urge to stick my tongue out. It was pretty hard, though.

84

Why was the Fraud Department after me? I tried to snatch the phone off him, but he swung it out of reach, leaving me frustrated, so I stamped on his foot and he let go of it, fast.

'Hello?' I said.

'Hello, Ms Grey, I'm calling from Barclays Bank Fraud Department. There's been some unusual activity on your account, and we need to make sure everything is all right,' an efficient-sounding woman told me.

'What sort of activity?' Maybe someone had got hold of my credit card details after all.

'Well, we have a payment here to Adrian Ponsonby for £500. Can you confirm if that is a valid purchase?'

I cringed. 'Unfortunately, yes.'

'And we have ten items yesterday for one hundred and nine pounds and ninety-eight pence each.' I could hear her tapping away on her keyboard. 'Strangely, they're all for the same payee, The Coffee Bean. Can you confirm if that is also a valid purchase?'

I sighed. 'Sort of. It was a mistake actually – well so was the £500 one – but...' I wandered into the corner of the room, put my hand round the phone, whispering. The Beefies' eyes followed me round the room like one of those creepy paintings that stare back at you from every angle.

'Well...I had a problem with the internet. What actually happened was: I was buying a present for a friend – I only wanted one – and the internet went a bit funny on me, and I ordered ten instead. Can you do anything?'

The Beefies snorted at this little revelation and then tried to turn it into a cough when I glowered at them.

'Well, if they are valid purchases, I'm afraid not. You'll need to contact the supplier and ask them to refund you. Sorry we can't be of any assistance, but if it is a mistake, they should be able to return the money via your card.'

Damn.

I grimaced. 'OK, then, thanks for phoning.' I flipped my phone shut. This time I held on to it tight. There was no way Eunace was getting his chubby paws on it again.

Everyone turned round as the door swung open, nearly knocking Beefy Number Two off his enormous feet. A petite woman walked in and stood behind the desk next to Eunace. I read the name badge pinned on her jacket. Eleanor Jones,

General Manager, it said.

'OK boys, I've just looked at the CCTV footage, and I can't see anything suspicious. 'Hello Ladies.' She smiled at us. 'Let me have a look in the carrier bags to see the merchandise, please.'

Eunace handed her the bags, and she rummaged around, pulling out the items we had bought.

'Hmm.' She pulled out the receipts, studying them with care. 'Looks like this is the culprit.' She pointed to the security tags which were still left on the clothes. 'I'm dreadfully sorry for this misunderstanding. We've got a new till assistant today, and it looks like she's forgotten to take the tags off.'

The Beefies looked uncomfortable, giving each other shifty glances.

'Well, we won't be shopping here again.' Ayshe stood up. I followed suit, shoveling our belongings back into our handbags.

'The least I can do is offer you a store voucher to spend as a token of our apology.' Eleanor handed us back our purchases.

'Well, um, OK. It would be nice to have some compensation for all the inconvenience.' I brightened up.

Eleanor reached into the desk drawer and pulled out a couple of vouchers and passed them to us.

'Once again, I would like to say how sorry I am. We don't need to tell anyone about this little misunderstanding, do we?' she asked.

I contemplated the fifty pound voucher, raising my eyebrows with interest. 'I don't think so, do we?' I looked at Ayshe for confirmation. Quickly thinking I could buy the cute slinky top I'd checked out when we'd first gone into the shop.

'No.' Ayshe studied her voucher and nodded her head in agreement.

'Good, then I'll escort you both downstairs.' Eleanor flashed her pristine white enamels at us.

As we swept out of the room, I leaned over towards the Beefies, who were hovering by the door, looking very ashamed of themselves.

'Neanderthals!' I hissed at them.

'Boob-groper!' Ayshe spat.

When we'd finally left behind the nightmare shopping trip, we spilled out of the store into the early evening darkness, bumping into our old school friend, Felicity. She was a tiny, mousey little thing who was very into the Bible and worked as a librarian.

'Hi, Felicity.' I wondered what she was doing in the middle of shopping heaven. She never bought any new clothes and always wore stuff from Oxfam.

'Hello, you two. I was just looking for something new to wear to your hen night.' Whenever she spoke, a giant mole above her lip twitched. It looked similar to a toasted Rice Krispie and had several, coarse, black hairs poking out of it.

'Oh, nice.' Ayshe grinned. 'Have you found anything yet?'

'No. Mummy says I should wear something more fashionable for a change.' She looked down at her shoes.

I studied her outfit, which consisted of a brown knee-length A-line skirt, covered by a navy blue mac, and a pair of the frumpiest shoes ever invented. Her hair needed a jolly good makeover too. Stuck in the 70s with a big, flicky, curly thing perched on the front and the rest of it was limp, lifeless and mousey. She was wearing a pair of pink, NHS glasses with pointy bits on the sides.

'I wouldn't go in that shop if I were you.' I jerked my head towards the shop from hell. 'I thought today was supposed to be about retail therapy, but I'm scared to go clothes shopping ever again.'

# Chapter 11

'Ah, it's Ali Baba.' Kalem grinned as I climbed into the Land Rover on our way to Clarissa's.

'Ha-bloody-ha. How could that shop have thought we were nicking something?'

He glanced over and looked me up and down.

'What?' Had I spilled something down my top?

'You scrub up quite well when you're not covered in wine.'

'Actually, you look pretty good for a change too. It's amazing what a bit of effort makes, isn't it?' I took in his checked Ben Sherman shirt and black trousers. He even had a pair of shoes on, instead of the usual working boots. His thick hair had been clippered and his angular jaw was clean-shaven, especially for the occasion.

'I am a bit worried about tonight. Clarissa used to be really nice at college, but she seemed a bit snobby the other night.'

'I'm sure it will be a very memorable night.'

'So what's Emine doing tonight?'

'Don't know.'

We pulled up in a street with a row of identical prim and proper detached town houses. All boasted block-paved driveways, sculpted miniature topiary trees, and strangely, all had dark-coloured people carriers and BMWs sitting in the driveways.

Clarissa had obviously been curtain-twitching, because as soon as we pulled up, she almost pole-vaulted out of the door.

'Helen!' She beamed at me then looked at Kalem: 'I'm sorry. I forgot your name. It was something a bit strange. Golom, wasn't it?'

'Kalem, actually.'

'Come in, come in. Charles is inside.' She wrinkled her nose in abhorrence at the sight of the battered old heap now taking up space on her drive and practically dragged us into the house. Her eyes darted around to see if anyone else in the neighbourhood was curtain-twitching.

'Hello.' Charles formally shook first my hand and then Kalem's.

'Here you go.' I handed Clarissa two bottles of red wine and a bottle of soda.

She peered at the labels with distaste. '"Soft and Fruity". Mmm, never had that one before.' She placed the bottles on a sideboard. 'Let me get you a nice drinky-poo. We've got a lovely bottle of expensive wine breathing in the drawing room that Clarissa has just opened,' Charles piped up.

Drawing room?

'Can I have mine half-wine and half-soda, please?' I asked.

'But you will spoil the clarity of the wine completely.' Charles looked appalled.

'Mmm, but I like it.' I gave a sugary-sweet smile, sitting down next to Kalem on a very soft brown leather sofa. It was so squashy, it pushed us together, and I could feel the warmth of his knee resting against mine. For some rather unexplainable reason, the hairs on the back of my neck rose.

Charles and Clarissa bumbled into the kitchen, fetching the drinks.

I whispered to Kalem, 'Oh, my God!'

He giggled at me, then pulled a straight face as soon as they returned.

'Thanks.' Kalem took the glass.

'That's quite alright, Golom.' She nodded at Kalem.

I took a sip of wine and nearly died. One, because it was foul and two because she had just called Kalem by the wrong name, again. Which I thought was quite hilarious.

'It's Kalem, actually,' he offered, but she ignored him.

'Let me give you a tour of the house.' Clarissa darted out of the room before we could say no.

We dutifully followed as she led us round the perfect conservatory, the immaculate lounge and dining room, and the equally flawless four bedrooms and two bathrooms. Everything was colour-coordinated in soft blues and greens, even down to the wonderfully plumped-up cushions and the fancy swags and tails on the Laura Ashley curtains.

Clarissa pointed out of the conservatory windows. 'Shame it's too dark to see the garden properly. We had it landscaped a few weeks ago, it looks positively exquisite. OK, let's sit at the table, starters are ready.'

Once we were seated at the table, which was crammed to the edges with napkins, gleaming glasses, Sabatier cutlery, and even seating cards, Clarissa started to bring out the food. By mistake

89

I'd sat in the seat marked for Kalem, although she had put a card with the name 'Golom' written on it. Clarissa picked up the card. Her jaw dropped when she realized we were in the wrong seats.

'Problem?' Kalem asked.

'No.' She swapped Kalem's seating card with mine.

'More wine?' Charles jumped up and refilled our glasses.

'This looks interesting.' I examined what looked like paté spread onto the thinnest piece of toast I'd ever seen in my life.

'It's menai pride.' Clarissa looked down her nose at us as she sat down.

I raised my eyebrow. 'What's that?'

'Mussel paté, dear,' she said.

I picked it up and took a bite.

Kalem picked up his knife and fork and attacked it with hunger but the toast was so crisp that it broke into tiny shards. He gave up and picked up the miniature pieces with his hand.

'You do eat mussels, don't you?' Charles asked. 'Some people find they're an acquired taste.'

'I've never had them before, but this is lovely,' I said.

'Charles was headhunted this week,' Clarissa exclaimed as she crammed more paté into her mouth.

I finished off my starter and licked my fingers. 'Who by?'

'Have you heard of the Al-Nasr Oil Conglomerate?' Charles asked in a smug drawl.

'No,' Kalem replied.

'It's a multi-billion dollar oil company,' Clarissa boasted.

'That's really good. When do you start?' I sipped my wine while trying not to breathe in as it made it taste slightly more palatable.

'Well...I've got an interview,' Charles added.

'Oh, so you haven't actually got the job?' Kalem licked his fingers.

Clarissa flicked her hand, dismissing his comments. 'It's just a formality, of course he'll get it.' She leaned over to Charles, patting him on the head.

'Well, that'll be quite an achievement, although personally I think there's more to life than working sixty-hour weeks at the sacrifice of spending quality time with your family,' Kalem said.

'That's an...interesting idea, but if Charles didn't get his huge bonuses, we'd never be able to afford all this.' Clarissa swept her hand round the room. 'What do you do, Helen? I seem to recall

90

you were doing something arty when we were at college.'
Clarissa poured me some more of the bloody awful wine, which
could have actually doubled up as paint-stripper – maybe it was
corked.

'Photography.'

'Do you work in one of those one-hour photo booth
thingamajigs?' Charles asked.

'No, I work for myself.' I fiddled with my hair. 'How about
you, are you working?' I asked Clarissa.

She shook her head. 'Oh, no, I don't need to work!'

Charles turned to Kalem. 'And what about you, Golom?'

'I'm not working at the moment,' Kalem said.

Clarissa turned her nose up. 'How absurd!'

I was feeling quite tipsy by this point and put a protective hand
on Kalem's arm, winking at him.

'What he means is that he's on half-term. He's a teacher,' I cut
in, giving her my best and most dazzling smile.

'Oh, I see,' said Charles, as he cleared the plates.

Kalem glanced over at me and put his hand over mine on the
table as they busied themselves in the kitchen.

A warm tingling slithered up my legs, but I thought it was
probably the wine affecting me.

'This is sea bass in a cream sauce, with crushed new potatoes
and petit pois.' Clarissa dished out the main course as Charles
kept the wine flowing.

'Great.' Kalem withdrew his hand from mine. 'You can't beat
fish, spuds, and peas.'

'Hardly, dear.' Clarissa gave a supercilious snort.

'What do you think of that painting?' Charles jabbed a finger
at the wall while shoving a whole spud into his gob.

It was disgusting. 'Lovely,' I said, I didn't want to be rude.

'It cost a fortune.' Charles said, mid-munch, pulling a
ridiculous face which made him look like a camel chewing a
scorpion.

'But do you like it? I mean, it's very nice having all this
materialistic stuff, but at the end of the day, does it make you
happy?' Kalem considered it with thought and shot Charles a
disgusted look at his jaw acrobatics but Charles was too
engrossed in his munching to notice.

Charles's table manners were probably loud enough to be
heard over a small earthquake.

91

'It doesn't matter whether you like it or not. It's the prestige of owning the art that actually counts,' Clarissa said.

'Have you got any children?' I said, downing some more of the dreadful plonk.

Clarissa pointed to some photos adorning a mahogany sideboard in the corner of the room. 'Yes, Casper and Charles junior,' she said without feeling, cold almost.

'Oh, so where are they tonight, at a friend's house?' I squashed a potato in the sauce and rubbed it around my plate.

'No, boarding School in Scotland,' Charles boomed.

'How old are they?' I asked as Clarissa shot me a disapproving look at my potato-rubbing antics.

'Eight and ten, those photos were taken ages ago.' Charles pointed over to the sideboard.

'I wouldn't be able to send my kids to boarding school. I'd miss them like crazy.' Kalem shook his head. 'In fact, I think when I have children I'd love to move to North Cyprus where my parents are from. There's hardly any crime and kids can learn more about nature instead of spending too much time playing computer games and keeping up with the latest fashions. Turkish Cypriots are very family orientated, and there's much more of a community spirit there, like the UK was fifty years ago.

'Well I went to boarding school, and I turned out all right. Anyway, there's nothing wrong with good old Blighty,' Charles whined.

Kalem finished his dinner, leaned back in his chair and stretched his long, toned legs before him.

'North Cyprus sounds lovely. All that sunshine, laid-back lifestyle, and beautiful scenery. The trouble in the UK is that people don't have time for each other any more. They're always too busy working and under too much pressure to perform. When I have kids, I'm going to look after them full-time,' I said, looking at Kalem in agreement. He squeezed my knee, making me glow with an unexpected excitement. I was quite enjoying this business of pretending to be a couple, and I loved all the affection he was showing me.

'More wine?' Charles looked at my empty glass and poured some anyway.

Halfway through the desert of chocolate and pecan tartlets, I felt a hot glow sweep over me. I fanned myself with my napkin, flushing profusely.

'Are you OK?' Kalem looked at me with concern as beads of sweat appeared on my forehead.

'I'm fine.' I stifled a nauseous feeling.

'You do look a bit green. Have you had too much to drink?' Clarissa asked.

I stood up. 'Actually, I feel a bit ill.' I rushed off, making a bee-line for the loo through the kitchen. But halfway there, I just knew I wasn't going to make it, so instead I veered over to the kitchen sink just in time to vomit into it.

Kalem followed me in, closely pursued by Clarissa and Charles. 'Are you OK?' Concern clouded his eyes as I gripped the rim of the worktop, feeling disgustingly sick.

'Oh, my God!' Clarissa's voice jumped several octaves. Her hands flew to her face when she saw the state of what was her previously pristine sink. If looks could kill, I would have been boiled alive, disemboweled, and sliced up into little pieces. Simultaneously.

'That's outrageous!' Charles muttered, then leaned over to Clarissa and whispered, 'People who can't handle their wine shouldn't drink so much.'

What a bloody cheek, I thought, when Charles had practically been pouring Cabernet Nitromors down my throat all night.

Kalem filled a glass of water, handing it to me, gently rubbing my back. 'How are you feeling?'

'Not very well.' I leaned back against him, feeling his arms encircle me from behind, supporting me.

'Have some water,' Kalem said.

I took a slow sip of cool liquid as he reached over for some kitchen roll which he dampened under the tap and then pressed to my forehead.

'Oh no...I think I'm going to be sick again.' I tumbled forwards over the sink. A tendril of hair fell over my forehead and Kalem swept it away from my face, stroking my head.

'I can't watch, I can't watch. It's disgusting!' Clarissa shrieked, pulling Charles out of the kitchen, where they hovered in the doorway, whispering to each other.

'Urrgh.' I collapsed onto a nearby chair and shivered as a chill of fever shook me. I was cold to the core but inside my body was on fire.

'Right, I'm taking you home. Stay there, I'll just get your coat.' Kalem strode into the drawing room, retrieved my jacket

93

and wrapped it round my shoulders.

'Are you going to clean this mess up, Golom?' Clarissa shouted at Kalem.

'No,' he snapped. 'Helen's not very well. I have to take her home.'

Clarissa huffed as loud as a steam engine. 'Had too much to drink, more like.'

Kalem gathered me up in his arms and carried me to the Land Rover. Carefully, manoeuvring the door open with one hand and resting me on the seat, he pulled the seatbelt over me and fastened it. Then, softly, he touched my face.

I rested my head on the door and opened the window, desperate for some fresh air. Everything was spinning and I wasn't sure that I was going to make it back home without depositing the contents of my stomach in the foot-well.

Kalem drove as fast as the ancient lump of junk would allow, shooting concerned looks at me.

'Stop!' I put my hand up. 'Going to be…' I clutched my stomach and doubled over.

Kalem pulled up at the kerb, just in time for me to fling the door open and throw up on the pavement. I sat there gulping for air, staring down at the bright red splatters.

'Here.' He handed me a tissue.

'Oh, my God, I think I'm bleeding internally. It's all red.'

'Come on, let's get you home. I'm going to call the doctor.'

Four and a half stops later – one was a false alarm – I'd been sick on half the pavements in town. When we finally arrived at my flat, Kalem carried me into the bedroom and placed me on the bed.

'Do you still use Doctor Lattimer?' He grabbed my phone book from the dressing-table, flicking through the pages.

I lay there trembling as he pulled the duvet up and around me, tucking me in fully clothed.

'Yes,' I whispered. 'Can you get me a bowl? Think I might throw up again.'

He returned carrying a plastic bowl, the phone pressed to his ear. Then he wandered into the kitchen, and I could hear his muffled voice. He came back a few minutes later with a glass of water.

'Doctor's on his way. He thinks you might have food

poisoning.' He sat down on the chair next to my bed, looking apprehensive.

I must have fallen into an exhausted sleep because when I came round, the doctor was sitting on the edge of my bed talking to Kalem in a hushed voice.

'How are you, my dear?' the elderly GP asked me.

I tried to lift myself up on to my elbows, but I couldn't quite make it and collapsed back down. 'Not too good.'

'I think you've probably had a dodgy mussel. It's amazing the amount of people who get food poisoning from seafood.' Dr Lattimer opened his big black leather case.

'But it was red. Do you think I'm bleeding inside?'

'Have you been drinking tonight?' Dr Lattimer asked.

'Red wine,' Kalem interjected, hovering by my side.

'Ah.' The doctor nodded his head. 'That explains the redness, then.' He pulled out a packet of tablets. 'Take two of these now and two again every four hours. I think you'll be OK in a few days.' He got to his feet and picked up his case. 'I think you should keep your eye on her,' he said to Kalem, patting him on the shoulder.

Kalem showed him out, then came back to sit on my bed as I leaned over to the bedside cabinet, picked up the glass of water and swallowed the tablets before flopping back onto the pillow.

'You heard what the doctor said, so I'm going to stay here with you tonight. I can't leave you like this.'

'Thanks.' I was in no position to resist.

And then I passed out.

I woke up a few hours later to complete darkness. I still felt awful. Picking up the bowl beside my bed, I threw up. Kalem, asleep in the chair next to my bed, shot up, almost toppling the chair. He perched on the edge of the bed, rubbing my back until nothing more could possibly come out.

'Reminds me of The Exorcist, all this projectile vomiting.' He carried the bowl to the bathroom, empted its contents and returned with it a few minutes later.

Wiping my mouth with a tissue, I attempted a smile. 'Why are you sleeping on the chair?' I patted the empty side of the bed. 'If you're going to stay, you might as well be comfortable.'

'Well, I've always wanted to get you into bed, but not really like this. And I know I'm not your type, anyway,' he drawled sarcastically, although for a second there was an edge to his voice, which sounded different, serious almost.

I patted the empty side of the bed. 'Come on. I know you're not likely to pounce on me looking like this,' I joked. 'If you're going to stay, you might as well be comfortable.'

The last thing I remember as I drifted off to sleep again was Kalem softly stroking my hand.

# Chapter 12
## Sunday, day 7 – Single Men Are Still Freaks

When I opened my eyes on Sunday morning, I was lying on my side. Kalem studied me with his intense brown eyes, which for the first time I noticed had an unusual pattern of green flecks running through them. He had a look I'd never seen before. Probably complete disgust.

'Did you know that you dribble and snore when you sleep?' he said.

I slapped him. 'Is that in-between the puking or at the same time?'

'You must have had a bad dream too, because you woke up suddenly, sat bolt upright in bed and shouted, "Duck! There's a sniper with a thirty-eight!" And then passed out again.'

'Blimey.' I smiled. 'What did you do?'

'Well, I ducked, of course.' He leapt off the bed. 'How do you feel?'

'Actually, I feel OK.' I sat up.

He rubbed his back. 'God, your bed's uncomfortable.'

'I like it.'

'Can you manage something to eat? I think you need something – how about a nice, greasy, fried egg sandwich?'

'Urgh!' My stomach gurgled at the very thought. 'Could I just have a slice of toast and a cup of tea, please?'

I could hear him bashing around in the kitchen, looking for cups and teabags as I heaved myself out of bed and wandered into the lounge on wobbly legs.

He pulled out a chair for me. 'Sit.'

'That's funny. You sound exactly like Ayshe does sometimes when she's being bossy.'

He came back in sloshing two big mugs of tea and balancing a pile of lightly buttered toast.

'Thanks.' I attacked two slices and slurped the tea. 'Think I must be dehydrated.'

'Are you going to be OK?' He finished his tea in a hurry. 'I've got to shoot off.'

My hand flew to my mouth. 'Oh, I forgot. Emine won't be very impressed, will she?'

97

He muttered something impossible to hear, leaving me alone, munching the rest of my feast and worrying about what had happened between us the night before. I mean, I was quite tipsy, otherwise I never would have held his hand during dinner. But then we had been pretending to be a couple after all, and he had reciprocated, hadn't he? But the strangest thing was that it had all felt quite natural. I wondered how many men would look after me so patiently during a throwing-up session of that magnitude. Certainly not Justin, that's for sure! But this was all totally ridiculous: Kalem was Ayshe's brother for God's sake, and he was involved with someone else. How would Emine feel about his late-night back-rubbing session with me? I was sure she wouldn't be impressed.

I tried to fling all thoughts of Kalem out of my mind, but it was just no use. They kept pinging back like a boomerang. Anyway, it was crazy. I didn't fancy him in the slightest.

'Pull yourself together. You're imagining things,' I muttered into the silence and busied myself tidying up the flat in preparation for Nick coming over.

It was only after I'd had a tidying splurge that I realized there was a message on my answer phone. I sat down next to it cautiously, hoping it wasn't going to be that lunatic again.

'Right, that's it. It's your last chance. If you don't come up with the money today, I'm going to send the Meat Cleaver up to see ya. Know what I mean? He's not called that for nothing, you know, and he won't take no for an answer.' And then he broke into a crazy kind of Vincent Price laugh, which went something like, 'Ooh hoo ha-ha-ha-ha, ooh hoo ha–ha-ha-ha.' The connection was severed abruptly. It was the bloody lunatic again. What the hell was he on about? A ripple of fear crept up my body. I fidgeted in my chair, biting my thumbnail, the music from the shower scene in *Psycho* playing in my head.

My mobile rang and I shot off the chair, an orchestra of drums pounding in my chest. 'Agh!' I screamed, reaching for the phone.

'Hi, it's Nick.'

I sank back into the chair, clutching my chest. 'Hi...Nick.' I fanned myself with my hand.

'Are you OK? You sound a bit strange.'

Why did he always seem to catch me at the worst moment? 'Erm...no, I'm fine.' I paused while my breathing returned to normal. 'Fine,' I repeated, which slipped out a little more high pitched than I anticipated. 'How are you?'

'I'm afraid something's come up, and I'm not going to make it today.'

'Oh...well these things happen, don't they.' Did I feel disappointed? I wasn't sure.

'I'd still like to take you to the boxing match on Friday, though. Is it OK to ring you in the week and sort out the details?'

'Yes, that sounds good. I'll speak to you later, then. Bye.'

By the afternoon, I felt one hundred per cent again. The unsteady legs were back to normal and my stomach only grumbled occasionally so I decided to visit Nan, something I'd done religiously every Sunday for years. She'd been ensconced in a nursing home after a brush with death following a chip-pan fire, which had almost caused a gas explosion big enough to topple the whole neighbourhood. It had even been on the news!

I was just dashing out the door when the phone rang.

'Hello, puke-monster,' Ayshe laughed.

I cradled the receiver to my ear. 'What a night! I'm fine now, though. Feel a bit ravenous still, but I've got Old Mother Hubbard in my cupboards.' I'd eaten the entire contents of my fridge after breakfast. The only thing left was a mouldy old piece of cheese, a jar of tomato purée, and a packet of hairclips – although I wasn't quite sure exactly what those were doing in there. I must have been having a freaky five minutes – aaagh! Maybe I was getting Alzheimer's too!

'Well, that is perfect because today's challenge is Sunday Night Food Shopping.'

'Why is food shopping a challenge? I always go food shopping.'

'Yes, but everyone knows that Sunday night is singles' night. It's the shopping equivalent of a dating agency.'

Did they? I'd never heard that before. 'Are you having a laugh?'

'Absolutely not. I think you should try the new Tesco that's opened at the end of the High Street. And they've got clothes in there too,' she breathed.

'Urgh! Don't mention clothes.'

'You're not seriously scared of clothes shopping now, are you?'

'No – yes – oh, I don't know.'

'Well, even more reason to go, then. You're supposed to be doing things to get your confidence back.'

I hesitated. Food shopping sounded all right. I could handle that with no problems. After all, I'd only been food shopping about ten million times in my life and nothing had ever happened before. 'OK, Miss. Whatever you command.'

'Text me when you finish, and I'll pick you up outside. Görüşürüz.' See you later in Turkish, she chimed.

I stopped off at a little shop on the way to the nursing home to pick up a couple of individual cartons of orange juice and some toffees. As I perused the aisles, I wondered whether the Sunday singles' shopping rule involved the corner shop variety as well, or did it just apply to supermarkets? Did it mean everyone who shopped on a Sunday night was single or just a small proportion? And who made up the rule in the first place? The possibilities were endless.

'Ah, Miss Grey.' Nurse Pratchett caught up with me as I headed up the corridor which had single, private rooms leading off on both sides of the walkway.

The rooms were directly opposite each other, which meant that each resident could look into the room on the other side. Often there would be slanging matches between them as they shouted at each other like inmates in a prison and only slightly more well behaved.

I twirled around a bit too fast and felt my stomach gurgle. 'Hi. How's my nan? Is everything OK?'

'She's fine.' Nurse Pratchett scratched her head. 'We've had to put a catheter in, though. She's not going to the loo properly. She doesn't like it, I'm afraid.'

Who would? I thought, as I hurried off to her room.

'Hi, Nan.' I breezed in and planted a kiss on her forehead.

The trouble with Alzheimer's was that sometimes she was completely sane and at other times completely gaga. It didn't help that she was getting very deaf lately so she shouted a lot, as well.

She smiled at me and sat up in bed. 'Helen!'

I wrinkled my nose at the strong smell of urine coming from her bed.

'What's going on here?' I picked up the bedclothes, looking underneath to see if the catheter had been leaking. 'Your bed's all wet, Nan. Did you have an accident? '

'What?' She looked at me completely mystified.

I waved my hand and plumped up her pillows. 'Never mind.'

'She did that!' She pointed through the doorway at the elderly woman in her room across the hallway. 'Dirty cow!' she said in a loud voice thinking it was just a whisper, nearly exploding my eardrum.

The woman looked up from reading her Mills and Boon. 'I've had just about enough of her,' she sighed.

'And as for that Nurse Hatchett—' Nan started again.

'Pratchett,' I butted in, handing her the toffees and juice.

'What, dear?' Nan eyed them with intense suspicion, as if they were loaded with Ricin.

'Never mind.'

I hoped I didn't end up like this, it would drive me mad! But then, if you were already mad, would you know it?

'Nurse Hatchett keeps coming in here and hiding a bag of piss under my bed!' she shouted at me. Her voice must have carried half a mile.

I could hear Nurse Pratchett snorting to herself in the corridor.

'Shush, she'll hear you,' I whispered. 'Anyway, don't worry Nan. It's not a bag of piss, it's a catheter bag.'

'Looks like piss! Why do I need a taffeta bag in here? I never go out.'

'No, a catheter bag!'

'What's that, then?' she looked fretful.

I thought I'd better get her off this subject fast. 'Have a toffee.' I pointed at them. 'You love them.'

'She stole my chocolate bar.' She pointed at the woman across the hall again who'd stuffed half a chocolate bar into her mouth and wiped the other half on her bedding.

'You don't even like chocolate,' I said.

'Go and get it for me, there's a love.'

'Here, have a toffee.' I opened the packet for her, sitting back to watch her fiddle with the wrappers.

'Oh, I'll have one later,' she huffed.

I studied her hair, which looked like it had been hacked to death. She had a lopsided fringe and half her hair was missing above her ears.

'Have the hairdressers been in again?' They usually let the college students loose to practice shampoo and sets on the poor unsuspecting residents.

'You could do with a hair cut, too.'

I ran a hand through my hair. 'I went on Friday!'

'About time too, you'll never get a nice young man if you let yourself go.'

'So, what's been happening this week, Nan?'

'A man got into bed with me last night.'

I was thinking about the same thing myself! 'Who was that, then?'

'He said his name was Albert, but I don't know anyone called that.'

'That's Grandad,' I said. 'It must have been a dream.'

'Couldn't possibly have been, dear. My grandad snuffed it years ago.'

I shook my head. 'No, my granddad; your husband.'

She beckoned me forward. 'I had to cancel my skiing holiday because I'm in here!' she bellowed.

'You've never been skiing.' I leapt back, my ears ringing.

'Yes I have. I used to go every year with Eddie.'

This was news to me. 'And who is Eddie?'

She considered this for a minute as if it was a trick question. 'You know, Eddie.'

I didn't have a clue who Eddie was. Maybe she'd been having an affair.

'And I used to go swimming once a week with David.' she let out a wistful sigh.

She sounded like she was a goer in her day! 'Who's David?'

'You know. David...what was his name?' She reclined against her pillows. 'Hassle.'

And then I knew what she was raving on about. 'You mean David Hasslehoff. You used to watch Baywatch every week.'

'No, I used to swim with him every week. Used to wear a lovely, red swimsuit, didn't I? Of course my figure was a bit better in those days.' She tilted her head, imagining herself running up and down the sun-baked beach with David chasing after her lustfully.

'What did you have for lunch?' I asked.

'Nothing. They don't feed you in here. I'm all skin and bone.' She looked down at her ample bosoms and plump arms.

'Of course they do.'

'No, they don't. She steals all my food!' She pointed at the Mills and Boon woman again who looked back at us and stuck her fingers up.

I inspected her top. 'Have you got that on back-to-front?'

'What dear?' she shouted at me.

'Your top, it's the wrong way round. Here, let me help you change it.' I grappled with her to get her top off and turn it the right way round.

'Ow,' she grumbled. 'Are you still seeing that young man of yours?' She asked me the same questions every time I saw her.

'Who?' I pulled her arms through her top.

'Chris.'

How could she remember my first ever boyfriend and not remember who I was?

'That was ages ago.'

She fiddled with her top. 'How are the children?'

'I haven't got any, Nan.'

'Why not? Does he have a problem in that department? Albert had a problem in later life. He used to make me wear a nurse's outfit sometimes.' She took her dentures out, studying them. 'What about that other fella. James or John or...'

'Justin.'

'He was lovely.'

'He was a cheat!'

'Well, why don't you get yourself a nice young man like Kalem?' She suddenly looked like her normal self again.

I blushed. 'It's a bit more complicated than that, Nan. You know that Yasmin and Deniz wouldn't approve of him going out with someone who wasn't Turkish Cypriot.'

'I always thought he was perfect for you.' She looked me up and down. 'Well, how about that other peculiar friend of yours? Charlene or something: the one who's always dressed in pink.'

'You mean Charlie. He's fine.'

'Is it a he or a she?' She tilted her head.

I didn't really know how to answer that one without getting into the finer points of weirdness. 'He's a he.'

'Well, why don't you go out with him, then? You could swap clothes.'

I was saved from answering – thank God – by Nurse Pratchett, who entered the room, carrying a tray of food. 'Here's your dinner, Lily. Your favourite: roast beef.' She lowered it onto the table and wheeled it over to the bed.

'Ooh, I love the food in here.' Nan sniffed at her Yorkshire pudding with delight.

I stood up and kissed her goodbye. 'I'll see you next week then, Nan.' And I left her to enjoy the food they never served!

# Chapter 13

By the time I reached Tesco that evening I was dying for a wee –
thought my bladder was about to spontaneously combust,
actually – so I tried to swiftly grab a trolley from the trolley park,
but all of them were stuck together. I tugged hard, but the front
one wasn't budging. Instead, the whole line of trolleys did a
Mexican wave at me. Frustrated, I yanked hard but still couldn't
get one of the little buggers to co-operate. I stood there for a few
minutes scratching my head, feeling ridiculous, until a hard
nosed woman with knuckle-duster rings came up and effortlessly
pulled the front one out – think I must have loosened it for her,
though. I managed to pull out the next trolley and deposited it
ready and waiting outside the loo area. Following the signs to the
toilets, I burst into the first door I came across. By this time, I
was doing a kind of half-sprint, half-trot, which rivaled that of
the hip-jiggling fast walkers in the Olympic Games. I dashed
into the nearest cubicle and weed for England. When I came
out; there was a small queue of men waiting outside the cubicle
door, eyeing me strangely. My cheeks burned scarlet. I'd been to
the loo in the men's!

I made a quick exit, only to find my trolley had vanished. So I
huffed back outside and grabbed the only one left which, not
surprisingly, was the reject that had a wheel with a mind of its
own. It must have had a bit missing somewhere as it made a loud
squealing noise like a mouse on ecstasy. The only way to steer it
in a straight line was to try and twist it in a diagonal manner so it
looked like I was purposely heading towards people, like a
kamikaze shopper. I repeatedly twisted my hips to get the thing
going in the right direction which probably made me look like I
had a severe walking problem or a wooden leg. Unless Paul
McCartney was shopping here tonight, I didn't have a hope in
hell of meeting anyone.

I started at the fruit and veg aisle, fighting with my trolley to
keep it going in a straight line and checking out my fellow
shoppers with a shifty glance. It was quite bizarre; there were a
few lone males and females around, but also a couple of big,
butch-looking women – one of whom looked like Eminem and
must have thought it was gay night shopping instead. There

seemed to be a kind of expectant buzz in the air.

I picked up an aubergine, giving it a quick squeeze, and then heard a crude titter going on behind me. How odd. I didn't think aubergine squeezing was in the least bit smutty.

Two men pushed their trolleys along, looking me up and down. Blimey, I thought, how come I'd never thought of this before as the place to meet someone? One of them smiled at me then busied himself looking at the carrots.

I plopped the aubergine in the trolley and wheeled it over to the oranges. After bagging a few of those, I noticed someone looking at me out of the corner of my eye. I glanced up and saw a really short guy carrying a shopping basket.

He shook his head at me. 'Some people will do anything to pull a bloke on singles' night.' He picked up some chillies and put them in a bag.

What the hell was he talking about? I hadn't done anything, yet. Or was there a certain singles' shopping etiquette, which meant that if you went for aubergines you were easy, but if you chose potatoes, you weren't?

'Pardon?' I asked.

'You know.' He scratched his eye.

'Mmm,' I mumbled and wandered off to the mangoes, looking over at him in confusion. His eye had turned bright red and watery. He rubbed at it furiously.

'Didn't anyone ever tell you not to touch your face after you've been handling chillies?' I thought he would be eternally grateful for this piece of information.

'I don't speak to floozies.' He stalked off.

What was the world coming to if you couldn't even have an innocent squeeze of a vegetable without someone getting the wrong idea?

I wandered into the dairy aisle looking for some milk. Only a few solitary cartons remained on the highest shelf, so I stretched up and tried to reach them, but it was no use.

'Here, let me.' A guy in a purple shell suit had just turned the corner and made his way over, leering at me.

'Thanks.' I smiled as he reached up and retrieved a few cartons. 'Two, please.'

He gave me a dirty little grin. 'Haven't seen you here before.'

'Well, it's only just opened, hasn't it?' I put the milk in my trolley.

'If you need any more help, just ask.' He gave me another lecherous sneer as he walked past, and then kept looking at my arse.

Whoa, creep alert! He was the last person I'd ever ask for help. Weren't there any normal men left in the world?

After collecting some cheddar, I reached for my usual carton of eggs, pausing in thought as I remembered what Kalem had told me about battery hens. Visions of poor little chickens being crushed to death in a big warehouse somewhere sprang to mind, so I picked up an organic carton instead and set off round the corner to the canned section, casually scanning the place for normal men.

As I stood there, wondering whether to buy baked beans and tinned tomatoes, I was shocked to spy Clarissa. What was she doing here on singles' night? And even more strange, why was she in supermarket uniform?

'Clarissa!'

She looked flabbergasted to see me. 'Helen! I thought I'd seen the last of you last night.'

My hand flew to my mouth. 'God, I'm really sorry about that. The doctor said I had food poisoning. Probably from a dodgy mussel. Apparently you have to be really, really careful with them.'

'That's impossible. Charles and I were fine,' she muttered with a glint of steel in her eyes as she piled up tins on the shelves.

'What are you doing here?'

'Oh, so you think you've caught me out, do you?' She glared at me with a tin of tomato soup resting in her hand.

'I...don't know what you mean. I thought you said you didn't work. Have you just started here?'

'Oh, I don't recall saying that. Was it before or after you threw up all over my kitchen?' She shot me a poisonous look.

I picked up a tin of beans. 'Sorry, I must have misunderstood.'

'I'm just um...um...helping a friend out.' Her mouth flapped ridiculously as she busied herself stacking the shelves.

Another member of staff wearing an identical uniform to Clarissa chose that well-timed moment to appear.

'I'm sorry to interrupt,' he said to me. 'Can I borrow this member of staff?'

'Of course.' I smiled at him.

'Right, then, Hyacynth Bouquet, we need you on the meat

107

counter, pronto!' He swiveled on his heels and stalked off. She threw the remaining tins on the shelf with enough force to cause a severe dent in it and scuttled away without meeting my gaze. As I waltzed off to the freezer section, I let out a soft giggle.

I perused the frozen veg, but there was only one packet of peas wedged at the bottom of a very tall chest freezer. Leaning over the top, I reached in slowly. Why did they make these things so high? I made a mental note to complain to the manager as I teetered on tiptoes, trying hard to grab the corner of the packet which was just out of my reach.

'Ooh.' I made a final stretch and just managed to snare it.

'Nice arse!' I heard behind me, instantly recognizing the dulcet tones of my neighbour, Clive, with the disgusting tooth-waggling habit.

'Shit,' I muttered to the peas before straightening up and spinning round.

'Oh, it's you!' He looked surprised, but carried on giving me a dirty little leer anyway.

'Hi, Clive.' I faked a smile, wondering how he thought he was going to pull anything, other than perhaps head lice, with those kinds of comments.

'Never seen you before on singles' night,' he smirked.

'Mmm.' The fake smile was glued to my face as I got an acrid waft of his foul-smelling BO.

'I used to go to Asda until this one opened, but there's definitely more choice in here.' He licked his lips. He was almost drooling.

'How nice – anyway, must dash. I can feel a severe heart attack coming on.' I darted off, throwing sneaky looks over my shoulder to make sure he wasn't stalking me from behind.

This whole shopping malarkey was taking its toll, but I was saved from complete boredom by the wine section, where I found a small stand giving away free samples – granted, they were only the minuscule thimble variety, but I figured I could stand there for a while and down a good few before anyone moved me along.

'We've got a special promotion on this week. This is the new Fanshawe's table wine. One bottle is only £3.99 this week,' said a very dapper sales lady who was caked in make-up. She had a complete Rocky Horror Picture Show going on all by herself. I hoped she had an industrial sized trowel at home: she was going to need it to scrape that lot off. 'Would you like to try it, madam?'

What a ridiculous question, of course I would!

'Absolutely.' I took a thimbleful of wine and downed it in two swift flicks of the wrist.

'What do you think?' She smiled up at me, and I thought her foundation might crack.

'I'm not sure yet, but I think you need bigger glasses. Can I try another one?' I thought I should get as many in as possible, really, just to give a well-rounded opinion.

I took an identical thimble without waiting for an answer. As I put it to my lips, I caught a glimpse of Clarissa striding up towards us.

'Clarissa! What do you think of this lovely wine, it's only £4?' I grabbed a thimble and held it out to her as she stormed past with a face like a smacked arse.

I hogged the stand for a while until the wine kicked in, giving me enough bravery to jump straight back on the clothes horse before I had any lasting psychological damage, and I headed off to the clothes section.

Picking up a few pairs of trousers, I deposited my trolley outside the changing rooms while I went to try them on. As soon as I walked into the cubicle I knew something wasn't quite right because my skirt was ruched up in a strange way. I twisted round, gawping in the mirror at my bum, which was completely hanging out. I'd inadvertently tucked the back of my skirt into my knickers when I'd trotted off to the loo and I'd been baring all and sundry to the whole shop all night. No wonder everyone had been checking out my arse and making smutty comments about it. I wondered how I could make a sharp exit out of there without seeing anyone that I'd already come face to bum with.

'Damn.' I flung the trousers on top of the trolley and made a speedy dash for the checkout.

I stood in the queue, not wanting to make eye contact with anyone. My best bet, I decided, was to stare at the guy in front's shopping on the conveyor belt. Which I did – well, until my eyes watered. One banana; one packet of jelly; one tub of crème fraiche and a tube of pile cream. How peculiar.

I could sense the presence of people filling up behind me, so I tossed my shopping onto the checkout as quickly as I could. It wasn't until I was halfway through that it dawned on me this wasn't my trolley at all. What was I doing with a bumper pack of nappies, an enormous packet of baby wipes, ten cartons of organic cranberry juice, and five packets of frozen broccoli florets?

The whole experience had worn pretty thin by this time so, to the amazement of the till assistant, I left the whole lot there and strode out of the shop with absolutely sweet FA.

On my way out to the car park, I spotted Kalem climbing into his Land Rover. I stopped in my tracks, my face flushing as I remembered the embarrassment of the night before. I was far too apprehensive to see him yet. If I stood still, maybe he wouldn't notice me. What was he doing here on singles' night, anyway? Why wasn't he at home with Emine?

I side-stepped slowly towards the trolleys, not wanting to make any sudden movements. Maybe I could hide behind them until he left. I'd nearly reached them when I saw his window wind down. He poked his head out, gazing at me in silence.

Damn. He's seen me.

'H, what the hell are you doing?'

'Nothing.'

'Hop in.' He jerked his head towards the inside of the vehicle.

'No, it's OK. I fancy a walk anyway. Nice night.' I tried to smile but my mouth decided not to work properly. I managed to lift the corners of my mouth a fraction, blinking rapidly, giving the rather fetching impression of a lunatic instead. I darted off behind the trolleys and stomped all the way home.

When I arrived, panting and red faced, I spied Charlie loitering with intent outside my door.

'Hello, sweetie. How was the singles' night shopping? What, no bags?' Charlie asked.

'Well, I won't be doing that again. Did you know that Sunday night is supposed to be singles' night?'

''Course! Everybody knows that.' He waved his hand.

'Did you want something?' I let myself in, and he followed on my heels like an excited little puppy.

'Well!' He clapped his hands together. 'Ayshe let me in on her little challenge for you tomorrow, and I was hoping you would let me tag along.'

'I don't even know what it is yet.'

'I'll give you a clue. It involves naked flesh.' He mimed an exaggerated Rik Mayall humping action, thrusting his crutch

110

backwards and forwards at me.

I'd had enough of naked flesh tonight to last a lifetime! 'What?'

'It involves male nudeyness.'

'What do you mean?'

He couldn't resist blurting it out any longer. 'A naked art class; drawing men's dangly bits; that kind of thing. Capeesh or not capeesh?'

'Capeesh. I don't know how she thinks these things up.'

'So?' he peered at me.

'So, what?' I'd forgotten the question.

'Can I come?' He jumped up and down like Zebedee with a spring loose.

''Course you can. The more the merrier.'

'OK, I'll knock for you at ten. Toodle-oo.' He skipped off.

# Chapter 14
## Monday, day 8 – Nudity Is Art

I wasn't sure exactly what woke me on Monday morning. It was one of three things: either Charlie singing I Will Survive at the tops of his lungs, the constant pounding on my door, or a totally explicit dream I was having about Kalem.

'I'm coming,' I shouted as I went to investigate the source of the banging.

I peered through the spy hole, hoping it wasn't Mr. Meat Packer – or whoever the hell he was – coming to get his money.

'Delivery for Ms Grey.' A couple of thuggy-looking delivery guys balanced a massive package in their arms.

'What's that?' I shouted through the door, just to be on the safe side. How did I know it wasn't the Vincent Price sound-a-like either?

One of the thugs read a label at the back of the package. 'It says it's from Adrian Ponsonby.'

I grunted. 'Oh, God.' I'd been in denial about the painting, hoping it would never actually turn up until after I'd popped my clogs.

'Where d'ya want it, luv?' one of them shouted from behind the door in a bored voice.

I opened the door wider and stared at the package for a bit. Frowning and scratching my head, I finally pointed to the cast-iron fireplace in the centre of the lounge. 'Here, please,' I said, gulping in total self-disgust.

They heaved it down and handed me a clipboard. 'Sign, please.'

After I'd scrawled my moniker on it, I handed it back and gawked at the painting, hoping if I stood there long enough and shouted 'Abracadabra!' in a really loud voice, it would vanish into thin air. Five minutes later, it still hadn't vanished, so I unwrapped it and leaned it against the wall. It should have been called Projectile Vomit, I thought, as it looked quite similar to the state of the pavement after I'd finished with it on Saturday night. I decided to leave it where it was until I could make my mind up as to what I could possibly do with it. Maybe I could make it into a coffee table or something. Perhaps if I just left it there long enough it might blend in with the room, and I would never notice it again.

Charlie had now given Gloria Gaynor a rest and had started a new rendition of Tina Turner in a totally non-Tina Turner way. How could anyone get any sleep around here?

I heard a muffled shout of, 'Shut that bloody racket up.' Probably the same grumpy person who hadn't liked my superior singing voice either.

I ambled into the kitchen to make breakfast. This consisted solely of the abandoned piece of cheese, which was the only half-edible thing left in the fridge, although by the time I'd cut off all the mould there was just a smidgen left. I made an iced coffee and then worried about my caffeine intake for the zillionth time.

Armed with coffee, I grabbed the phone and anxiously tapped in the number for The Coffee Bean, pacing until someone picked up. After explaining my rather unfortunate predicament about the multiple cappuccino ordering spree, they promised to refund nine out of the ten orders and assured me they would only send out one. They were very good about it – they didn't even laugh, although I bet they did, as soon as I hung up. I breathed a hefty sigh of relief and promised myself I would never ever buy anything online again. It was just too scary.

When Charlie finally shut up and knocked on my door, I was raring to go, but my stomach kept growling at me in hunger.

'Yoohoo.' He rang the doorbell. 'Didn't disturb you with my singing, did I?'

'I think you disturbed the far reaches of Outer Mongolia.'

'Was I good? I've been practicing.' He swung a pink handbag.

'Fabby. Don't think I could tell you and Gloria Gaynor apart.' Who was I to disillusion him?

Today Charlie was dressed conservatively – well, for him anyway; for anyone else it would have been completely over the top. He pranced up the road, with me in tow, wearing a fluffy tiger patterned jumper with the words BITE ME emblazoned across the front and some tight, denim jeans. The outfit wouldn't be complete, of course, without the sock, which he'd squeezed into its usual place.

\*\*\*\*

113

'Where are the nudey art classes?' Charlie asked when we arrived at the information desk in the college. He could hardly contain himself.

'You mean life drawing?' The receptionist squinted over the top of her glasses. She looked a bit of a dragon with evil little eyes and a pinched-up mouth.

'Yep.' Charlie nodded.

'Room five, down the hall.' She pointed and I could have sworn a puff of smoke erupted from her mouth. 'It's the fourth door on the right.'

'Oh, goody.' He skipped away and I pretended I wasn't with him.

Half a dozen middle-aged women and a couple of older men, all looking a bit arty, sat on plastic chairs in the brightly-lit class room. They were arranged in a circular pattern for maximum viewing. Easels were set up in front of them, with a selection of pencils and charcoal on trays underneath. They all looked very serious and completely in their artistic element.

Charlie sat down and I arranged myself next to him. In the corner of the room the teacher stood with his back to us, talking to a striking-looking, thirty-something guy, wearing a long, brown bath robe.

'Cor, he's not bad.' Charlie leaned over and whispered to me.

'Shush.' I giggled, studying the pencils with interest.

'OK, we'll just wait a few more minutes to see if anyone else turns up and then we'll begin.' The teacher turned round and addressed the group. Slowly, his eyes travelled to mine.

I gasped. It was Kalem.

He strode across the room towards us. 'What are you doing here?'

'Well, this is Helen's challenge for the day,' Charlie answered. 'And I just wanted to see a willy!'

'What are you doing here? I didn't think you taught life drawing?' I asked

'I'm just standing in for the regular teacher who's off sick.'

'Well, I hope you're not expecting me to come up with a Michaelangelo masterpiece. I can't draw to save my life,' I said.

'Right, let's get started then.' Kalem made his way to the centre of the room. 'OK, everyone, unfortunately Bob can't make it today, so I'm taking this class. For those of you who haven't seen me before, my name's Kalem.' He looked round the room. 'Now, I'm sure some of you haven't picked up a paintbrush or a pencil since your school days, but don't worry. Drawing is about individual expression, there is no exam or competition with anyone else. Anyone can learn to draw.'

'Apart from me,' I whispered to Charlie. He hadn't seen my unusual skills yet.

'No, I'm serious.' Kalem must have heard me. 'Anyone can draw. But it really doesn't matter what you draw. Practice makes perfect, as they say.'

The man in the bathrobe calmly slipped it off, revealing his defined muscular body and six-pack. He picked up a chair and placed it in the centre of the room, sitting down with his rather impressive wedding tackle on full display.

'Oh, I say!' gasped Charlie.

My eyes widened as I examined it closely. God, it was huge! How could he walk round like that and not do himself an injury?

'Wow,' I muttered.

'This is Paul.' Kalem motioned to the model. 'Some of the best art is actually unplanned and spontaneous. Art should be fun, not regimented. You just need to go with your instincts and let them flow uninhibited.'

'I wouldn't mind getting uninhibited with him,' Charlie said.

'If you break down what you are drawing into smaller and more angular lines, this will help you see the real object. Now, there are popular methods for teaching drawing such as the grid method, whereby you break the picture up into smaller blocks and draw each block individually. But for this week, as there are probably a few regulars here,' he smiled at a woman who was hanging on his every word, 'I think we should just make it fun this time and let you draw away.' Kalem swept his hand round the room.

'I want to get cracking.' Charlie was about to pop with desperation.

'If you have any questions, I'll be wandering around the room, so please just ask.'

I picked up a pencil, gawping with fascination at Paul. Where did I start? Was it best to begin with the head, or the feet, or even the wedding tackle? Biting the end of my pencil, I studied him, which wasn't hard because he really was rather gorgeous. Looking round the room, I gazed at all the other artists who were pensively admiring him in an artistic kind of way, not in a pervy

115

kind of way like me. Charlie was off and away with no such problems, getting fast and furious with his charcoal.

Deciding to start with the main outline of the body, I pulled a thoughtful face and concentrated on his shape. I stretched my arm out and closed one eye, holding my pencil up high in front of Paul. I didn't know exactly what it was meant to achieve, but I'd seen other people doing it, so I copied them.

'I am so good at this.' Charlie swept his charcoal across his paper. I didn't want to look in case I unwittingly copied it, and he got the hump.

I slashed the pencil over my page, trying to draw the outline of his body. After twenty minutes, I sat back and surveyed my work. It was not good. It looked very similar indeed to the Michelin Man, so I  pulled the paper off in frustration and screwed it into a ball, sulking for a bit while I waited for a flash of inspiration. Charlie hummed away to himself.

Take two wasn't much better. This one looked like the Michelin Man who had been on a recent diet, but still had tubby tendencies. Oh well, I thought, at least a Michelin Man was better than nothing.

My phone suddenly meowed and all the arty people looked around for a cat. One of the women must have been allergic to them as it produced a sneezing fit. Leaning into my bag, I flipped it open. It was Ayshe as usual.

'Don't forget family henna night tonight. Leaving at seven. XXX.'

I bent down to throw it back into my bag, but as I got up again, my shoulder clipped the edge of my picture. It went flying and hit the drawing of the lady sitting next to me. My jaw dropped as I witnessed her picture hit her neighbour's, which in turn banged into the next one and then the next in a concertina effect, just like a pack of well-stacked dominoes. Paul watched the whole event unfold with amusement from the centre of the room as all the serious arty people glowered at me.

The blood drained from my face. 'I'm so sorry,' I said to everyone, glancing over at Kalem, who stood, transfixed to the spot, gazing back at me with a glassy, statue-like mask on his face.

Slowly, he dropped his gaze to the floor and looked at it in horror. He crouched down and busied himself picking up the jumble of easels scattered across the room as the rest of us spent

116

the next ten minutes picking up our respective pictures. When we'd put the artwork annihilation back into some kind of order again, Kalem circled the edge of the room towards me.

I wiped a bead of sweat from my upper lip.

The rest of the class shifted away from me, dragging their easels and chairs out of and beyond knocking-over reach as I sat in stunned silence, willing the floor to open up and swallow me.

Kalem crept up behind me, his jaw throbbing. He bent over, lips touching my earlobe. 'What the hell do you think you're doing? Are you trying to get me sacked?' he whispered.

His breath tickled my eardrum. I gulped and shook my head.

'For God's sake, lay off the caffeine!' he hissed in my ear and walked over to the other side of the room, as far away from me as he could possibly get.

'Here, I think this is yours.' Paul got up from his chair and handed me a piece of charcoal, whilst I scrabbled around on the floor collecting the stray pencils which were still strewn all over the place. It was a bit unfortunate I was crouching down because his wedding tackle veered dangerously close to my face as he handed it to me.

'Thanks. Sorry about that.' I averted my eyes to avoid a close encounter of the willy kind and sat back down, glancing about in case another accident just decided to happen around me.

Charlie leaned over to me, scrutinizing my work. 'Excellent,' he muttered at it. 'That man is hung like an elephant!'

'Yes, but it's the size of it when it's erect that counts,' I said.

Then he looked slightly puzzled. 'So what you're saying is…it gets smaller when it goes hard, then? Because that is already colossal!'

Paul met my gaze and looked very smug. I slouched down, hiding behind my easel. When I popped back up he was gazing into space, so I started on take three, which took a couple of hours to bring to its full, stunning, work-of-genius potential. Now I went completely the other way, and it was more of an anorexic Michelin Man.

Kalem wandered over to Charlie, studying his drawing. 'You might like to try drawing the whole subject next time, instead of just the penis.'

I glanced over at Charlie's very eye-catching piece. He'd taken up the whole paper with a ginormous willy. He leaned back admiring it, looking very pleased with himself.

117

One of the arty looking women glanced over at Charlie's drawing and gave a disapproving snort. Several frosty looks flew our way too.

Kalem glanced at the clock. 'I'm sorry, folks, we're going to have to wrap it up now. You're welcome to take your artwork home with you or you can leave it here to finish off next week.'

I thought I'd leave mine and then everybody would be extremely jealous.

Charlie started rolling his up. 'I'm taking mine. Think I'll frame it.'

Paul, the-well-endowed, was suddenly overcome by a bout of shyness and stepped back into the bathrobe. He wandered over to my easel, studying it with interest.

'That's a very...interesting perspective. Will you be back next week?' He grinned at me.

I glanced at Kalem, who shook his head at me in silence, miming violent throat slitting actions.

'Probably not,' I said.

'I will be,' Charlie butted in, then dragged me out of the door. 'Come on, I'm famished. Shall we get a sandwich?' he said to me, his picture wedged securely under his arm.

'Absolutely, I haven't had anything proper to eat for ages.' I was ravenous.

We formed a disorderly queue at the sandwich bar and waited among the fellow lunchees. I ordered a melted brie baguette and Charlie opted for a plump-looking sausage roll. He had willies on the brain. There were some small booths along the sides and some bistro tables in the centre of the room. As we headed towards the only empty space left, I saw Emine and a well-suited man coming out of a booth on the opposite side. I stopped in my tracks and grabbed hold of Charlie's arm, nodding in her direction. She hadn't seen me, so I scrutinized her carefully. She was the complete opposite to me: very girly, whereas I was always more of a tomboy. While she was tall and willowy, I was short and – well, not exactly plump – especially after I'd now lost weight – but more sort of...un-willowy. And – ooh, maybe I should try and tame my messy curls and go for the poker-straight look like her. There was no doubt about it, she was beautiful with a wonderful figure and a permanently orange spray-on tan – I'm sure her teeth were bleached too – but to Ayshe and me, she always seemed a bit false and very shallow.

118

She looked at her companion, giggling and fluttering her eyelashes at him. I admitted to myself that although I'm not the most experienced when it comes to men, even I recognized a heavy dose of flirting when I saw one.

'Who's she with?' Charlie murmured. He was worse than a woman when it came to gossip.

The man put his arm around Emine's waist, and she gazed up at him with a lusty look in her eye as they moseyed out.

'I wonder if Kalem knows what she's doing while he's at work,' I whispered, tightening my grip on Charlie's arm.

# Chapter 15

I squeezed myself into my new skinny jeans, now that I was skinny – well, skinnier than I'd been before, anyway. I cut the tags off my new slinky top – courtesy of the freebie voucher – and shimmied into it. After applying some subtle eye make-up and lip-gloss, I scrunched up my hair a bit with some wax. Sod the super-sleek look: I didn't have time for straighteners now.

I tottered up to Ayshe's just before seven.

'Are you lot ready?' I shouted.

Ayshe swung the door open. 'Come on,' she grumbled to Atila and Kalem.

'You know what it's going to be like. Your dad will be pissed again and come out with something completely embarrassing.' Atila balanced a cake tin carefully on one hand. 'Especially as the men have to go in one room to drink Turkish coffee and brandy, and the women have to go in another and do their henna thingamabob. I don't even like Turkish coffee.' His hair flopped in his eyes, so he flicked his head back in order to see again.

When I saw Kalem, an awkward feeling niggled in between my shoulder blades. After what had happened on Saturday night, I was suddenly beginning to feel very uncomfortable around him.

'Hi.' I licked my lips anxiously, but he was his normal self and didn't even notice me gnawing on my thumbnail.

When we rolled up at Yasmin and Deniz's house the place was already heaving with family, shouting and gesturing wildly with their hands. To the casual observer, it would've seemed like they were having a row, but this was just an ordinary Turkish Cypriot conversation. Most people were milling around in the huge lounge with its big French windows and original wooden floorboards, sanded with care and restored to their former glory. An antique Turkish rug, a family heirloom passed down through generations, adorned the centre of the room. Two tables had been put together at the far end of the room and covered with a beautiful woven cream tablecloth. They were so laden with food they looked like they were about to collapse. Chairs had been arranged around the outside of the room so people could eat on their laps.

'Merhaba.' Yasmin kissed us all in turn, then hurried off to the kitchen to bring out yet more food.

I followed her and handed her a couple of bottles of wine and soda. 'Here you are.' I smiled at her, and she touched my face with the palm of her hand.

'How are you, darling?' she asked.

'I'm fine. Food looks great,' I said as my stomach shouted at me.

Kalem came wandering into the kitchen and stole a piece of bread from the basket his mum was about to take into the lounge. 'God, I haven't eaten all day,' he said with his mouth full.

Yasmin slapped his hand away. 'Doesn't Emine ever feed you? Where is she anyway?'

I looked at him with interest, waiting for an answer, wondering if she was still with Mr. Business Suit. He mumbled something with his mouth full, but it was inaudible.

'She's a strange girl that one.' Yasmin tutted, handing him the basket. 'Here, take this into the lounge, darling.'

'Have a look at this!' Atila came in, took the lid off the cake tin and showed it to Yasmin.

'Ooh.' She clapped her hands together. 'What's that, raspberry coulis on top?'

'Well, I've been trying a new mix which has got some kind of alcohol in it, and you have to try and guess what it is!' Atila gushed. He was always talking shop with Yasmin, who adored cooking herself. This was evident by the amount of delicious stuff piling up in the lounge.

'Did I hear the magic word "alcohol?" What's the time? Is it whisky-o'-clock yet?' bellowed Deniz.

'Hi, how are you?' I asked Ayshe's dad.

'I'll be all right when I get some whisky down me.'

'Hi, Dad.' Ayshe gave him a big hug.

'All right, you lot?' Leila, Ayshe's cousin, appeared in the kitchen.

Leila and I were both going to be Ayshe's bridesmaids. Leila was lovely, with olive skin, gorgeous silky, dark hair and a beautiful face, but her voice was so cockney, you wouldn't believe it could come out of a woman who looked like an angel.

There were hugs all round again.

'I'm starving. When's the grub up?' Leila patted her stomach.

'I think everyone's here. OK, come and help yourselves,'

Yasmin shouted and a hungry swarm of people rushed to the food. A herd of stampeding buffalo had nothing on this lot.

'Where's that Emine?' Deniz hollered past me to Kalem as we waited in the food queue.

'Don't know.' Kalem picked up a piece of cucumber and munched on it as we moved along single file.

I loaded my plate with meze, pitta bread, helim cheese – which made your teeth squeak when you ate it – various types of salad and güveç, a traditional Turkish stew. This was the first decent meal I'd had in ages and boy, was I making the most of it.

I flopped down in a chair next to Ayshe and Leila and started stuffing my face, balancing the plate precariously on my knee. I definitely approved of Yasmin's cooking, and the only times I had eaten properly since the Justin saga were either at Yasmin and Basil's house or at Ayshe's flat.

The room was silent for a while as everyone tucked in, apart from Yasmin who was reading the coffee cup of her cousin, an elderly spinster.

Yasmin tipped out the grains of Turkish coffee into the saucer and gazed at the black sludge with a look of deep concentration. 'I definitely see rings! Yes, I'm sure of it. Mark my words: you'll be getting married before the year is out!'

I threw sneaky glances at Kalem, who had now finished his food and played with one of his nieces. He looked so at home, hiding his face behind his hands and then whipping them away to her delight. Next he stole her Barbie from her and started role-playing, pretending that he was Barbie and talking in a high-pitched voice. He danced the doll's feet up and down her leg, talking to her in Barbie language. He caught me looking and smiled, which made my stomach lurch and do an unexpected back-flip. I averted my eyes in case he could read my mind and knew how I was beginning to feel about him. He would make a really good dad one day, I mused.

'Is that how Emine talks?' chortled Deniz.

'Stop it now.' Yasmin slapped him on the arm. 'You've had too much whisky as usual.'

'I've never had enough.' He stumbled off to the kitchen for a refill.

'So where we going on the 'en night?' Leila asked Ayshe.

'We're going for a meal at that big Chinese, The China House. They have a disco on a Wednesday night, so we can have a boogie, too,' Ayshe said.

I felt bad because I hadn't really helped to organize much for her wedding. But then she was so super-organized, she wouldn't have let me anyway.

'We went there once, a bit out of the way but the grub was nice. 'Ere, Mehmet, it's good in there, innit?' Leila shouted across to her husband who was too engrossed in a conversation about V8 engines to answer her.

Deniz zigzagged into the room with a very large glass of whisky and sat next to me. 'Now the children have gone upstairs to play, I have to ask something.' He put one hand on his knee. 'This has been bothering me for ages, and I want an answer from the men.' His eyes darted round the room. 'What is the toilet etiquette in a men's loo?'

Ayshe and I cracked up as Atila slapped a hand to his forehead.

'Eh? Wot you talking 'bout?' Mehmet wondered, also in a cockney accent which rivaled that of his wife.

'Well,' Deniz leaned forward, 'Mehmet, if I give you a scenario, tell me what you would do.' He paused. 'If you go into the men's and there are five urinals, which one would you go to?'

'The end one,' Kalem shouted.

'Middle one,' Mehmet decided.

Deniz looked around for any more offers.

'The end one,' Atila agreed, throwing his hands up in the air. If you can't beat 'em, join 'em.

'Right.' Deniz put his finger up. 'But...what if there was someone in the end one?'

'The other end one.' Kalem looked up at his dad and shook his head.

'Yeah, same.' Mehmet nodded.

'I'd have to agree with that.' Atila had a horrified look on his face, wondering where this whole conversation was going to end up.

Deniz waved his finger again. 'Well – and here's where it gets interesting – what if there was someone in the middle one?'

'What, someone in the middle one and both end ones, or someone in the middle one and one end one?' Atila was perplexed and so was everyone else I think.

Deniz considered that for a moment. 'What, two people in one end one together, or one person in each one end?'

Ayshe and I burst out laughing. 'Let's say, one person in the middle and one person at each end.' I decided to speed things up. We'd be here all night at this rate.

'OK, what would you do, then?' Deniz threw the question out to anyone who knew what the hell he was talking about.

Atila considered it. 'I'd go in the cubicle.'

'Yeah, me too.' Mehmet nodded.

'Ooh, that's a hard one. Is the person in the middle just starting or just finishing?' Kalem broke in, which confused Ayshe's dad even further.

'I'm not sure. Does that matter?' Deniz scratched his head.

'Of course!' Kalem threw in.

Deniz thought about this for a moment. 'OK, just starting.'

'Are any of the ones at the end finishing?' Atila asked.

Mehmet considered this for a moment. 'Good point, mate.'

'One's starting and one's finishing,' I piped up, looking around.

All the men were deep in thought for a few minutes.

'Aah, but which one's which?' Deniz wagged his finger at everyone. Atila tapped his forefinger on his lips, deep in concentration, and Kalem threw me a look as if to say, can you believe this? 'I need another whisky. Things were never this complicated in the old days in Cyprus when it was just a hole in the ground.'

Yasmin began shooing all the men out and into the dining room.

'OK, I think this is hardly the type of conversation we want for a pre-wedding celebration. It's time for the henna ceremony.' She walked behind them, rounding up the stragglers and clapping her hands.

Ayshe went to get changed into a traditional costume and came back wearing a hand-made, deep-purple, floor-length velvet dress, decorated with gold sequins and beads. The sleeves were too long for her and flared out at the cuffs. A veil the same colour covered her face.

Leila took my arm. 'I know you've never done one of these before. Just follow wot I do.'

Yasmin put on a CD of traditional Turkish music and all the aunties and cousins sat around in the chairs clapping and smiling. Leila linked her arm with Ayshe, so I followed suit on the other side, and we walked her round the room several times. Next, Yasmin placed a chair in the centre of the room and pushed Ayshe gently on to it. Leila grabbed me along with two other women and led us to the corner of the room where there were four bedspreads and four large rectangular pieces of material. She picked up a bedspread, motioning for me to do the same. All four of us then carried them on our shoulders, dancing round the room. Yasmin picked up the material and laid one sheet flat on the floor in front of her daughter. Once we'd finished dancing, Leila placed her bedspread on top of the material. The bedspread was slightly smaller than the material and some of the women stood up, folding the edges of the material over the top of the bedspread. I watched with fascination as Yasmin handed out needles and thread to them. Some of the women began to sew the edges of the material to the bedspread, whilst the others clapped to the beat of the music. Once the whole thing had been sewn up, it was my turn to put my bedspread down. I arranged it over the top of another sheet of material and took a needle and thread. The sewing continued until all four bedspreads had been completed, then Yasmin produced an earthenware pot and covered it in a silk scarf. Leila took the pot and began dancing around Ayshe, shaking it in time to the music. She handed the pot to one of the other women, and they did the same. When it was my turn, I copied them, getting into the swing of things and gyrating to the music while all the others looked and carried on clapping. As I swung round, the pot slipped from my grasp and fell to the floor, landing on the antique rug where it decided to crack into pieces and spew forth its contents. The henna inside was greeny-brown and had the consistency of thick paste. My eyes widened to the size of saucers, and I immediately knelt down to try and scoop it back into the broken pot. Leila and a few of the others came to my assistance as Yasmin stood, trance-like, with her hands pressed so hard to her cheeks I thought we'd have to prise them off with a crowbar. We managed to scoop up most of it, and I rushed to the kitchen to find a damp cloth. After several attempts to wipe the rug, it became apparent that nothing was going to shift the stuff. Instead, I'd made even more of a smeary, brown pattern in the middle of the rug.

'Oops.' I looked up at Yasmin, who was now standing over me, eyeing the stain. 'I'm so sorry.'

'It's OK, darling.' Yasmin had come back to the land of the living, but her voice was a bit strained. 'Don't worry.' She patted my hand.

'Oh God, I'm really sorry.' I cast my eyes downwards, biting my thumbnail. A wrinkly old woman in a head scarf giggled at me. She pinched my cheek hard and garbled something in Turkish which I didn't understand, giving me a gappy-toothed grin. I only knew a few words I'd picked up from Ayshe, so I couldn't tell if she was calling me a complete idiot, or saying it was the best henna party she'd ever been to, and she hoped I'd be invited to the next one.

'Don't worry. We'll just have to walk round it for a while.' Yasmin was being very kind, but I felt terrible.

'Let's carry on.' Yasmin took charge again, scooping up some of the henna from the broken pot and rubbing it into the centre of Ayshe's palms. Next she took some silk fabric and wrapped her daughters' hands in them as Leila brought out a tray full of mixed nuts and passed them round. Some of the women took handfuls, then threw money on top of the tray. I couldn't tear my eyes away from the big splodge on the rug.

After that, the night ended abruptly, probably because Yasmin wanted to scrub the carpet to death with stain remover.

'Let me help you clean it up,' I whispered to her as Ayshe went to wash her hands and get changed.

'No, it's OK,' she insisted.

After lots of kissing all round, Ayshe, Atila, Kalem, and I bundled ourselves into the car and drove home in silence, leaving me to fester about what a complete hash I always made of everything.

'Where did you learn your trail-of-destruction skills? Is there a school for it?' Kalem finally broke the silence, fixing his mocking eyes on me. He must have thought I was a total idiot.

Why did I always muck everything up? I thought glumly. I bit my fingernail and prayed to be beamed up to planet Zob.

126

# Chapter 16
## Tuesday, day 9 – I'm Going to Be Healthy

During the night, I had recurring nightmares which involved paintings, rugs, and Kalem. I was trapped in a room surrounded by Yasmin's splodgy rug, the projectile vomit painting, and a giant inflatable banana – not sure where the banana fitted in, really. The picture caught fire – wishful thinking – and the room was engulfed by flames. Picking up the rug, I tried to batter out the fire. But instead it caught alight and spontaneously combusted, leaving only a pile of ashes on the outside and the big stained part in the middle miraculously intact. Then Kalem burst through the door shouting, 'What the hell are you doing nooooooooooooooooooooooooooooooow.' The 'now' part went on forever in slow motion and was a bit freakish. Next, he proceeded to batter me over the head with the painting until it broke – that was the good bit – then he called me something, which sounded like, 'fuckwit', and shot out of the door and into the arms of Emine who was calling me a 'boyfriend-stealing-bitch.' I was quite shaken when I woke up, I can tell you. Maybe I'd eaten too much cheese.

I grabbed the phone, calling Ayshe's number to dish the dirt on Emine and Mr. Business Suit. The exchange went something like this:

Me: 'I saw Emine in town yesterday with some guy, and he had his arm round her.'

Ayshe: 'What?'

Me: 'Yes, in the sandwich shop.'

Ayshe: 'Did they look like they were…you know…seeing each other, then?'

Me: 'Absolutely, she was all over him like a dose of chickenpox.'

Ayshe: 'Poor Kalem! Do you think I should tell him?'

Me: 'Well, I think he needs to know. I remember what it was like to find out Justin was doing the dirty on me.'

Ayshe: 'Urgh! I can't believe it. I never liked her. I'll tell him, as soon as I get a chance. What a bitch!'

Me: 'What a trouty-pouty bitch.'

Ayshe: 'What a trouty-pouty, fake, orange bitch!'

As I stood outside the door of some prospective clients later that morning, I knocked tentatively, listening to the sounds of an argument inside. This didn't bode well for a future marriage, I thought.

'Hello, you must be Helen.' A young woman answered the door who didn't look more than eighteen. 'Come in.' She closed the door behind me and led me into a small lounge with a log fire simmering in the fireplace.

'Hi, I'm Bulldog.' A stocky, rugby-playing kind of guy with cauliflower ears and a squashed-in nose stood up and gave me a rugby-tackle handshake, almost crushing my hand in the process. 'Do you want some tea?'

'No, I'm fine actually.' A new hand would be nice, though, I thought, lowering myself down into a rather scary, psychedelic-looking armchair.

'I'll have some. Katie!' he shouted, even though she was right next to him. 'Get me some tea.'

'I'm not deaf. You get it, I did the last one,' Katie said.

'No, you didn't.'

'Yes, I did.' Katie sighed and stalked off to the kitchen.

'So, have you got much need for computers?' he asked.

'Well, I have photographic software, send emails, use it for the net. That kind of thing.'

'I've just started a computer software business. If you need any software or anything let me know.'

'OK.' I pulled out some sample photos, wedding books and a price list of my photography packages.

Katie came back in carrying a mug of tea. 'Here you are, darling.' She handed it to him.

He took a big swig, then spat it out. 'Urgh! No sugar. You know I have sugar.' He glared at her. She glared back and went to put some sugar in – or maybe arsenic.

'I've had no sleep for weeks trying to get this business up and running.' He prodded the fire with a poker and sat down on a three-seater sofa, which was an equally psychedelic number.

'No, starting a business can be pretty tiring at first. It took me five years of hard slog to build up my business after I'd decided to branch out on my own. Luckily, word of mouth played a big part in getting new clients, and now I'm pretty busy. It also helps that I'm a woman. A lot of brides feel more comfortable with me than with a male photographer.'

After Katie had obliged with the arsenic, she perched herself right at the opposite end of the sofa. They didn't look very much in love to me.

'Here you go.' I handed Katie the portfolio. 'This is an example of the type of photos I take. Usually, I do a mix of traditional formal pictures and also more modern spontaneous ones which, as you can see, are very natural and capture the moment without being too posed. There's a lot of call for these kinds of pictures now.'

Bulldog pulled it from her hands and studied it.

She shot him a look of complete exasperation. 'I was looking at those.'

'No, you weren't.' He flicked through, crossing his legs, so she had to stretch over him to look at it.

'Yes, I was.' To my amazement, she snatched it back. This had certainly never happened to me before.

'No, you weren't!' He grabbed it back again.

'Why don't you both look?' I suggested.

With much reluctance, they moved closer together to study the photos. 'I like this wedding book, not the traditional albums,' Katie said to Bulldog.

'Yes these have been very popular lately. Your chosen photographs are printed into a modern hard-back book and tailored to your own personal design.'

'I don't,' he snapped at her.

'Well, I do.' She pulled the book out of his hand.

'Oh, you always have to start, don't you?' He frowned at her.

'No, I don't.'

'You could always have both.' I tried to be diplomatic.

Bulldog stood up abruptly and sat on the other armchair. 'You always get what you want, don't you?'

'No, I don't,' she muttered, still looking at the photos. 'You got what you wanted when I caught you snogging that girl in the pub last week!'

I felt a tense, nervous headache coming on and rubbed at my forehead, wondering why on earth these people were even thinking of getting married. Fingers of fear clamped their grip over my heart. If I'd stayed with Justin, is this how it would've ended up? Stuck in an unhappy, unloving rut? A marriage

129

doomed to failure before it even began?

'Are you OK?' Bulldog looked at me.

Apart from you two, yes. 'Fine.' I tried to think up an excuse to leave. 'Think I might have a virus or something.' I carried on rubbing my head for effect.

'Haven't you got AVG?' he asked.

'Sorry?' What the hell was that? It sounded a bit nasty, like TB or VD.

'Virus software. A lot of my customers don't even have it. I've established my own kind of software programme for viruses, as well, it's very state-of-the-art.'

Then it clicked. 'No, I think I'm OK, thanks.' I tucked my hair behind my ear. 'Well, why don't you have a think about things? Did you say you were getting married next September?' I looked from one to the other.

'No, we're not.' Bulldog stared at her.

'Yes, we are.'

'Well, you've got ages, then. Have a think and then call me.' Or not, I don't care, honestly.

'You said September! Don't you remember, that night when you proposed, and you were pissed?'

'No, I didn't. I said, "We'll see."'

'No, you didn't.' she glowered.

'Yes, I did.'

I couldn't take any more of it and was relieved when my mobile meowed giving me a break from it all. 'Excuse me.' I opened my phone and read the text from Ayshe, whilst they carried on with their migraine-inducing banter.

'Today's challenge – be ready at seven – wear something casual.' It said.

'OK, why don't I leave you a price list, and you can call me if you decide on something.' I leapt up to make a sharp exit, gathering my stuff.

'Oh, that's right, chase her off. Always chasing people off, aren't you?' she hissed at him.

'No, I'm not.'

'Yes you are,' she spat, following me to the front door.

I yanked it open and walked out. 'OK, call me if you want,' I murmured, trotting off as fast as my little legs would carry me.

'Don't forget about the software,' Bulldog shouted after me.

****

I wandered to the supermarket to pick up a few bits. Even the mice in my flat were turning their twitchy little noses up at the lack of food. Three bags of shopping later, I trundled off towards home, lost in my own world of thoughts, dying for a coffee and a super large headache tablet.

'H.' Kalem pulled up beside me. I really must have been thinking hard. I hadn't even heard his chugging old beast pull up.

'Kalem.' I lifted my hand up to wave but the shopping was too heavy and I nearly ripped my elbow off.

'I would say jump in, but you might telepathically cause some kind of accident to me or my baby.' He patted the dashboard.

'Ha-ha.'

'Come on, get in.' He stretched over to the passenger side and opened the door for me.

I deposited the bags in the back seat and climbed aboard. 'I feel so bad about last night.'

'Don't worry. Mum managed to get the worst out, and the rest of it kind of blends in with the pattern.'

'Really?'

'Nah, only joking. She said something about never inviting you back there again.'

'Shit!'

'No, It's OK. The stain really did come out...well most of it.'

I didn't know whether to believe him or not now. 'Really?

'Yes,' he said in a firm voice as he veered off the main road and onto a dirt track.

'Aargh, are you allowed to go down here?' I shrieked, taking in the Road Used as Public Path sign.

'Thought you might like a bit of off-roading,' he said, as we bumped along a very narrow muddy track.

'Ooh, God!' I got jolted about and almost had a severe case of whiplash.

Branches scraped along the side of the vehicles like nails on a blackboard as we ploughed on over fallen logs and down trenches. At one point, I thought we were going to smack into a silver birch tree but Kalem gracefully manoeuvered the vehicle round it and carried on down into a sloppy ditch, which looked like an old river bed. The track soon widened, and we passed some luscious green fields on either side, where sheep and cows munched away peacefully on the thick, velvety grass. We finally

131

came to a secluded wooded area where he parked and jumped out. Walking round to my door, he heaved it open.

'Come on,' he said.

I jumped out. 'Where are we going?'

'For a walk in the nice fresh air.' He started off across a field.

'Ooh, I love walking.'

'Ha, you hate it!' He wandered off with his hands shoved in the pockets of his combats.

We walked for a while through the deserted forest, our footsteps echoing on the crunchy leaves. Eventually, we came to a wooden sty, and he climbed over first. As I stepped up onto it, he grabbed me by the waist to lift me over. His face drew close to mine, and I felt his warm, sweet breath caressing my cheek. Gazing into his eyes, I stiffened. Perspiration tingled on the palms of my hands. I couldn't move.

'Come on, what are you waiting for?' His voice broke the spell.

'Um…nothing.' I composed myself, stepping down.

We plodded along through the woods and after about twenty minutes something caught his eye. 'Look.' He pointed at a little calf next to a big black and white cow, ambling along in a gently sloping muddy field in the distance. Might have been a bull, though, it looked huge.

'Ah, how sweet,' I cooed.

'Did you know that cows actually have wide-angle vision and can see about three hundred degrees around them. But they have 3D vision when they are looking directly ahead?'

'Oh yes, 'course I did.'

'And did you also know that some people are harnessing Cowpat Energy? They've got massive amounts of methane.'

'Seriously?'

'It's true.'

I had visions of cows blowing up like balloons and shooting off spontaneously into outer space.

'How do you know all this, then, Mr. Cowpat Man?' I glanced at him out of the corner of my eye and admitted, once again, how perfectly gorgeous he was. God, what was happening to me? I was even starting to ignore the faded, army-green trousers and his knackered old boots. This could only mean one pretty serious thing: I was having a nervous breakdown!

The new and unusual feelings that had been creeping up on me were getting stronger, and I couldn't understand why he was having this strange effect on me suddenly. There were only three problems:

1) He was involved with someone else.

2) He was Ayshe's brother and, although his family was wonderful, they would never approve of him being with someone who wasn't Turkish Cypriot.

3) He thought I was a complete idiot.

We eventually came to a lake, rolling down from a distant stream. Perching ourselves on a fallen tree stump on the edge of the water, I spied a handful of swans with their thick winter plumage. They gazed at us with slight interest and then went back to preening themselves.

'Look.' He pointed upwards.

The fluffy cotton wool clouds were hanging, seemingly motionless, in the brilliant bright blue sky. I squinted against the low winter sun.

'What? I can't see anything.' I shielded my eyes with my hand.

'There! It's a barn owl. You can tell that by the beige-coloured back and wings and how it's pure white underneath.'

I caught sight of it and watched as it flew off into the distance. We were strangely quiet for a few moments in the stillness; then Kalem looked over at me.

'What?' I felt uneasy, my throat dry and constricted. Was he going to tell me what a complete disaster freak I was again, as usual?

He took a deep breath. 'What did you ever see in that bloke?'

'Who? Justin?' I pulled up my knees and hugged them.

'Mmm.' He looked over to the lake with a strange expression on his face, almost pensive.

I sighed. 'Well, things were good in the beginning, until he decided he preferred sleeping with his boss instead of me!' I paused for a moment. 'But I guess he's done me a favour in the long run, I'm starting to realize how selfish he really is.'

'Well, we're not the same people as we were in our twenties. If we haven't learned from our mistakes in the last ten years, then there's not much hope for us, I suppose.' He smiled at me.

'No, you're absolutely right. If I was exactly the same person now that I was ten years ago, then I'd have learned nothing in

133

life.'

'So what do you want now, then?' His eyes met mine, cautiously.

'Someone down-to-earth. Someone funny, that I can have a laugh with. Someone who actually cares about me.'

'But why are you carrying on with this stupid challenge thing? You're not likely to meet a decent guy by going speed-dating and God knows what else, just a complete bunch of superficial jerks.'

'Ha! You're a fine one to talk. What about Emine? She's as superficial as they come, isn't she?' I thought about her sneaking around with Mr. Business Suit. I nearly blurted it all out and almost had to gnaw my lip off to stop myself.

He looked at his feet. 'Look...I wanted to–'

And then my phone burst into life, biting into the tranquility of the countryside.

'Sorry, I have to get this, it could be a job,' I said. 'Hello?' I stood up.

'Hi, it's Nick.'

'Hi,' I replied, looking over at Kalem.

'I'm just checking everything's OK still for Friday? Do you want to meet somewhere for a drink before the boxing match?'

'That sounds...lovely. How about we meet at the Watermill?' It was a trendy little wine bar in the High Street.

'Perfect. Is seven-thirty OK?'

'Yeah, Friday, seven-thirty at The Watermill,' I said, but what I really wanted was to be spending the evening with Kalem.

'OK, great. I've got to go, work's still manic. See you Friday, then.'

'Bye.' I hung up.

Kalem suddenly jumped to his feet and an awkward silence fell over us. 'Come on, we should be getting back. All your frozen stuff will be thawing out.'

# Chapter 17

'Kalem!' I pulled the door open that night as soon as the doorbell rang, ready and waiting for my next challenge. 'Where's Ayshe?'

'Actually, I came up with your challenge tonight so I thought I'd take you.'

'Oh, well where are we going?'

'Have you heard of Gloria Cox?' he said as we wandered down the hall.

I thought for a moment. 'No.'

'You know, the big healthy-eating guru. She's written that book, Change your Life, Change your Diet. Everyone's going mad about it.'

'What's that got to do with anything?'

We got into the Land Rover parked along the driveway to the car park. He performed a flawless three-point turn, then narrowly missed Charlie's super-girly Smart car, which had pink, feathery cushions on the dashboard.

'Well,' he glanced at me as we motored off down the road, 'she's doing a book club reading tonight at that big bookshop in town. I thought with all this change-your-life stuff that you're doing, you might need a bit of help to change your diet, too. Let's face it, you haven't exactly been eating properly since you split with Justin.'

'Well, no, I haven't, really. Wherever do you get all these challenge ideas from?' I asked as we pulled up outside the book store.

He shrugged. 'I was worried about your diet. You drink too much coffee and you need to find out about organic produce and be more environmentally aware of what you eat.'

I glanced at him thoughtfully as I slammed the car door shut. 'Well, thanks for taking such an interest in my diet. I am feeling a bit hungry now you mention it. Will there be any food there? Hopefully, they might have some cream cakes.' I grinned.

He didn't answer. He was already pulling the door open and heading inside.

We stepped into the huge bookshop and were directed upstairs to the rear where a small crowd had gathered in their function room. Bottles of water and glasses were laid out along one side of the room. No alcohol, though, and not a single cream cake in sight – damn, this was serious!

'There she is.' Kalem pointed at a petite, slim woman with shoulder-length, bouncy blonde hair and effervescent blue eyes. Her skin looked flawless and wrinkle free, but she must have been in her late fifties. She absolutely glowed with vitality. If this was what healthy eating did for you, then sign me up.

A mixed horde of healthy wannabes sat, waiting for her to begin, although judging by the size of some of them, there was positively no hope in this lifetime. One of them was even stuffing a super-sized Mars Bar down his throat.

We grabbed a seat at the back and waited along with the other patient people.

'Hello, everybody.' Gloria practically ran round to the front of the room, bursting with life. In fact, she had so much energy, she could have blown up a few buildings with no explosives whatsoever. She took up a position in front of a podium. 'For those of you who don't know me, I'm Gloria Cox, the author of Change your Life, Change your Diet.'

'Of course we know who she is. She's absolutely wonderful,' whispered a super-skinny stickwoman whose head was much too big for her body, making her look like a microphone.

'Now, I'm not going to go into great depths about the contents of my book because obviously I want you to go out and buy it!' Her eyes swept the room, giving us all a cheeky little twinkle. 'But I do want to talk to you about several important things, which will hopefully give you the inspiration to change your life and change your diet.'

I wondered how many times she would pummel that catchphrase into us.

'Now, the most important thing is that a diet is not actually a diet.'

'That's where I've been going wrong,' whispered Stickwoman.

'What is it, then?' shouted out a large beer-bellied bloke.

Gloria formed her mouth into an O shape as she thought about it, which made it look like a polo and was rather curious. 'Well, it's a whole lifestyle change. You can't just go on one of these faddy diets for a few weeks or months and expect it work long-term. Remember a diet is for life, not just for after Christmas.'

'Oh damn, that's a shame,' someone muttered.

'Shush.' Stickwoman turned round and gave a disapproving glare.

'Now, if you read my book, it gives you a whole variety of foods you can eat with no limits. They are all healthy foods which you can eat and not put weight on.'

'Are Mars Bars on the list?' asked the Mars Bar King.

'Unfortunately not.'

'What about chips?' someone else shouted.

'No, we're getting on to the wrong track, totally. The foods in, Change your Life, Change your Diet, are all super-rich foods packed with nutrients.' She hesitated and made that polo shape again. 'They are organic and unprocessed foods, super-foods, which include algae and wheatgrass.'

'Urgh, why would I want to eat grass?' I asked.

'It's not grass. It's wheatgrass.' She tiled her head, smiling.

'Can you just eat wheatgrass and nothing else?' asked Stickwoman.

I leaned over to Kalem. 'It looks like she's been doing that already, she's going to waste away soon.'

Gloria gave a little chuckle. 'Of course not, you need a healthy, balanced, variety of food. OK, moving on, then. Your body gives a lot of signs, which show the state of your health. For example, the tongue, face, nails, eyes and hands can all show signs that your body is not happy. Other examples are things like foul-smelling stools; these indicate that your digestion system isn't working properly.'

'Yuck,' Mars Bar King did a little piggy-grunt.

Kalem and I chortled.

'I know, it's not pleasant, is it? And if you examined your stool, it would give you a very clear indication as to what's going on inside.'

'Fabulous, I'm going to do that from now on,' Stickwoman muttered.

'Another example would be an itchy bottom.' Gloria did the polo thing again.

'I get that. What does it mean?' Beer Belly Bloke looked worried.

'Well, it could be a case of piles or worms. Alternatively, it could be that you are sensitive to a particular kind of food.'

'Gross,' I said.

'This brings me on to the next thing which is intolerances to certain foods. A lot of people now are becoming sensitive or intolerant to certain things, particularly wheat and dairy products. A lot of additives can cause problems too, and that's why it's very important to choose organic and unprocessed foods.'

'Can you get organic Mars Bars?' Mars Bar King enquired.

'No,' Gloria snapped. I think she was getting increasingly fed up with him. 'Does anyone here suffer from food cravings?'

'No.' Stickwoman shook her head violently.

'Chips and curry sauce,' Beer Belly Bloke yelled.

'Well, food cravings can be a sign of food intolerances,' she informed us, ignoring them. 'Did you know cows today produce about six times more milk than they did ten years ago?' She scanned the room.

'Oh, that's awful,' Stickwoman cried in disgust.

'Why?' shouted Beer Belly Bloke.

'Well, it's because of all the hormones and other chemicals, which are given to them to produce more milk. That means when you consume it, you are also taking in all these unwanted things, as well. And these are things that you could be intolerant to. So it's all about choosing milk, grains, fruit and vegetables, which are organically produced with no harmful chemicals or pesticides. Now, there are foods that are very full of nutrients and will give you bags of energy.'

'Sugar?' I asked.

'No.' She regarded us all with complete exasperation. She must have thought we were a complete bunch of no-hopers. 'For example, mung beans are absolutely packed with nutrients.' She composed herself and carried on.

'If I just ate mung beans all day and did lots of exercise, would that be OK?' Stickwoman asked her.

I thought she was joking at first, but she looked too excited by the prospect and I realized she was dead serious.

'Well, no – we get back to the healthy-balanced-diet rule again.' Gloria nodded at her. 'Another one is parsley, which has more vitamin C, gram for gram, than an orange.' The polo thing was going on again. 'It's very important to eat regularly. It's no good skipping a meal and then bingeing later. You have to get into the grazing mentality, and by this, I mean, eat little and often. Now, another chapter in the book covers items to avoid,

138

such as caffeine and alcohol.'

I didn't think I wanted to hear this part.

'Has coffee got caffeine in it?' someone asked.

I pretended I wasn't listening and Kalem dug me in the ribs to listen up to the great guru.

'Of course.' Gloria raised her voice, looking like she was about to flip any minute. 'Now, as many of you know, caffeine is a stimulant.'

I stuck my fingers in my ears muttering, 'La-la-la-la! I can't hear you.' I didn't want to hear anything bad said against my two favourite things.

'It can increase your blood pressure, and stimulates the body's adrenal glands, making you stressed and anxious.' She paused.

Kalem pulled my hands away, glaring at me.

'It also makes you tired and inhibits the absorption of other vitamins and minerals.'

'What? Like parsley?' asked Stickwoman.

'No, parsley is a food, not a vitamin.' The calmness was beginning to crack. 'Now, alcohol puts a huge strain on the liver and digestive system.'

I put my hands up to my ears again to hear no evil, but I could still hear her.

'It can cause the degeneration of cells and numerous other related problems.'

'Damn. I like coffee and alcohol,' I whispered to Kalem.

He pressed his finger to my mouth. 'Be quiet and listen for once.' His fingertip lingered for a few seconds on my lips, and I thought that maybe I should keep talking, just to feel his touch on me, although I didn't think I'd get away with it as Stickwoman was giving me some kind of scary death glare.

'There are a lot of foods that also cause stress to the body, such as salty and fatty foods. Processed foods contain many additives and preservatives. Cow's milk is another, and if people find they can't tolerate it, they can switch to soya or goat's milk.'

'Does goat's milk taste of goats?' shouted someone.

'Well...No.' Gloria let out an exasperated sigh. 'Equally, there are foods which do the opposite and combat stress.' She glowered at Mars Bar King before he could say the dreaded two words.

'WHAT?' Stickwoman shouted.

'I have a list of them in Change your Life, Change your Diet.'

We weren't going to get a sneaky preview of them. 'The book also gives you information on how to detox.'

'Is that like Botox?' I asked.

'No, it's a method of ridding the body of all the toxins and other substances that build up over time. It can stop you feeling tired, depressed or irritable, and can stop you suffering from headaches and other ailments. I have included a list of them in Change your Life, Change your Diet.'

'Give us a clue?' Beer Belly Bloke cried out.

She wagged her finger at him. 'You'll just have to read the book now, won't you? Another important thing is exercise, and I can't emphasize that enough.' She narrowed her eyes at Mars Bar King and Beer Belly Bloke. 'It is essential for weight loss and to get your body functioning correctly.'

'Urgh,' I groaned. Whoever invented exercise should be shot.

'And the final topic of tonight,' Gloria went on, glad it was almost over, 'is colonic irrigation. This is also known as colonic hydrotherapy, and the procedure is similar to an enema, only a lot more powerful.'

There were horrified looks all round.

'A tube is inserted into your anus and sterile, warm water is then sent into your colon and lower bowel.' Gloria ignored the astonished crowd and carried on with an excited look on her face. It was almost as if she was imagining having colonic irrigation right there and then.

'Ew!' Mars Bar King waved his hand in front of his nose.

'It is a wonderful experience and everyone should try it. It can help to clean out years' worth of faecal deposits, toxins, mucus and gas. Some people are very surprised at what comes out – in fact, one person I know had whole Brussels sprouts flying up the tube!'

Mars Bar King would probably have whole Mars Bars shooting out.

'Urgh! No way am I doing that! My bum is definitely an out-hole. I'm not sticking anything in an out-hole!' I mumbled to Kalem, shaking my head.

'Well, that about wraps it up for tonight. I will be signing books for purchasers in the next few minutes.'

'I'm going to get one,' I said to Kalem and leapt up to be the first one in the queue. After hearing horrible things about itchy bums and up-ya-bums, I decided that I really must give myself a kick up the bum and be more healthy. A full-scale panic started as most people scurried off to buy a copy. Stickwoman elbowed me in the ribs with her boney arm and pushed in front of us as several others became riotous, vying for a slot in the queue.

In the end, after much pushing and shoving, Kalem and I both bought a copy just as Mars Bar King sloped off without one – he was probably going to stock up on another family pack of choccies.

'I've just thought of the ideal challenge for you tomorrow,' Kalem said to me as he dropped me off outside the flats. 'Go up to Ayshe's when you get up, and I'll be waiting for you. We're going to the gym!' He laughed.

'The gym!' Hmm, I supposed that the good news was that I'd get to spend more time with Kalem, but the bad news was I'd have to do something I'd spent most of my life trying to avoid: exercise. 'Well...I guess I could give it a go. Thanks for taking me tonight.'

'What are friends for?'

I pulled the door open. 'Yeah, friends.' I whispered under my breath.

I read the entire contents of the book from cover to cover when I got home that night. I was too interested in scratchy body parts and furry tongues to let it slip from my grasp for a single minute. I could see that what she was talking about did make sense and resolved to start a new lifestyle change by doing more exercise and trying to switch to an organic diet.

It wasn't until I'd finished my reading mania that I noticed a message on my answer phone.

'It's me again. It has come to my attention that I've been leaving messages on the wrong number. So...no hard feelings and just forget everything I said. Know what I mean, eh?' It was the whacko nutter again. I put my hand to my chest in relief. At least that cleared up that little mystery.

I hoped.

141

# Chapter 18
## Wednesday, day 10 – I Love Exercise

I was up bright and early the next morning raring to start my new healthy lifestyle. I was extra keen to get started as during the night I'd had a dream in which my liver split into two large chunks and fell out of my body. That couldn't possibly be a good sign. I even tried out Gloria's suggestion of starting the day with a glass of hot water and lemon juice.

I decided that a trip to the gym might not be such a bad thing after all, as long as I wasn't expected to wear skin-tight cycling shorts and a leotard that went up my bum. I was seriously upset that I'd thrown my old joggers away. They would have come in mighty handy, and I would look just the ticket – well, apart from the manky coffee stains down the front.

So instead, I threw on a pair of old leggings, which were stain-free, and a baggy white T-shirt. Then I dusted off my slightly mouldy trainers which had been stagnating in the back of the wardrobe and shook them upside down in case there were any mice droppings inside. At last I rammed them on and jogged up the stairs to Ayshe's.

'Ugh.' I banged on the door. 'Come on! Get up.' I put my hand on my heaving chest.

'Hiya.' Ayshe opened the door, chewing on a bacon sandwich.

I took it off her. 'Hey! You're not allowed that. Is that organic bread?' I looked at it. Could you even tell the difference by looking?

'No.' She frowned. 'What are you up to?'

I picked the bacon out of the sandwich and threw it on top of the greasy grill-pan, leaving only the toast behind on her plate.

'Hey, what are you doing? I was enjoying that!'

Felix eyed the bacon with a hungry look on his face.

I wagged my finger at her. 'Have you read that Gloria Cox book?'

'No.'

'Well, if you had read it, you wouldn't be eating that.' I pointed to the congealed bacon. 'It will give you severe wind and liver failure. You can eat the toast, though.'

'Thanks, but it's organic bacon. Kalem brought it with him.'

she muttered with an indignant look on her face. 'Want a coffee?'

'No thanks.'

'OK. Who are you and what have you done with Helen?'

'Ha-ha. I'm going to be much healthier from now on. I'm actually glad that Kalem thought up the Gloria Cox challenge. I'll be a changed woman in no time,' I said as she stuffed the bacon back in-between the two slices of toast and carried on eating it – much to the disgust of Felix, who threw us a filthy look and growled in annoyance.

'Yum.' A crazy grin spread over her face as she scoffed the lot.

Atila came wandering into the kitchen with one side of his hair stuck to his head where he had slept on it. 'Got one of those for me?' He peered at the bacon sandwich.

'You're not allowed it,' I said.

'Why not, is it off?'

'Haven't you read Gloria Cox's book either?' I pointed at Kalem's copy on the table.

He picked it up and studied it. 'Load of old mumbo-jumbo. You don't complain when you're having one of my orgasms, do you?'

'What, those chocolate things? Ooh, yeah, they're gorgeous. Are you going to whip one up for us after we get back from the gym?' I started salivating.

'Who's going to the gym?' Ayshe asked.

'Helen and I are.' Kalem emerged from the bathroom, smelling of a mix of engine oil and deodorant – which wasn't as horrible as it sounds. It was actually rather heady, like a chemical pheromone reaction pulling me towards him.

Atila laughed. 'Helen, in the gym! I'd like to see that.'

'Well, let's get up there before I change my mind.' I jogged on the spot for about one minute, then collapsed on the chair, breathing deeply.

'If you manage a whole session in the gym, I'll have a reward waiting for you tonight. I was thinking of trying out a new recipe this morning for an aphrodisiac cake.' Atila raised his eyebrows at me, grinning. 'And that's definitely going in my sexy cookbook.'

****

143

'Hi Kalem. Haven't seen you up here for a while,' a very over-muscled gym instructor greeted us when we arrived at the leisure centre.

He wore thigh-hugging, black Lycra cycling shorts and a vest top. His legs were so huge they rubbed together when he walked, and as he leaned on the reception desk, his biceps rippled.

'Wow, awe-inspiring.' I nodded to his arms.

He flexed them. 'I know. The ladies like it.'

'I've been doing a lot of walking in the countryside. I only come up here when the weather's bad,' Kalem said to him.

I wondered to myself whether all this weight training made their willies shrink. I'm sure I read that too much exercise could reduce them to amoeba-sized proportions.

'OK.' He grabbed a form and handed it to me. 'Fill this in, please. You have to do an induction first. You can show your girlfriend round if you like,' he said to Kalem.

I blushed, studying the questions on the form, so I wouldn't have to point out that I wasn't his girlfriend. After the usual name and contact details came the hard ones.

1) Sex? Answer: thanks, but no.

2) Age? Answer: thirty but look much younger.

3) Occupation address? Answer: anywhere.

4) Occupational position? Answer: standing, but occasionally sitting down.

5) Do you have a heart problem? Answer: probably will in a minute.

6) Do you suffer from breathlessness during exercise? Answer: sometimes during sex, but that was a long time ago.

7) Do you suffer from palpitations or unusual heart flutters? Answer: only when I think about someone special.

8) Do you have any back problems? Answer: only when I did a handstand when I was very drunk.

9) Are you allergic to anything? Answer: men who cheat.

10) Have you had any operations? Answer: I think I had a lobotomy once, but I can't remember.

11) Do you enjoy a healthy eating programme? Answer: yes, started an hour ago.

12) Have you suffered from any illnesses? Answer: hangovers.

13) Do you suffer from any other problems? Answer: accidents frequently happen around me.

144

I handed it back to him, and he studied it with interest, occasionally shaking his head and looking up at me in disbelief.

'Right, come on, then. I'll take you round the equipment.' Kalem led the way into the gym.

Floor to ceiling mirrors covered one wall and various exercise benches were laid out in rows. There was a huge stack of free weights in the corner, ranging from tiny, weedy ones to monstrously large, hefty-boy ones. Several of the Hefty Boys, with muscles which rivalled the gym instructor, huffed and groaned as they lifted weights in pairs, shouting out the number of repetitions they had done and checking themselves out in the mirror.

The middle of the room housed quite a few treadmills and exercise bikes and a funny looking skiing thingamabob. A couple of trendy-looking fit women jogged away on the treadmills without even breaking into a sweat. The rest of the area was taken up by free-standing weight machines and exercise mats.

'OK, I'll show you how to use these machines, and you can get the hang of them. Then next time you come, I'll show you some of the free weight exercises. Right, this one here is the leg press.' He selected the lightest weight possible and sat down in the chair. 'Put your legs flat on this plate, then press them forwards and bring them back slowly. Your turn,' he said to me as he got off.

I copied him but it was a struggle trying to press my legs down. 'Ooh, God,' I griped. 'That's a bit hard!'

'Next one is the lat pull-down which works these muscles in your back.' He ran his fingers along the sides of my back. 'Also works your arms. This is a good one for the girls.' He sat down on a chair facing the machine and pulled down a bar on a pulley system.

After he'd jumped off, I sat down and tried it out. 'Which muscles does it work again?'

He stood behind me, running his fingers along my back again. 'These.'

I smiled to myself dreamily, facing the wall. 'Mmm, nice.'

'Pardon?'

'Er…I mean it's nice that it works those muscles.' I pulled on the bar until my arms began to ache.

'Don't worry, everyone's like it at first. Just try and do about

145

ten goes of each machine this time round, and then you can increase it a bit every time you come.'

'Aargh!' One of the Hefty Boys slammed down a heavy weight on the floor in a tantrum and strutted round it while he looked about to see if anyone was gazing at him in awe.

We wandered over to another machine. 'This one is the bicep curl machine.' Kalem sat down, put his hands round a bar in front and pulled it towards him.

I feasted my eyes on his arms.

'Hurgh!' screamed one of the Hefty Boys and shot us an angry look.

'Think he needs to lay off the steroids,' I whispered to Kalem.

'We need to do a warm-up first,' Kalem said after he'd spent an hour showing me most of the equipment.

Oh God, what was that? A hundred laps of the car park? A quick sprint to the juice bar?

'And how do we do that?' I asked.

'Anything aerobic, let's try the treadmill for ten minutes.' He wandered over to show me how to work the complicated-looking contraption as the Hefty Boys glared over at me like I was fresh meat.

We hopped on to the treadmills next to the two trendy, fit-looking women who'd been at it for ages and still hadn't shed a jot of sweat. They were fully made-up with bright red lipstick and smothered in eye make-up, but there wasn't a smudgy smear of mascara in sight. We could hear them talking about how many lunges and sit-ups they could do now. One of them mentioned the figure three hundred, but she must have been telling a porky.

I started a slow walk.

'Oh, by the way, Ayshe wanted me to tell you that she's not wearing one of those veils or L plates tonight. She said she wouldn't mind a stripper, though, as long as it's not a big fat roly-poly-a-gram.'

'Well, she'll just have to wait and see. She nearly got a pot-belly-a-gram. Angie wanted Barry to be the stripper for tonight!' I snorted to myself and Kalem pulled a horrific face.

'You know your challenge for tomorrow – Ayshe said it was a surprise? Well, you have to make sure you're ready at nine for a whole day out. And bring some casual gear and a swimsuit. It'll be great, you'll love it.'

We walked in silence for ten minutes, and I was dying to ask whether Ayshe had said anything to him about Emine yet, but I didn't want it to seem like I was pushing in case he got suspicious, so I bit my lip hard to stop the urge to blurt out anything incriminating. I could still remember about twenty years ago when one of Kalem's cousins married an English guy and the whole family was up in arms about it. There was a massive hoo-hah about her getting involved with someone who wasn't Turkish Cypriot, so I didn't think they'd be too impressed to learn what was going on now inside my head. And none of her family had ever gone out with a non-Turkish Cypriot ever again. Kalem's family had taken me into their lives unconditionally when my parents died, as if it was their duty; their calling. How could I repay them for that by falling in love with Kalem and causing another family scandal?

We upped the tempo to a tiny jog as I stared into space, daydreaming about Kalem until his voice brought me back to reality.

'Huh?' I panted as sweat poured into my eyes and my T-shirt stuck to my back like a second skin.

He got off the treadmill and walked behind me mumbling something I couldn't hear. I craned my neck round to listen to him, but as I was walking forwards and looking backwards, my feet suddenly developed a mind of their own and before I knew it, I'd caught the edge of the treadmill and flown off the back of it, landing in a crumpled heap on the floor.

'Ow!' I shot up as quick as I could, hoping no one had witnessed my humiliating sharp exit – almost a back-flip – from the bloody thing. I rubbed my bum covertly – didn't want it to look as though I'd actually hurt myself. 'They're a bit dodgy. Don't think I'll be going on one of those again.' I gave it a dirty look, wondering how big the bruise would be tomorrow.

The trendy, fit women next to us sniggered.

'Ooh, I'm so sweaty.' I stretched the damp T-shirt off my skin, wafting it backwards and forwards as rivulets of perspiration trickled down my back and in between my boobs. I was not a pretty sight and did a mental cringe. If all my embarrassing moments rolled into one didn't put him off me, this certainly would.

'Let's go on those leg thingies.' I pointed at a couple of machines next to each other with a seat and some stirrups that the gym instructor had shown us.

147

We sat down in the seats, stretched our legs out in front of us and put them in the stirrups. There was a little lever to pull to separate the stirrups, which were pressed tightly together. I pulled the lever and my legs flew wide open.

'Ooh,' I gasped. I'd forgotten to select a lighter weight and the stirrups were so heavy I couldn't bring my legs back together again. I felt like I was about to have a smear test in front of a large audience.

Kalem cackled, as did the trendy, fit women. I looked over to see if anyone else had noticed. The Hefty Boys grunted in the corner – I wasn't sure, though, if it was a laugh or whether the growth hormones were kicking in.

'Can you help me?' I leaned over to Kalem, who was using his machine perfectly.

He got off and changed the weight on mine to a lighter one. And then I was off, swinging my legs open and shut like there was no tomorrow.

'Have you had enough yet?' Kalem asked. 'I must admit that I'm quite impressed. I thought you would've given up by now.'

'I can't give up yet. I'm determined to be super-fit from now on. Why don't we go over there and do some stuff that they're doing?' I pointed to the free weights that the Hefty Boys were using. 'They won't bite, will they?'

We watched the Hefty Boys for a bit, then I decided I couldn't possibly manage to copy what they were doing, unless I wanted my arms to fall off, so I picked up a few of the weedy weights and moved my arms up and down in a unique wobbly fashion.

'You're doing it wrong,' Kalem said.

'Oh.' I thought I'd got the hang of it.

'You're supposed to do it like this.' He moved his arms out to the side until they reached shoulder height and then brought them back down again in a slow, fluid action. 'Here, like this.' He wrapped his hands around my wrists and maneuvered my arms up and down. 'That's it.'

Maybe I could learn to love this exercise business after all. Helen Grey, Miss Fitness 2009.

Twenty minutes later we sat side by side on some mats in the centre of the room, and I tried to copy Kalem as he did some stretches. The only trouble was that he appeared to be doing some kind of freaky advanced yoga moves. He sat on the floor, balancing on his bum with his legs open wide in the air like a pair of scissors. I sat gawping as I tried to imitate him. After a couple of attempts, I collapsed over on to my back, giggling profusely. Then he tried a strange double-jointed arm movement where he yanked his arm behind his head. I really didn't fancy having a go at that one for fear of a shoulder dislocation and complete agony, so I gave up and lay like a starfish on the mat.

'I didn't know you were so good at Yoga,' I said.

'There's a lot you don't know about me.' He turned to me slowly, fixing his intense eyes on mine for a second before he jumped up. 'Come on, I think you've done enough for one day.' He grabbed my hand, jerking me up from the floor so that I tumbled towards him, into his arms.

And at that moment, I was close enough to feel his heart drumming in his chest; close enough to see his pupils dilate, and I wanted to kiss him so badly I could feel the frustration oozing from my pores. It felt like I was spinning out of sync with the earth, wobbly and light-headed and fuzzy at the edges.

'I don't think they allow snogging in the gym, it's very distracting. You never know what sort of accident might happen when you're distracted,' Kalem said, which jump-started the rational side of my brain to kick in, overriding my emotions bouncing around in all directions.

I pulled back sharply before he realized what I was thinking and the moment was over and lost, disintegrated into a million other lost moments that we can never get back.

'Snogging! What a ridiculous thought,' I said, willing my voice to sound convincing.

'We can go back and have an orgasm now after all that hard work, or a bit of aphrodisiac thingy,' Kalem said, leading the way out of the gym.

But I seriously doubted he was thinking of the same kind of orgasm that I had in mind.

# Chapter 19

''Ere, 'as this got carrot in it?' Leila shouted to Atila, stuffing a piece of cake in her mouth.

Ayshe, Leila, Angie, Felicity and Charlie were all milling around in the kitchen having a pre-dinner drink as we waited for the limo to arrive at seven-thirty.

Kalem and Atila – who were also going on Atila's stag do that night – were busy hiding in the lounge from all the women and Charlie.

'I'm allowed carrots; that book said so.' I finished my piece off.

'No, guess again,' Atila shouted through the door.

'Ginger?' Charlie screeched.

All the girls – except Felicity, of course – were dressed up in party frocks and heels, although I wasn't going out without my faux fur coat – it was really nippy out there. Charlie, trying to blend in, was wearing a pink-checked kilt with a pair of chunky boots and a glittery white T-shirt which said 'I'm Free' on it. I couldn't see if he was complete with sock, and I didn't want to pull the kilt up for fear of what I might find lurking underneath.

'No,' Atila shouted. 'Kalem, get me a beer will you?'

'Why can't you get it?'

'I wouldn't be safe going in there with all those cackling women.'

I tried to prise open the cork on a bottle of champers, but it didn't want to co-operate. I didn't particularly want to break my fingernails; I'd been trying, lovingly, to restore them since chewing them to non-existence after the Justin saga.

Kalem crept up behind me and tried to yank it out of my hand. 'No way am I going to let you open that. You never know what sort of disaster will happen.'

The fiery heat of his fingertips brushing over mine caused an explosion in the nerve endings of my fingers and the bottle slipped from my grasp, sending it crashing to the floor.

'Oh, God!' I grabbed a dustpan and brush and began to sweep up the pieces of glass.

'Helen, what's wrong with you?' Ayshe gave me an odd look, grabbing a handful of kitchen roll and mopping up the sticky champagne slick on the tiles as Kalem opened another bottle of champagne, expertly popping the cork which plopped neatly into the sink.

A whole kitchen roll and two dish cloths later, Ayshe held out several glasses for him, and I tried to hide behind the door, embarrassed. If I just ignored him maybe I would stop having all these ridiculous feelings about him, which were clearly not reciprocated. But it was pretty hard to do that right now: he looked particularly gorgeous tonight in a white shirt and jeans which fitted him with perfection and accentuated his rather fit body.

'Have you got a licence to take Helen out?' He grinned at me.

'Ha-ha.' I sank back against the door frame as he collected a few cans of beer from the fridge.

'You're dangerous,' he said, squeezing past me, brushing his chest against mine.

Good job I had my coat on as my nipples were springing to attention like a couple of missiles.

I wrapped my coat round me tighter, just in case anyone could see, and found the handcuffs I'd bought for Ayshe in my pocket. 'Here you go.' I giggled suggestively at her. 'You can spice up your love life now.'

'Ooh, great!' She looked at them. 'I'm not wearing them out tonight, though.'

'I would.' Angie raised an eyebrow and studied them.

'Yeah, we know you would,' Ayshe cackled, putting them on the kitchen work-top.

'If you don't want them, I'll have them.' Charlie picked them up, examining them with delight.

Felicity couldn't even bring herself to look at them.

'Where are your mates from work?' Angie asked Ayshe.

'Oh, they're going to meet us at the restaurant. And Mum's not coming, she thinks it will be a bit too outrageous for her; she has to put up with enough outrageousness from Dad'

'Banana?' Charlie cried.

'Huh? What are you talking about?' I asked him.

'In the cake. Is it banana?'

'No,' Atila replied.

'I think it's got mace in it,' Felicity piped up and her hairy Rice Krispie twitched.

'When are you going to make me one of those orgasm things?'

151

Angie shouted out to Atila.

'Ha! I don't think you need any extra orgasms,' I snorted.

Felicity blushed, excused herself and went off to the loo.

'I get an orgasm from the Hoover now,' Angie said.

I dreaded to think how. 'How lovely.' I pulled a face of mock disgust. 'Remind me never to borrow your Hoover.'

'I've also discovered a new super Rabbit – and you'll never guess what – a couple of weeks ago my eldest, Libby, found it in my drawer and asked me what it was.'

'You're joking!' we said in unison.

'No.' Angie shook her head. 'Naturally, I told her the first thing that came to mind, which was that it was a bead-maker. And then the other day she sneaked it to school for show-and-tell without my knowledge and duly told everyone it was her Mummy's bead-maker! I don't think I'll get invited to a parents' evening ever again!'

Our cackles of laughter permeated the kitchen.

Atila cringed. 'Oh, for God's sake. Shall we get out of here?' he said to Kalem, jerking his head towards the door. 'I can't stand all these shrieking females.'

As they clambered round the sofa to get out the door, Kalem caught my eye and threw me a mischievous grin on his way out.

'Potatoes,' Atila shouted as he closed the door.

'Ooh, err, how queer! I've never heard of potatoes in a cake before.' Charlie was lost for words.

'So Felicity, how's the Librarianism going?' I asked when she returned.

'It's great.' She shrugged. 'I love looking at all those books, especially the Bible.'

'I read that book once, thought it was great! When are they going to bring out Bible Two?' Angie said with a straight face. 'I bet you've been looking at the porno books, really, haven't you?' She gave a throaty laugh. 'The quiet ones are always the worst.'

I laughed so much that I managed to spray champagne all the way down the front of Felicity's drab, shapeless, grey, 1970s pinafore dress. 'Ooh, I'm so sorry.' I searched for a cloth.

'It's OK. I'll go and rinse it.' She trundled off back to the bathroom.

'Oops,' I said to everyone, putting my hand over my mouth.

'Why does that say 'I'm Free' on it?' Ayshe pointed to Charlie's top. 'I thought you were seeing Marco?'

152

'This week I am mostly not seeing him. He can be a right little bitch, you know.'

'Where are we eating, have you booked a table somewhere?' Felicity questioned when she returned with a big wet patch down the front of her dress.

'The China House – you know the one out in the sticks where you can eat as much as you like.' Ayshe downed her champagne as the limo driver sounded his horn in the car park below.

'Does that include men?' Angie guffawed.

'Come on you lot.' Leila rounded us all up and bundled us out the door.

As we piled into the white Hummer limo, I spied a chilling bottle of Moet. 'Ooh, look.'

'Come on, quick, open it!' Charlie said.

'Only if you absolutely insist,' I chortled. The champagne was going to my head on an empty stomach.

We all drank a toast to Ayshe. 'Cheers.' I grinned as we chinked glasses.

'Down the hatch,' Felicity offered.

'Şerefe,' Ayshe said, Turkish for cheers.

'Chin-chin.' Angie dribbled some champagne down her spectacular cleavage which was threatening to explode out of her dress all by itself, wiping it off absent-mindedly.

'Bottoms up.' Charlie crashed his glass against ours with a glint in his eye.

'Charlie, you have to clear this matter up for us. Do you – or do you not – stuff your pants with a sock?' I drawled.

'Wouldn't you like to know?'

'YES!' we all shouted – even Felicity, who was beginning to relax a bit under the influence of the alcohol.

'Well, I'm not sharing.'

'Oh, go on mate,' Leila shouted.

'No.' He stuck his nose in the air and refused to tell, leaving us all in everlasting wonderment.

Amid raucous laughter and joking – and, of course, copious amounts of alcohol – we blitzed out of town with the windows down. As we sped along a deserted country road, the limo slowed down and came to an abrupt standstill.

'Oi, where are we?' Leila wound the window down and looked out.

We all fought for a position near the window to have a look-see. ''Ere, this ain't the Chinese,' Leila said.

We were parked up outside a café which said: The greasy spoon – Truckers and Bikers welcome.

'Ooh, blimey,' Charlie muttered. 'Is this where we're going?'

'Sorry, folks, there's a problem with the limo, and I need to check it out.' The driver got out and wandered around the car, looking at the tyres and kicking them from time to time.

'I went out with a trucker once,' Charlie said. 'He was a bit of a brute.'

'Sorry girls, looks like we've got a flat tyre. I've never changed one on this vehicle before, and I'm not sure where the wheel-brace and jack are. I'm just going to make a call to the office.' The driver sighed, scratching his head.

'Oh, no,' we groaned.

'Maybe we should call the restaurant and let the others know we'll be late,' I suggested.

Ayshe fumbled around in her bag for her phone and then frowned. 'No signal. Anyone else got one?'

Leila and I looked at ours,which were the same. Charlie hadn't brought his because he didn't want Marco to ring him, and Felicity was too much of a technophobe to even possess one. The driver pulled out his mobile and held it up in the air to get a better signal.

'Must be a black spot,' he mumbled. 'I'll try the phone in the café.'

'You don't think they'll bite, do you?' Felicity asked.

'I hope so.' Angie threw her head back and laughed.

A few minutes later the driver reappeared. 'The phone in the café's broken. Would you believe it?'

'Oh, well. Let's sit in here for a bit and have some more drinks.' Ayshe wasn't bothered.

We were all starting to feel a bit drunk by then and could really have done with something to eat to soak up all the champers.

'I'm starving,' I grumbled. 'I can't wait for some kung po prawns. They make the best in The China House.'

'I like the seaweed.' Ayshe nodded.

'It's not real seaweed, is it?' Felicity asked.

'No, it's sewage.' Charlie sniffed and pinched his nose.

Felicity looked horrified.

'It's spring greens or something. Atila had it on the menu

154

once. It was yum,' Ayshe told us.

"'Ere, you not 'ad a Chinese before or summut?' Leila asked Felicity.

'No, Mummy doesn't like Chinese.' Felicity still lived with her mum at the age of thirty.

'Don't know what you're missing.' And then I shivered. 'Brrr, it's getting a bit cold in here with no heating on.'

'Listen girls, I'm going to walk up the road and see if I can get the mobile to work, or find a payphone or something.' The driver said.

'Shall we go into the Café? It's freezing out here?' Ayshe asked everyone.

The consensus of opinion was a yes, so we tottered off in our best party frocks and heels into the dirtiest greasy café known to truckers and bikers. As we wandered in, we glimpsed a handful of Hell's Angel types at one table, with empty plates stacked in front of them, containing the remnants of coagulated fry-ups. They were all pierced and tattooed to death with big ZZ Top beards and long ponytails. Two of them were in the midst of having a pretty serious arm wrestle, grunting noises filled the air.

A couple of the other tables were filled with some hill-billy looking truckers, wearing checked shirts and baseball caps, also nursing the standard fry-up and mugs of dishwater-dirty looking tea.

'Ew.' I wrinkled up my nose.

At the counter stood a leather-clad, helmet-wearing biker, surveying the scene with interest.

'He looks like an animal.' Charlie pointed to one of the Hell's Angels.

And with that, they all looked up and studied us.

'Hello, girlies,' one of them said, and then he looked at Charlie, trying to work out if he fell into that category. 'Lost are we? He smirked, giving us a flash of his filthy-looking teeth, which were very wonky, as well, and looked like dilapidated headstones in a graveyard.

Some of them looked a lot like the cast out of the film *Deliverance*. I could hear the banjo music reverberating somewhere in my head, and was a tad worried they were going to ask us to squeal like pigs, although I'm sure Charlie would have quite liked it.

Felicity hid behind me. 'Do you think they'll kill us and steal all our money?'

'Don't be ridiculous! This isn't the middle of Texas, where you can go for miles without seeing anyone, and all the bikers stick together to rob and murder people. Everyone knows where we are,' I whispered, hoping that was true. But I was a bit doubtful. I was sure I'd heard of some funny kind of ritual these guys got up to, but I tried my best not to recall it from the depths of my memory for fear of shitting myself.

'This ain't The Ritz, you know.' One of the Bikers examined us. 'Wot you doing 'ere?'

Leila, recognizing a fellow cockney, did the honours and elected herself group speaker. 'Broken down, mate.' She eyed him with suspicion. 'We're just off on a 'en night. What's it gotta do wiv you lot, anyway?'

'Oh, bugger,' I muttered.

'Help, Mummy!' Felicity squeezed her eyes shut.

'Hey, look after these girls, they're alright,' the guy at the counter informed the others in an authoritative voice.

We all looked to our saviour who picked up a triple bacon lard-burger to go and strode towards us, clanking metal rimmed biker boots along the floor.

'Whatever you say, Bulldog,' one of the bikers said, cowering in the corner.

I breathed a hefty sigh of relief and mouthed the word 'thanks' to him as he gave us a salute and headed out the door.

And then to our surprise, the Hell's Angels started roaring with laughter, slapped their hands on the table so hard that it was in danger of collapsing and asked us to join them for a cuppa.

'Better still, there's some bubbly in the limo. I'll go and get it,' Angie suggested, eyeing up one of the bikers who was so hairy he looked like a bear.

'Oi, you!' One of them with a pierced lip, eyebrow, nose and forehead – and probably a few other things – pointed to Felicity. 'Come and sit next to me.'

Felicity screwed her eyes up, shaking her head. 'Please don't kill me, please don't kill me.'

'Come on.' Mr. Piercings moved further up the seat and let her squeeze in next to him, looking down at her moustache and hairy mole in fascination. 'I love hairy women.'

Felicity let out a nervous snort. 'Oh, do you?' she replied in a timid mousey squeak.

'Not 'arf.' He gave her a crazy-looking grin.

'Oi Gaffer, get us some mugs, will ya. We're gonna pour a toast,' the Bear growled at the chef when Angie came back bearing gifts of red wine.

'We've finished the good stuff, we'll have to start on this.' Angie held up two bottles of plonk.

'That champagne stuff is bollocks, anyway.' One of them sniffed.

'So which one of you lot is getting hitched then?' asked the Bear, looking between us all. 'I bet it's you?' He pointed at Charlie, narrowing his eyes.

Charlie blushed. 'It's not.'

'Is,' insisted the Bear.

'Not,' insisted Charlie.

The chef came out of the kitchen in a grubby apron, containing more grease than the fry-ups on the plates – which was an enormous feat in itself. He carried a tray of pint glasses and laid them in front of the bikers, making himself scarce again as they poured the wine into them.

'Next time, more bacon!' one of the Hell's Angels roared at him as he shot back into the kitchen.

Mr. Piercings put his arm round Felicity, almost crushing her to death.

'Ooh, you're rather strong.' She gazed up at him.

I looked at Ayshe, amazed. It seemed like there was a possible romance blossoming here.

'Can I come on your 'en night?' Mr. Piercings smiled down at Felicity. He had a big lump of egg stuck to his beard which wobbled when he spoke.

'Sorry, no. You're a man,' Ayshe said.

Mr. Piercings pointed at Charlie. 'Well wot's 'e doing 'ere, then?'

'Charlie's only a pretend man,' I filled them in.

'Oi, do you mind!' Charlie retorted.

'So what do you do, then?' Angie flirted with the Bear.

'Go on, 'av a guess.' He looked at her.

'Geoff Capes impersonator?'

'Something that involves crushing people to death?' I asked.

'Wrong, try again.'

'Ice-cream man,' Angie offered.

'Wrong.'

157

'Ping-pong tester,' I cackled.

'Nursery nurse,' he said, and everyone fell about with laughter.

'You change baby's nappies and stuff?' Angie asked. 'Well, I would never have believed it. I used to go out with a bloke who liked wearing nappies – he had a bit of a nappy fetish.' She waved her hand as a saucy smile crept up her face. 'But that's a whole different story.' She gave the Bear a lustful stare and adjusted her bra strap.

Mr. Piercings gazed down at Felicity like she was the best thing since the nose-ring was invented. 'Can I 'av your number?'

And to our complete surprise, Felicity, who had never even been on a date before in her life, handed it over quicker than you could say Harley Davidson.

For a split-second a peculiar feeling of déjà vu chilled my bones. I quickly shook it away. 'God, what's the time?' I demanded with a sudden urgency, grabbing Ayshe's wrist and looking at her watch. I'd just remembered the stripper was supposed to be arriving at the restaurant at about nine.

'Half past eight. What's that driver up to?' Ayshe got up and leaned out of the doorway, gazing into the car park. 'He's coming,' she shouted back to us over her shoulder.

'OK, girls, sorry for the wait. I've fixed it now and you can carry on your merry way.' The driver, covered in oil, wiped his hands on a dirty rag and led the way to the limo.

# Chapter 20

After we'd managed to prise Felicity away from the dirty clutches of Mr. Piercings, we finally arrived at the traditionally decked out restaurant dead on nine. Our rowdy little hoard was led by an overawed Chinese waiter to a table in the centre of the room, much to the annoyance of the nearby tables and cosy couples who had been hoping for a romantic night out. The place was styled with black and white checked floor tiles and red Chinese lanterns dangled from the ceiling. Chinese scriptures adorned the walls and the table cloths were carefully coordinated in reds and whites. A huge tropical fish tank took up most of the bar area and this led on to the spacious dining room, where the subdued lighting made for a relaxed dining experience. A conservatory to the rear housed a dance-floor and a sound system which was set up for a disco that they held every Wednesday night. I think they must have crammed in a few extra tables for the occasion as they were very tightly packed together.

A middle-aged couple on the next table studied us with interest as we sat down.

'Hello.' Angie waved at them, and they turned away.

'I'm sorry, but your other guests have already left,' the waiter informed us.

'Oh, no! My work crowd has all gone; they must have thought we weren't coming. I'll text them and see if they'll come back.' Ayshe pulled her phone from her bag.

'Never mind, more food for me. I'm going to keep ordering the starters, I love them.' Charlie patted his stomach.

'Ooh, this looks good.' I started to play with the swivelling carousel contraption in the centre of the table which meant we could whirl food around with wild abandonment.

'Gotta get crispy duck,' Leila insisted.

'Does that say kung poo prawns?' I showed my menu to Ayshe. Either it was a typing error, or I was more under the influence than I thought and was already seeing double.

'Perhaps you would like some drinks to start?' the waiter suggested, pen poised.

'Not 'arf,' Leila rattled off our order.

'Wonder what this is.' Ayshe eyed her menu. 'Fang dang

dango.' She looked round for any offers on the subject.

'Never heard of it. What about this, katrap pong?' I wondered.

'Do they just do egg and chips?' Felicity asked.

'No, you've got to try something,' Ayshe insisted. 'What about tea-smoked chicken?'

'I smoked tea once in college. It was foul. Tasted like shit,' Charlie said.

When the waiter returned, we ordered a whole heap of starters and a few main dishes to be getting on with.

'Can we try some fang dang dango, as well, please?' Ayshe asked him.

'Ah, you like dog, then?' He snorted as he wandered off, scribbling on his pad.

I pulled a disgusted face. 'Urgh, I'm not eating that!'

When the appetizers arrived, we tucked in with glee. I swung the swivel table round to grab a spare rib, and it knocked my fork flying on to the floor. I swiftly bent down and retrieved it.

'Forking hell!' I squawked at my own joke, closely followed by everyone else, apart from Felicity, who looked completely bewildered.

'I don't get it.' Felicity frowned, scratching her head.

Half way through a crispy, golden wanton, I glanced over to the bar area. Hiding behind the fish tank, between a large catfish and a very brightly coloured angel fish, I spied a policeman standing with his back to us, talking to a waitress.

'How queer. What's he doing here?' Charlie whispered to me.

I smirked. 'Wait and see.'

My phone started meowing and I held it under the table to read it.

'I am your strip-a-gram waiting at the bar. Please rendezvous with me and point out the hen.'

'Just going to the loo.' I shot up.

As I got closer to the bar, I realized the policeman was actually Paul-the-Well-Endowed from the art class.

'Well, hello again.' My jaw dropped.

'Hi.' he beamed. 'What a coincidence. How are you?'

'I'm good, thanks. The girl with the long black hair and the black dress is the one getting married.' I pointed over to Ayshe.

'OK. If you go back to your table, I'll be over in a minute.'

'I know you!' Charlie pointed at him as Paul approached our table a few minutes later. 'You're the one who's hung like an

160

elephant. Are you a policeman? You can arrest me any day.'

Angie's eyes suddenly lit up, and she feasted them on his crutch like there was no tomorrow.

Ayshe knew exactly what was coming and turned an interesting shade of crimson. Several of the other diners looked on with interest. I seriously hoped it wasn't going to put anyone off their spring rolls.

Suddenly, the song YMCA blasted out of the stereo, and Paul wiggled his butt and gyrated his hips in front of us. Charlie leapt out of his chair, following close behind him singing the complete rendition of the chorus and miming the actions in his exaggerated style while Paul tried to get as far away from him as possible. This just seemed to excite Charlie more.

'Ooh, you are playing hard to get.' Charlie managed to catch up with him and began bumping Paul's backside with his own, which caused the whole restaurant to erupt in a fit of giggles.

'Get off me!' Paul shoved him away and carried on with his routine as Charlie yanked at Paul's uniform.

'Ooh, that's on a bit tight. Get it off. Get it off.' Charlie tugged harder, but it wasn't budging.

Paul's routine then turned into a Saturday Night Fever kind of dance as he pointed his finger in the air and then back down again, with Charlie manhandling him.

'Oi, stop it.' Paul stifled a laugh, trying hard to maintain a professional façade.

'Get 'em off,' Leila and Angie chanted, clapping in time to the music.

Paul started undoing the buttons on his shirt whilst thrusting his hips in Ayshe's direction as Charlie pulled at the shirt from behind.

'Get it off,' he shouted in Paul's ear.

Then Angie shot out of her chair and grabbed Paul's face in her hands, pushed it in between her mammoth boobs – wiggling them around for good luck – and practically suffocated him in the process. Paul's arms flailed behind him as he pulled his head out, gulping for air. The poor guy was being accosted from the front by Angie and the rear by Charlie.

'You lot are nuts!' Paul shouted over the music, managing to get his top off unaided and get into the hip-swivelling action again, undulating back and forth repetitively. He launched himself on to Ayshe's knee, jiggled around a bit, and then he sat

161

on Angie's lap. Felicity tried to hide under the table, but she couldn't escape quick enough and he managed to jump on her before Charlie dragged him off, pulling him down onto his own lap where he held him tight. Paul struggled to get out of his clutches when at last Angie tugged on Charlie's arm and the captive managed to break free. Then he stood in front of Ayshe and whipped his trousers off in one fluid action – I think the Velcro down the sides must have aided his spontaneous exposure.

'Is that real?' Angie stared in disbelief at the sight of Paul-the-Well-Endowed, bulging in a bright red, sequined thong.

'Absolutely.' Charlie's eyes widened. 'I'd recognize that humongous thing anywhere.'

'Shush,' Paul whispered. 'People will get the wrong idea.'

'Oh, golly.' Felicity was perspiring so much that her glasses slid down the end of her nose.

Charlie thought he'd try to assist Paul by ripping off the only piece of kit he still had on, but Paul was having none of it. As Charlie tugged harder, Paul tried to run away, and a big tug of thong ensued.

'Get him off me!' Paul looked at us for help.

'Come here,' Charlie muttered.

There was a big ripping sound as the thong split and came off in Charlie's hand. Some of the other diners looked shocked and averted their eyes. Even Angie was gob-smacked at the size of it and nothing surprised her. Felicity almost fainted and clutched her chest. That left Leila, Ayshe and me – we were all were doubled over, howling with laughter so much that my stomach hurt. Paul quickly cupped his tackle in his hands and then gave a big wave to everyone in the restaurant. As he ambled off to get changed, Charlie gave him a slap on the bum and chased after him.

''Ere, I thought you woz lookin' to meet a new fella.' Leila poked me. 'What about that stripper?'

'He looked all right to me. I wouldn't kick him out of bed,' Angie said. 'Especially not with the size of his donger. Haven't seen one that big before, and I've seen my fair share, believe me.' She nodded knowingly. Angie worked as a nurse in the vasectomy clinic and was always telling us funny stories about different shapes, sizes and other general qualities of penises.

'Well, there's someone else I'm interested in, actually.' I

162

giggled, but didn't want to give too much away and the drink was making my tongue a bit loose.

'Who?' Angie sat forward.

'I'm not saying.' I folded my arms across my chest.

'That Nick you've got a date with?' Ayshe asked.

'No, not telling.' I gave them a sly grin.

'I'll get it out of her.' Ayshe put her arm round me and kissed me on the cheek.

After the excitement of the stripper, our main courses arrived. We devoured them like a flock of velociraptors and were still munching away when the disco started.

'Where's Felicity gone?' I asked, realizing that I hadn't seen her for about fifteen minutes.

'Loo, I think.' Angie swallowed a mouth full of chow mein.

Charlie came back looking flushed and sat down for about a second. 'I'm going to dance.' He leapt up and launched himself onto the dance-floor, where he pranced around singing full blast in a completely over-the-top kind of way.

'It's raining men! Hallelujah it's raining men!' Charlie grabbed the microphone off the DJ and shouted on the dance-floor.

I furrowed my brow at one of the dishes. 'Is that the dog thing?' No one had touched it.

'I'm not eating it.' Leila grimaced at it.

'I'd rather eat a red hot poker,' I said.

Charlie pulled his top up, rubbing his belly whilst belting out, 'I'm too sexy for my shirt, too sexy for my shirt!'

'Where's that Felicity?' I looked around for her, swaying slightly.

'I'll look in the bogs.' Leila wandered off in search of her.

'Ain't no mountain high enough!' Charlie burst out. We all turned to see him attempting to drag an elderly woman – who was right in the middle of enjoying her chicken and sweet corn soup – off to the dance-floor with him. She prodded him in the groin with her walking stick and he toppled onto the floor.

'She ain't in there.' Leila sat down again and then looked at Felicity's chair. ''Er bag's 'ere.' She bent down to pick it up, peering under the table. 'She's fallen asleep under 'ere.' She poked Felicity with her foot. 'Oi, get up.'

Felicity mumbled something, which sounded like, 'Fuck off'. But couldn't possibly have been, coming from her lips.

163

We all lifted up the table cloth to have a look. 'Come on, get up, we're going for a boogie.' Ayshe and I both poked her in unison.'

'Dancing Queen!' Charlie yelled in the background.

'Where am I?' She rubbed her eyes.

'Can't 'andle 'er bevvies,' Leila said as we all got up and headed off to join Charlie, leaving poor Felicity under the table.

I gave the DJ ten out of ten for stamina as he chased Charlie around the dance-floor, trying to put a stop to his one-man karaoke show. Due to my gym-sore legs and the amount of wine we had consumed, I pranced around for a couple of hours like a geriatric on crack.

# Chapter 21
## Thursday, day 11 – You Can Never Have Enough Knickers

I thought I was dying when I woke up the next morning. No one could have such a bad headache and not have a brain tumour, surely. Note to self: Never, ever drink that much again! The room was still shrouded in darkness and the central heating hadn't yet kicked in, so it must have been early. I turned over and a searing pain shot through my right eye, but the good news was that the room-spinning had vanished. My tongue felt like I'd been having a secret carpet licking session in my comatose sleep. I snuggled tighter under the duvet, willing the banging in my head to miraculously disappear. When it hadn't gone after fifteen minutes, I prised my eyelids apart. Reaching inside the bedside cabinet, I pulled out some whopping great painkillers, strategically hidden there for just such an occasion. After downing a couple of them – and an extra one, just in case – I managed to return to the land of nod. The next time I woke, a grey haze peeped through the gap in the curtains and rain drummed hard against the window. A bolt of lightning illuminated the room and thunder grumbled towards me in the distance.

The pneumatic drill banging inside my brain had disappeared and the room was now stiflingly hot, so I kicked the covers off my feet, turned onto my side and studied the wardrobe, wondering about what would happen when Kalem found out about Emine.

Would he manage to forgive her and try to salvage their relationship? Or would he not want anything to do with her? Would that leave the door open for me to try and wedge my foot in, or would his family forbid it? Just because I'd suddenly developed some kind of bizarre obsession with him, it didn't follow suit that he would be having the same ideas about me. Apart from the night at Clarissa's, where I wasn't sure if it was part of the act, or whether it had meant anything to him, everything between us was as it always had been. Friends. It was strange, but I couldn't even tell now when these sensations had

165

started to creep up on me. I'd been so busy trying to get on with my life-changing plan that I hadn't really noticed when things had changed. One minute he was ordinary Kalem, Ayshe's brother, who wound me up constantly. And the next, he had become someone I could see myself spending the rest of my life with. Could I be falling in love with him?

I made a mental list of exactly what it was I liked about him. He was ravishingly attractive with his chiselled good looks, but he was so much more than that. He was funny, caring, he adored children – as I did – and he appreciated the simple things in life. But best of all, he'd always been there for me. In fact, he was the complete opposite of Justin.

I couldn't see how it was ever going to go anywhere, though, and if I risked trying to tell Kalem about it, it could ruin everything between us and also upset Ayshe – which would go down like a meteor straight through the head. It was all very, very scary.

So, I thought firmly to myself, what I need to do is put these insane deliberations out of my head and concentrate on getting on with my life. After all, I rationalized, that was why I'd started this whole challenge thing in the first place. But it would be easier said than done, and it didn't make me very happy.

I swung my legs over the side of the bed and realized they were still killing me from my impulsive bout of exercise at the gym. I mooched around the flat with difficulty – a foggy head and a miserable, dark mood didn't help matters – and started to make tea and toast. Well, I tried to make some tea but had to give up after I absent-mindedly put the tea-bag down the spout of the kettle instead of into the mug. I chewed my toast in a trance, staring through sensitive slits – which used to be my eyes – at the bleak world outside the window. It was very quiet this morning. I hadn't heard a peep out of Charlie, so he must have still been away with the fairies.

Ayshe told me I had to bring a swimsuit for today's challenge, so after I'd woken up a bit, I rummaged around trying to find one. I came across a mouldy old thing, which on closer inspection was threadbare around the boob area, making it almost completely see-through. That went straight in the bin. My second attempt was more successful and produced a black halter-neck bikini, purchased in anticipation of a summer holiday with Justin that never happened. I must have stuffed it down the back

166

of the drawer and forgotten about it. Even the price tags were still on it. I shoved it in a hold-all along with a towel and some spare knickers, just in case. After reading Gloria Cox's book I realized that you never know when you might be affected by a bout of incontinence; plus I didn't have a clue what we were up to today. I threw on a black T-shirt, a warm fleecy jacket and some tatty-looking leggings, which had started life as smooth, skin-tight lycra but were now reduced to a bobbly, baggy-bum consistency. Pulling my hair up into a top knot, I inspected myself in the mirror with disapproval.

The night before had taken its toll. Bags had appeared under my eyes and blobs of make-up stuck to my eyelids, which had the rather unattractive effect of making me look like I had one big eyelash on each eye. I scrubbed my face with a flannel and scrutinized my skin – oh, God! What the bloody hell was this? I'd developed about ten wrinkles overnight. Putting my fingertips beneath my eyes, I stretched the skin down nice and taut – damn, that didn't work. You could still see them. I had to buy some anti-wrinkle cream immediately. I'd better start now, I thought, and catch them early. I'd read somewhere they can creep up on you overnight, and I could be looking just like one of those wrinkly looking Shar Pei dogs quicker than I could say collagen serum. I stuck out my tongue, frowning at the white lines on it. Urrgh, I must read through the Gloria Cox Bible again and find out what that meant. Outwardly, I hadn't changed in the last eleven days – well, apart from the odd grey hair and a few winkles – but inwardly, I now knew what I really wanted.

A huge bouquet of velvety, blood-red roses greeted me as I pulled open my front door. Retrieving the fragrant bundle from its resting place on the floor, I searched for an accompanying envelope and ripped it open, reading it in disbelief:

Dear Helen,
I'm really sorry about the other night. I can't live without you.
I promise I'll change if you just give me one more chance.
All my love
Justin XXXXXX

Slowly, I lifted the flowers to my nose, drinking in their spicy perfume. Was it true? Could he really change? Had I made a

167

mistake? I wished – not for the first time in my life – that I had a magic crystal ball. Because if I'd known then what I know now, I would've kicked myself for being so stupid.

After putting them in some water, I traipsed up to Ayshe's very slowly for fear that any sudden movement might bring the early morning Kango back to life and make my aching legs worse. Ayshe wasn't in a much better state when I arrived.

'God, my head.' The palm of her hand rested on her forehead. 'Good night, though, wasn't it? I can't believe Felicity got a date.'

'I know, she'll probably be married before me,' I muttered. 'I hope we're not doing anything energetic today.'

'Don't worry, we can take it easy. We're going to a health farm.' She smiled. 'Ooh, remind me not to move my face, it hurts. I think my brain's bruised.'

We drove slowly up the long winding driveway which led to Felsham Hall Health Farm whose glowing reputation preceded it. State-of-the-art pioneering beauty treatments and a famous list of clients made it second to none. The setting was beautiful: large panoramic gardens, mature trees and vast acres of manicured lawns. Stepping out of the car and into the rain, we crunched over the mossy gravel and found ourselves in a very impressive, stark, white hallway with a sweeping marble staircase in the centre and a check-in desk to the right.

'May I help you?' A flawlessly made up lady stood behind the desk. Her long blonde hair was pulled so tightly into a bun that it made her eyes slant upwards.

'We're booked in for a spa day,' Ayshe informed her.

She took our names and scanned the register. 'You have been booked in for a traditional Mediterranean steam bath massage, a seaweed body wrap and a pedicure. This is your timetable.' She handed us a sheet of paper, pointing to a list. 'If you go to the treatment waiting area five minutes before your appointments, they will call you from there. The rest of the day you can use the swimming pool, sauna and steam room, and take any of the fitness classes listed on this sheet.'

'Very nice.' This was just the ticket: a lovely, lazy, relaxing day to get rid of the hangover.

'The changing rooms are over there.' She pointed across the hall. 'There are dressing-gowns and towels for your use during

168

the day, and lunch is served between twelve and three.'

'OK, thanks.' We gathered up our forms and headed off to get changed.

'Wow, these dressing-gowns are a bit soft. Mmm, they feel lovely.' Ayshe picked one up and looked at it.

'How do they get their things so white?' I examined the soft, fluffy towels.

'Look at all these beauty products.' Ayshe picked up a tub of rejuvenating cream from a selection of various tubs and sniffed it.

I grabbed a miniature pot of anti-wrinkle cream and applied most of it in one go, rubbing it in eagerly until my skin shined with grease.

I swung round to Ayshe. 'Have the wrinkles gone now?'

'Don't know what you're worried about, anyway. I can't see any.' She stared at my super-slimy face.

'Shall we go to the pool first and lounge around there?' I suggested. 'Don't feel like doing anything energetic until I've woken up, and my legs are agony. They're a bit better now that I've warmed up a bit, but walking downstairs is a definite no-no.'

Ten minutes later, armed with our swimming gear and towelling bath robes, we lay side by side on comfy sun-beds in the warm conservatory around the pool area. Murals of Mediterranean gardens had been painted on the walls and large exotic palm trees in terracotta pots were dotted around. To the side of the pool there was a jacuzzi together with a freezing cold plunge pool that I definitely wasn't going in – no way! Some more changing areas led off to the side with a steam and sauna room. Two men lounged on sun-beds in the opposite corner of the room. The older one, in his fifties, was asleep with his mouth open, emitting a curious ticking sound from the back of his throat. The other one had his Speedos pulled up to his man-boobs and was thoroughly engrossed in a paperback.

'What about yoga?' Ayshe studied her sheet.

My gaze flew up to the ceiling. 'I had an embarrassing experience during yoga once. Don't fancy repeating it, really.'

'What?'

'I farted.'

'Probably everyone farts during yoga.'

'Yes, but it wasn't out of my bum.' I gave her a wry smile.

169

'How about a step class?'

'Too energetic.' I still felt grumpy and tired, which wasn't helping to lift my mood. 'How did Atila's stag night go?' I closed my eyes

'He strolled in around four, so I think he had a good time. The most important thing is that he came home fully-clothed, not handcuffed to some inanimate object, and completely untarred and unfeathered, which is always a bonus on a stag do. The only problem was that Dad got so confused about the public toilet etiquette thing, he locked himself in one of the cubicles and then couldn't get the door open for an hour.'

'Mmm, crazy.' My eyelids began to get heavy, and I drifted off into a semi-sleep.

'Oh, I almost forgot. I spoke to Kalem about the dreaded Emine.'

I perked up all of a sudden. 'Oh, yes.' I did my best impression of being casual. 'What happened?'

'He said she could do whatever she liked. He finished with her ages ago.'

'What? Why didn't he say anything?' I sat up.

'You know what he's like, he hates discussing things like that.'

How could he not tell anyone? 'Why did he dump her?' I was all ears.

'He said she was "a jumped-up, superficial tart", but then we knew that anyway. Don't know why it took him so long to find out.'

'I'd agree with that.' I smiled to myself.

'I think he's interested in someone else.' She looked at me.

A crushing feeling gripped at my chest. 'He didn't say who?'

'No, he wouldn't tell me. I tried to force it out of him, but he wasn't having any of it.'

'Oh.' I plopped back on the lounger, my thoughts reeling.

Who was the mystery woman? It was bound to be someone refined, gorgeous and calamity free. And how was I supposed to pretend I was happy for him when I wished it was me he was with? Maybe it was the sister of one of his mates, like the tall and stunning Zerdali with the huge doe-like eyes, cascades of brown hair and legs which went up to her armpits. She was absolutely gorgeous with a husky voice that made everything sound seductive, and she was really nice too – which was seriously annoying. She was basically a woman's worst nightmare. I bet she didn't have grey hair and wrinkles.

I felt a weight of dread descend on me. If there was no hope for me and Kalem, should I take this 'change-your-life' stuff one step further and change it completely? Maybe I should move abroad somewhere to keep as much distance between us as I could. After all, I could do my photography anywhere, and this challenge had shown me that there was definitely a big, wide world out there waiting to be discovered.

'Come on.' She leapt up. 'Let's do a few laps.'

I grunted. 'You're obviously feeling better, then.'

'Much, now come on.' She took my hand and pulled me up.

'God, that's a bit cold.' I stalked into the pool and did some splashy breast-stroke.

'It's lovely, it will wake you up.'

We managed a gentle warm up, chatting as we glided up and down. But I couldn't shake off the sinking feeling which was beginning to wash over me like the chilled water.

We swam for another ten minutes doing a leisurely back-stroke, and then I could hear a dirty titter coming from the two men on the loungers.

'What's up with them?' I whispered to Ayshe.

'Don't know. Ignore them,' she said as we came to the end of the pool and swam off again.

I concentrated on the lights in the ceiling so that I knew roughly when I would get to the edge of the pool and not whack my arm on it like I'd done the first few goes. As we drew closer to the men again, one of them said, 'Cor. That's a bit of all right.'

'Urgh! Dirty old men.' Ayshe gave them a disgusted look, then carried on swimming.

'Go on, come to Papa,' one of them whispered to the other.

'What are they talking about?' I faced my head to Ayshe as we lay on our backs.

'Who knows? Bunch of perverts I think.'

'That's quite impressive.' one of the men went on.

I glanced over at them and saw them leering at me. 'For God's sake, what are they looking at?'

'Ignore them.' She pushed off from the edge again.

When we'd finally had enough, I held onto the bar at the edge and floated on my back, letting the water hold me up with ease.

'Oh, I know what they were looking at!' Ayshe glanced at my

171

chest and pointed to my boob.

I looked down. 'What?' Then I realized that my right boob had wormed its way out of my bikini top and was on full display. 'Aagh!' I stuffed it back in and turned my back on the men. 'How embarrassing.' A wave of shame almost drowned me.

'Could have been worse, I suppose. It might have been your bottoms,' Ayshe cackled.

I slapped her on the arm in mock horror. 'Come on, let's go to the sauna,' I hissed.

After a sweaty half hour in the sauna we hurried off to find some lunch before our treatments began. The dining room was empty when we arrived so we helped ourselves to the impressive buffet which provided rabbit-food healthy options and fully-laden calorific ones. I loaded up my plate with an organic chicken salad. Ayshe had gone for grilled salmon with roasted vegetables and a banana. She eyed my plate.

'What?' I frowned.

'Wow! Gloria Cox must have talked some sense into you. That's the healthiest thing I've seen you eat for years.'

'I know. I told you I'm trying to take it all seriously.'

'Kalem would be really proud of you.'

'Yes, he would.' I beamed.

'Oh, my God, I can't believe I'm really getting married on Sunday,' Ayshe gushed as we sat down.

'Ooh, I know. I'm so happy for you.' I put my hand on her arm.

'Kalem's going to pick the flowers up for me on Sunday morning and bring them round the house while we're getting ready. And I wanted you to take some casual shots at the flat before we leave for the Priory.'

I rubbed my hands together. 'I can't wait to get started on your wedding book. I promise to have it done by the time you get back from your honeymoon.'

'I've been practicing my new signature. It's really odd when you've had the same one all your life, and then you suddenly have to change it. Shame he hasn't got a nice surname, though – I mean, I'm going to be Mrs. But.'

'You'll be the butt of all the jokes, then, won't you! Ha-ha. Or, you could keep your old name, I suppose, or have a double-barrelled one.' I bit into my chicken.

'Mmm.' She hesitated. 'I don't think Mustafa-But sounds too

good, though. Sounds a bit kinky!'
   'Charlie would absolutely love it!'

# Chapter 22

I studied my timetable as we waited in the treatment area. I was first up for the massage and Ayshe was booked in for the seaweed wrap at the same time.

'I wonder if it makes you lose a few pounds. It says here it's supposed to detoxify you and make you lose inches, apparently.' Ayshe read the information sheet.

'Maybe I could have one a day.'

'Ms Grey.' A giant of a man, built like a Russian shot-putter with a foreign accent, called out my name and motioned for me to follow him.

He led me into what looked like a miniature Turkish Bath room. There was a round marble bench in the centre of the dome-shaped room, and jugs of water, presumably to increase the steam power, were placed at regular intervals around the outside. The concave ceiling had round holes cut out of it, which were fitted with multi-coloured stained glass, so the room took on a soft, tinted glow.

'Can you tek off your undervare and wrap zis towel round you and lie face down 'ere, pleeze.' He pointed to the centre of the bench. 'I'll be back.' He sounded like Arnold Schwarzenegger.

I stripped off my bra and knickers, placing them on a chair in the corner of the room. Didn't really want to mess with shot-putting Arnie. I could feel the warmth rising up from the marble, permeating my skin, and I began to feel very drowsy. When he stepped back into the room, he placed a big bowl of thick, soapy water next to me and dunked a round sponge into it. Then he was off – sponging me dynamically with the mixture which was actually rather nice and soothed my painful muscles. He began on my legs, working his way up to my buttocks. I jumped a bit when he got too close to my bits and bobs, but if he noticed, it didn't bother him, and he carried on up to my shoulders and back, which was heavenly. I nodded off, mentally whispering Justin's message over and over in my head. When Arnie asked me to turn over onto my back, I woke up disorientated, wondering who was massaging me. I rolled over, holding onto the towel to protect my modesty and then fell back into a relaxed, dreamy state again as he travelled up my legs once

174

more. Again he was getting a bit too close to my nether region for my liking, and this time he abandoned his sloppy sponge in favour of his own, firm hands. I opened my eyes and glared at him suspiciously, but he ignored me and carried on. After another twenty minutes, he whistled a version of, We Wish you a Merry Xmas and finished off with my arms.

'You can reeelax and stay 'ere for five minitz,' he said before heading out the door.

After a few minutes, I sat up feeling light and feathery. I slipped out of the towel and pulled on my bra. But...wait a minute...where were my knickers? I looked under the chair. Nothing. Strange, I could have sworn I left them there. Had I brought them with me? Or had I left them in the changing room? I frowned, eyes scanning the room for any sign of them. I shook my head. I was losing the plot. I'd had so much on my mind lately, I'd probably just forgotten to put them on and had left them in the changing room after all.

When I got back into the waiting room, Ayshe had already finished her treatment and was flicking through a beauty magazine.

'How was it?' she asked.

'Um...interesting.' I flopped down next to her. 'How about the wrap thingy?'

'Good, I think I've lost half a stone.'

'Really?'

'Nah,' she tittered as the shot-putter called her name.

Another woman sitting next to me leaned over and whispered into my ear, 'Have you just had that Mediterranean massage?'

I turned to look at her. 'Yes,' I whispered back. 'Have you?'

She leaned in closer. 'Did you lose something in the treatment room?'

'As a matter of fact, I did. Did you?'

'Yes,' she gasped. 'My knickers!'

'Me too!

'How disgusting. Right, that settles it, we need to speak to the manager. Come on.' She charged off towards the reception desk with me bringing up the rear. 'Excuse me, could we have a word with the manager, please?' she said to the waif-like teenage girl with tragic-looking eyes sitting behind the counter.

'What seems to be the problem?' the Waif's voice was so quiet it was almost a whisper.

175

'We've both just had one of the Mediterranean massages, and we had our knickers stolen!'

The receptionists' eyes widened. 'Really, madam?'

I nodded in agreement. 'Is that part of the massage?'

'Not at all. I'll get the manager right away.' The Waif dashed off and left us both standing there, simmering away like hot springs.

'I'm not letting him get away with this!' the woman shrieked.

I looked round the waiting area and a few of the other women who were milling around drew closer. 'Did you have your knickers stolen in the Mediterranean massage?' one of them asked.

'Yes, you too?' I said.

'Absolutely, it's disgusting, the man should be sacked.'

'And I did, too,' another woman piped up.

'I am the duty manager here. What seems to be the problem, ladies?' A short, dumpy-looking woman addressed the group. The buttons on her blouse strained under the weight of her abundant bosoms and her eyebrows had been plucked to almost non-existence, giving her a look of constant surprise.

'My knickers have been nicked,' the first woman informed her.

'Mine too,' I added.

'And mine.'

'Mine too.'

'And my friend's in there now. Hers are probably being stolen as we speak and—'

'These are very serious allegations. Which masseur was it?' she interrupted, a sombre expression locked in place.

'The one in there.' And with this the first woman pointed to the room containing the Turkish Bath as the waif hovered by, biting her nail.

Just then, a loud scream errupted from the steam room: 'Aagh! What are you doing, you pervert?' Ayshe came running out, clutching her knickers to her chest.

'You too?' the first woman said.

Ayshe nodded. 'I've had loads of Turkish Bath massages, and no one does that!' she fumed.

'I can only apologize profusely, I'm afraid that  member of staff is new. He came very highly recommended.' The manager shook her head. 'Does anyone want to involve the police or can we deal with this internally?'

'Only if you sack him,' the first woman said.

'I agree.'

'I want to make a complaint to the police,' I said.

'Here, here.'

'Me too,' Ayshe snapped. 'He shouldn't be able to get away with it. I'm going to call the police.' She tugged her mobile out of her bag and dialed 999.

'Hello, what's your emergency please?' the police controller asked.

'I've had my underwear stolen.' Ayshe glared at the manager.

'Were you in them at the time Madam?'

'What? Of course I wasn't!' Ayshe said.

'Do you know the offender? Do you know where he is?' the police controller went on.

'Lock him in the steam bath.' the first woman said to the manager.

'We're going to lock him in the bath,' Ayshe informed the controller.

The manager, deciding she could have a riot on her hands, thought it was best to comply.

'What's your name and address, please?' the controller enquired.

Ayshe rattled off her details. 'Do you need my phone number?'

'If it is the same number you are calling from then we have a record of it. Where did the incident happen?'

'In the bath.'

'Why was he in the bath with you?'

'Because he was giving me a massage!'

'Sorry, I don't understand. You were in the bath and this man was giving you a massage, and then he stole your knickers?' the police controller asked.

'No, no. I'm at Felsham Hall Health Farm. I was having a massage treatment and the masseur tried to steal my knickers. I'm supposed to be having a nice, relaxing day!' Ayshe's voice reached a high crescendo

'Oh, I see. OK, we will have a police unit with you in about half an hour.'

'Right, thanks very much.' Ayshe slammed her phone shut. 'Someone's going to come up,' she told everyone.

'Well, if you're making a complaint, so am I,' the first woman spat.

'Me too,' I said. How dare he have a jolly when we were in a vulnerable state.

'OK, ladies. Perhaps you would all like to go into the snug room and wait. Follow me, please.' The manager led us to a quiet sitting-room. 'When the police arrive, I will send them up. Can I get you something to drink – on the house, of course?'

'Wine and soda please.' I flopped down into a deep, leather Chesterfield and folded my arms across my chest.

'Brandy.'

'I'll have one too.'

'I need one for the shock.'

'Wine, please,' Ayshe said, stony-faced.

'I would like a cigar too, please,' I added, as I ran a hand rather manically through my hair.

'You stopped smoking!' Ayshe looked at me.

'Well, occasionally I have a sneaky one under moments of extreme stress. And I think this qualifies.'

The manager abandoned us, closing the door behind her with a firm click.

'Filthy animal,' I spat.

We went into ranting overdrive until Miss Abundant Bosoms came back looking very uncomfortable. Silently, she placed a tray of drinks and a couple of giant Churchill cigars on the coffee table in front of us. I grabbed a cigar, yanked the wrapper off and gave it a quick sniff – urgh, it smelled of sheep shit – oh, well – needs must.

Forty-five minutes later, two policemen arrived. The older one had the most poppy-out eyes I'd ever seen and bright-red, ruddy cheeks and the other one looked about twelve. They sat down with us and took our details. There were serious looks all round.

'So, after the massage, your knickers all disappeared. Is that correct?' the older one asked whilst the younger one took notes in a small, black notebook.

'Yes,' everyone agreed in unison.

'And they were left in the room with you whilst you were having the massage?' the younger one interrupted.

'Yes!' the first woman answered.

'Did he use any force or offensive weapons to get the knickers?' The older one gazed at us, and I thought his eyeballs were going to ping out.

'Only his hands,' I fumed.

'Can you explain exactly what he did, please, madam?' the younger one asked.

'Well, I left my underwear on the chair and when he finished my massage, they'd vanished,' I said.

'Yeah, same for me.'

'That's about right.'

'Yes, they were definitely there before the massage.'

'I actually caught him trying to take them. I tried to pull them off him, and he ripped them,' Ayshe added.

'Can you describe the...' the younger one coughed, 'hmm...knickers, please.'

'Mine were navy blue cotton. Size twenty, from Marks and Spencer.'

'Black cheeky knickers with the words "Do you wanna play?" on the back,' I said.

The younger one glanced up briefly, then repeated what I'd said as he scribbled it down.

'Mine were magic knickers,' one of the women said.

'Pardon?' PC Poppy-eyed asked. 'What are magic knickers?'

'The kind that hold your flabby bits in. When I bought them, the shop assistant assured me they would make you look two sizes smaller,' the first woman told him. 'They don't work, though!'

'Well, they certainly disappeared,' the younger policeman said. 'Maybe they were magic.'

She glared at him. 'Can I get them under the Trade Descriptions Act or something for telling lies?'

'Sorry Madam, that's a civil matter. Where's the offender now?' PC Poppy-eyed asked.

'Locked in the steam room,' Ayshe volunteered.

The policemen stood up. 'OK, we'll go and talk to him and come back in a moment.'

I downed my drink. Puffing furiously on the cigar, I tipped my head back and blew a trail of blue-grey smoke up to the ceiling. 'Gross,' I muttered to no one in particular. 'And I've missed my seaweed wrap and pedicure.'

After twenty minutes, they returned and took a statement from each of us.

'He's admitted the whole thing. He had a locker full of various women's…erm, articles. We're going to arrest him for theft and we will be in touch with you ladies shortly to indentify your underwear,' the younger one informed us.

'Thanks.'

'Pig! Oh sorry, not you, officer,' I stammered.

'Thank you, officers.'

'I should hope so too,' the first woman said as the manager skulked back into the room.

'I'm very sorry about all this. Before you leave, we will be handing out complimentary passes from the check-in desk for another day at the spa.'

'I need to have a seaweed wrap.' I said, still harping on about it as I stubbed out another cigar.

'Thanks,' Ayshe muttered, as we headed off to get changed.

# Chapter 23

'Whaaat!' Atila screeched when we spilled the beans on the knicker-nicking masseur.

'I know. Can you believe it?' Ayshe stormed around the flat like a balloon that had just had all the air let out.

'What did the police say?' Atila held his arms out for her, and she stepped into them, resting her head on his shoulder.

'They arrested him.' She sniffed.

'Are you OK?' He looked at me. 'Do you need a cuddle, too?'

I nodded, feeling sorry for myself, and joined them in a big group hug.

'Well, I'm not going there again, even if we did get a complimentary pass,' I said. 'Good job I took a spare pair of knickers with me.'

'Maybe I'll go.' Atila let go of us and poked at the spaghetti sauce. 'See if I get my boxers stolen by a big butch Swedish woman masseur.'

'By the way, I haven't said thanks for paying for me to go as well. It was a wonderful day – apart from the weirdo and the lack of seaweed treatment.' I took a spoon from the worktop and tasted the sauce.

'Actually, I didn't pay for yours.' He pulled four pasta bowls from the cupboard and filled them with linguine.

Grabbing some cutlery from the drawer, I shot him a questioning glance. 'Who did, then?'

'Kalem.'

'Why?' I frowned.

'Dunno, he insisted.' Atila shrugged as the doorbell rang. 'Oh, that's probably him now.'

Ayshe stomped off. 'I'll get it.'

'Whaaat?' Kalem said as soon as she had filled him in. 'Have you reported it?' He walked into the kitchen, looking from Ayshe to me, apprehension clouding his eyes. 'Are you both OK?

'Yes and yes.' I slumped down at the table, exhausted.

'Will you have to go to court?' Kalem lowered himself into a chair next to me.

'I'm not sure.' I shrugged, then grated some parmesan on top of my pasta. 'He admitted it, so probably not, which is good.'

Kalem put his hand on my arm and gave me a look which I couldn't quite work out. 'I feel terrible.'

'Why?' I gulped hard as a surge of electricity shot up my body.

'Well, I was the one who suggested it to Atila. I thought it would be a nice surprise for you both.' He took his hand away.

'And you paid for me?' I wound some pasta in between my fork and spoon but it fell off and splattered onto the table. 'Oops.' I reached for my napkin.

Kalem pushed me back down. 'No, I'll do it.' When he'd soaked up the mess, he looked down at his meal. 'Yes, I paid for you.

'Thanks very much, it was very kind of you, but why?' I gazed into his eyes. 'I could have paid for myself.' Did he have feelings for me after all?

'Well...I thought with all the ridiculous things you've been doing lately, you could do with a bit of time to relax your mind, as well as your body, and get your life into perspective. What better place to do that than at a health farm? You are like a sister to me after all, and Atila wouldn't let me pay for Ayshe, so I thought I'd do the next best thing. Even I didn't think you could get into any trouble there.' He shook his head. 'Boy, how wrong I was.'

So that was it. A brotherly gesture. Disappointment flooded through my veins.

'You'll never guess what else Helen got up to today,' Ayshe said.

I elbowed her in the ribs.

'Hmm, let me guess.' Kalem put his fingertips to his temples. 'She single-handedly set the building on fire?'

'No,' Ayshe grinned.

I frowned at her.

'She staged a political coup?' Kalem asked.

'She flashed her boob at a couple of old perverts!' Ayshe giggled.

'What?' Kalem shrieked at me. 'Are you on drugs?'

I coughed. 'It's not what you think. It was an–'

'What the hell were you thinking?' A vein pulsed in his neck.

I gasped. 'Well...it was an–'

'You're obviously not content with bloody streaking round

182

Tesco and mooning over the frozen veg; you have to go one step further and flash the rest of you off to some dirty old men.' He narrowed his eyes at me.

A lump rose in my throat. I swallowed. 'Oh, so you um…saw that then, did you?'

'Saw it?' Kalem leapt off the chair, his six foot frame looming over the table. 'Saw it? The whole bloody shop saw it!' His voice cranked up to an ear-splitting decibel.

I opened my mouth and a nervous giggle slipped out.

'You're insane!' Kalem shouted, throwing his napkin on the table. He glared at me with a fiery heat in his eyes. A minute passed. No one said anything. And then he strode out the door.

I gaped at the empty doorway, wondering about his very vocal and out-of-character display of animosity towards me because of what was, after all, an accident. Either it meant he thought I was some kind of compulsive naturist. Or worse…a lunatic. Or…even worse…he hated me.

We picked at our food half-heartedly in eerie silence.

'Well, that was a conversation-killer,' Atila muttered eventually

'What's up with Kalem?' Ayshe threw me a questioning look.

I shrugged. 'I don't know.'

She reclined in the chair, folding her arms. 'Well, something isn't right. He's not normally like that.'

'He has been acting a bit weird lately.' Atila nodded.

'Is there something going on between you two?' Ayshe said to me.

Oh crap! Ayshe could usually read me like a book. Had she guessed my secret?

'No!' I said, hoping I didn't look as guilty as I felt. 'Maybe Atila knows what's wrong with him.' I glanced at Atila, trying to deflect the conversation away from me.

'Beats me.'

'If nothing's going on, why are you looking so guilty?' Ayshe concentrated her gaze on me with thoughtful eyes.

I shifted in my chair. 'I'm not.'

'Did something happen the night of the dinner party?' she carried on.

'No!' I said, painfully aware that I was beginning to sound like a stuck record

'I know what it is.' She narrowed her eyes slightly.

183

Double crap! I averted my gaze and fiddled with my napkin.

'You two have had a row, haven't you?'

I breathed an invisible sigh of relief. 'No.'

'Hmm.' Ayshe didn't sound convinced.

'So, that clears that up. Kalem's acting weird, but we don't know why,' Atila said.

'I think I need a drink.' Ayshe cleared the half-eaten plates and brought out some wine for all of us. 'So, are you looking forward to your date with Nick tomorrow?'

Although I'd liked Nick, now my emotions were all topsy-turvy and facing in a completely unexpected direction, I didn't know what to think anymore. 'I suppose so.' I gulped my drink, thankful that she'd finally changed the subject.

And then it hit me. What had been the whole point of this life-changing challenge? I realized I had gone completely off-track. When I thought about it, that was exactly what this thing had really been about: forcing yourself to do out of the ordinary things, regardless of whether, deep down, you really wanted to or not, because one thing would always lead to another, and so on and so on. Everything you did always had a knock-on effect, and when you got down to it, the trouble with life was that it would always be full of unexpected inconsistencies. When Ayshe used to tell me, 'you never know what's round the corner', part of me used to hate her for it because – well, wasn't that always what people who were happy and contented said to people who weren't? She had Atila and her life was moving on. She was getting married and would live happy ever after. Hopefully. But what I really needed to do, regardless of how I felt about Kalem, was to just get busy with my life, and maybe then I could just forget about him.

'Right, let's talk about the wedding for a change.' Ayshe rested her hand on Atila's knee.

'What, again?' Atila muttered.

'So, Saturday night, you are staying with Kalem.' She poked him in the leg. 'And Helen is staying with me. Sunday morning at o-seven-forty-five hours precisely, we will arise,' she sniggered.

'You mean get up.' I twirled my hair around my fingers, whilst I concentrated on her.

She nodded. 'Exactly, this thing has to go like clockwork.'

'You're not arranging one of your bloody board meetings,'

184

Atila said.

'I know, but these things have to be organized well, you know. I don't want to be late to my own wedding – I know it's the bride's prerogative and all that, but still, I want to be on time.'

'Go on, then, what happens after you arise?' he asked.

'Helen brings me breakfast in bed.' She looked smug.

'What? That's not in the rules is it?'

She tilted her head. 'I think smoked salmon and scrambled eggs should do it,' she garbled on without pausing for breath. 'Then we've got all morning to do hair and make-up and girly stuff. Leila is coming round at twelve. Kalem's picking up the flowers at twelve and bringing them here. No doubt Mum and Dad will be popping in.' She hesitated. 'Oh, I hope Dad doesn't start drinking until after the service.'

'I think your dad's funny when he's had a few. He could liven it up a bit.'

She ignored me and steamed on. 'You've got to take piccies while we're getting ready.' She pointed at me. 'And then off to the Priory for three o'clock. Now, because you'll be doing photos during the ceremony.' She pointed at me again, 'Leila will be sorting out the bridesmaid stuff when we get there.' She sat back, finally complete. 'Is that all understood?' She looked at everyone for confirmation.

'Yes, miss.' I saluted her.

'I've got to pick the dresses up tomorrow, as well. I forgot to mention that bit. And you've got to get the suits.' She pointed at Atila.

'And I've got a pre-wedding surprise for you in town on Saturday morning. So be ready at eleven. OK, Mrs. But?' I pointed at her this time and stood up. 'I'm going to shoot off. With all the excitement today, I need to sleep for a week.' I yawned and kissed everyone Turkish-style on both cheeks.

Very early the next morning I woke with a start. I studied a patch of street light dancing on the wall of my bedroom for a moment before turning onto my back. I tried to drift back into a very yummy dream I was having about Kalem, but much to my annoyance, muffled shouts from Charlie's flat next door kept interrupting me.

'Help me.' I thought I could hear. I pulled the duvet over my head and tried to ignore it, but he was getting louder.

'Help!' Charlie cried. 'Help me!'

'Oh, for God's sake! Why can't anyone get any sleep round here?' I stormed out of bed and banged on his door in my fleecy pajamas and fluffy hamster slippers.

'Who's there?' Charlie wailed.

'St John's Ambulance. What's the matter with you?' I shouted.

'Is that you, Helen?'

'Of course it's bloody me. Now you've woken me up, open the door and tell me what the matter is.' I banged on it again.

'I can't open it. I'm stuck,' he yelped. 'You'll need to get your spare key and open the door.'

'Right – back in a minute.' I stomped off to retrieve it from a jumble of keys in my kitchen drawer.

'Who's there?' Charlie asked when I forced the key in the lock and pushed the door open.

'It's me again.' I looked around the lounge for him. 'Where are you?' I wandered into the kitchen.

'Bedroom, but I warn you, it's not a pretty sight.'

I flung open the door to his bedroom, which was dark apart from a small sliver of light coming through the heavy, lilac, crushed-velvet curtains, and came face to face with Charlie. When my eyes had adjusted to the light, I saw his lily-white body laying spread-eagled on the bed, legs and arms akimbo.

I stood agog, rooted to the spot at the sight of him handcuffed to the bed, naked except for a feather duster placed tactfully over his todger. He gave me a wicked grin.

'What have you been up to?' I erupted with laughter. 'I recognize a pair of those handcuffs. They're the ones I gave Ayshe!'

'I know. I nicked them off her. Can you let me out?' He struggled with the handcuffs, but they didn't budge.

I edged closer to him, trying to avoid eye contact with the duster. 'Where's the key?' I put my hand over my mouth and stifled a laugh.

'There.' He jerked his head towards a very shrieking Liberace-looking gold and purple chair.

I fumbled around on the chair, picking up some socks and a pair of leather hot-pants with the very tips of my fingers. A tiny little key plopped to the floor. Retrieving it, I walked around the bed, undoing all four handcuffs as I went. 'There.' I smirked at him. 'Good night, was it?'

'Well, it started off good. Then this happened, and he went off and left me. I've been like this all night,' he muttered, holding the duster to his crutch and swinging his legs off the bed.

'Who?' I wanted the gossip. 'Marco?'

'We had a bit of a tiff.' He rubbed at his ankles and wrists, which were a nice shade of arctic blue. 'That's it! I've had it with him!'

'Would you like me to make you a nice, hot cup of sweet tea?'

He looked at me with a hang-dog expression. 'No, I'll be OK. Thanks, Helen.'

I stood up to leave. 'OK, see you later.'

'TTFN.' Charlie paused, mid-thought. 'And don't tell anyone,' he hissed at me as I closed the door behind me.

# Chapter 24
## Friday, day 12 – First Dates Are Full of Surprises

I was still giggling to myself an hour later, as I walked along the High Street on my way to see Nan. I wouldn't be able to go on my normal Sunday jaunt to see her, so I wanted to get a quickie visit in before the wedding.

'Hello, Nurse Pratchett. How are you?' I asked when I reached the nursing home.

The unmistakable perfume of boiled-to-oblivion cabbage wafted up the corridor.

'Your nan thinks she's got Elton John in her wardrobe today.'

'Nurse, Elton John's come back. Can you get him out again?' Nan shouted at the top of her voice from her room.

'See.' Nurse Pratchett rolled her eyes.

'I'll go and get him out,' I said, wandering off to her room, heels squeaking on the lino.

'Hello, Nan.' I swung round the doorway and planted a kiss on the cheek. She smelled of Lily of the Valley and TCP, which was not a particularly nice blend.

'Who are you?' She pursed her lips together, looking at me like I was the devil.

'Helen. You know; your granddaughter.' I pulled open the wardrobe to check for Elton, just in case Nurse Pratchett and I were the mad ones and my nan was the only sane person in here.

'Oh,' she sighed, pointing at the other wardrobe. 'He's in there. Nurse Hatchett keeps taking him out, but he keeps coming back.' She flopped against her pillows. 'Some times he sings to me, you know.'

I stood back and let her see there was nothing there. 'See, he's come out of the closet now. There's no one there.' I sat on the chair next to her.

She leaned forward, squinting. 'I love Elton. I wrote a love letter to him once. He never wrote back, though.'

'Well, I expect he's been a bit busy.'

'Helen!' She suddenly recognized me. 'Hello, dear.' She patted my hand.

'How are you then, Nan?' I took my hand in hers and gazed at her liver spots and wrinkly face.

188

'I think I've got a hernia.'

I crinkled my nose up. 'And how did you get that? Swinging from the chandeliers again, were you?'

'Don't be ridiculous, weight-training, of course.' She went into a trance-like state. 'I can remember when me and Malcolm were at it behind the potting shed on the allotment. I nearly got a hernia then, as well.'

'Who's Malcolm?' I asked, not really sure if I wanted to hear this.

She stared out of the window. 'He was my first love, until that hussy Sylvia from down the road stole him. Evil witch. I never got over him.' She shook her head. 'He didn't felt the same about me after she got her hooks into him.'

'So what did you do, Nan?' I stared at a rabbit outside nibbling some grass.

'Well, I married Albert instead, although I never forgot about Malcolm. Albert was a very good husband, you know, but if you want my advice, don't settle for second-best.' She cast a knowing look in my direction. 'You have to wait for the right one.'

'What if he's unavailable like Malcolm?' I heaved a frustrated sigh.

'Then you'll have a broken heart like I did.'

Great. Just what I wanted to hear.

'Have you lost weight?' she growled at me all of a sudden, which made me jump and almost blew my ear off.

'Um...a little.'

'How's that other knobbly-kneed girl?'

'Ayshe? She's getting married on Saturday. I'm going to be a bridesmaid.'

'Always a bridesmaid, never a bride.'

All right, don't rub it in. 'How's the food this week?'

'I wanted to make an omelette but Nurse Hatchett won't let me.'

'She'd kill us all,' Nurse Hatchett muttered in the corridor.

'You know what the fireman said after you left the gas on and nearly burnt the house down that time, don't you? You are not allowed near a cooker.' I shook my head.

'Are you from environmental health? Because I found a lizard in my dinner the other day.'

'I'm Helen.'

'No you're not. She's huge!' She sat forward, studying me hard.

'No, she's not...I mean, no, I'm not.' She had me doing it now. Pretty soon I wouldn't remember who I was any more.

'How about sneaking me in a curry next time you come, hmm?'

'You hate curry.'

'No, I don't. I hate it.' She gave me a strange look, as if I'd just force-fed her a whole ginormous plate of the stuff. 'See that man over there?' She pointed across the hallway. The Mills and Boon lady from last week had been replaced by an old man who was lying on his back, snoring like a frog with a magazine half open, resting on his chest. 'He loves me.'

'And how can you tell that?' I raised my eyebrows.

'Oh, you don't believe me, huh? It's true. He's always shouting at me and making jokes about me behind my back. But I can hear him, you know. I'm not deaf!' She paused. 'That's how you can tell, you see. When they pretend they don't like you, really they do.' And then she fell asleep.

I daydreamed, gazing out of the window, wondering about what she'd just said.

Five minutes later, revived from her power nap, she was as fresh as a daisy. 'Helen! When did you get here?' she shouted into the quietness, making me jump again.

'Ages ago.'

'Quick, get Elton John out!' She pointed at the wardrobe.

I jumped up. 'OK, OK, don't panic.' I opened the door, pretending to shoo him out. 'All gone, see.'

'Thank God for that.' She put her hand to her chest. 'I'm allergic to goats.'

'Yes, Nan.' I nodded and plonked myself down again

'Do you remember when I took you, Ayshe and Kalem out to Hyde Park for the day and you dropped your ice cream down your knickers?' She seemed to be lucid again. Maybe she only had selective madness.

'No. I can't remember that. How old was I?' I loved hearing stories about when we were younger.

'About six, I think.'

'So, what else did I get up to then, Nan?'

'Well, there was one time when you threw up all over Yasmin's carpet. You would have been about ten, I suppose.'

190

I seemed to be making a habit out of ruining Yasmin's carpets.

'Yes, I remember. Ayshe and I had a homemade, peppermint-cream eating competition to see who could guzzle the most. It had been foul.'

'And the time when you fell off the roundabout and broke your foot and Kalem carried you all the way to casualty. Why are you so accident-prone?' She scratched her head.

'I'm not.' I was in denial.

'If I remember rightly, you nearly set yourself on fire once with a magnifying glass, didn't you?' She fiddled with her bony fingers.

I snorted. 'Hardly! That would be impossible. And anyway, you can't talk. You nearly blew up the whole street.'

'I did love looking after you when your mum and dad died. You knew that, didn't you?' Her face softened all of a sudden. 'But it was lucky that Yasmin and Deniz sort of adopted you into their family. Their house was always like a second home to you. You know, I can remember the time when Kalem said he was going to marry you when you grew up.'

I didn't remember that one. 'Did he?'

'Oh, yes. I always thought you'd make a nice couple.' She eyed me. Maybe she was just pretending to be a nutcase, and, really, she was perfectly on the ball. 'He came to see me recently.'

'When?'

She waved her hand. 'Oh, I don't know. Might've been last week, or was it last year?' She shook her head. 'Anyway, he said it again. He said he wanted to marry you.' After that revelation she dozed off again.

'Nan,' I whispered. How could she go to sleep after she'd just told me that? 'Nan?'

Could it be true? Had he really said it? Or was it just the ramblings of a senile woman? No, it couldn't possibly be true. After all, Nan thought she was having an affair with David Hasselhoff. Those weren't the kind of thoughts of a sane person. I picked at my thumbnail, lost in a trance. I couldn't let myself believe it was true. I would just be torturing myself. I shook my head. It isn't true. It isn't true. Shut up brain.

I had to do something to take my mind of things until Nan woke up and I could ask her. To kill time until she came back to the land of the living – if that was ever possible – I sent Ayshe a

191

text.

'Did you remember to pick up dresses?' I asked.

'Yes, doing it now,' came the reply.

'Going on a bridesmaid de-fuzzing splurge tonight. Was thinking of shaving my bits off and having a Hollywood. What do you think?' I sent back.

'Ayshe's popped out to get dresses, but I think it's a fantastic idea,' was the next reply.

The colour drained from my face. 'Who's this?' I fired back, whizzing my fingers across the buttons.

'Kalem. Ha-ha,' he replied. It just had to be, didn't it?

How embarrassing! He was the last person I wanted to know about my hairy bits. How many more humiliating situations could I possibly get into with Kalem to put him off me for life?

I snapped my mobile shut with a heavy sigh and glanced over at my nan. Her snoring was competing with the man across the hall, so I decided to make a quick getaway whilst the coast was clear. If she couldn't even remember who I was, she'd never remember what she'd just said when she woke up. I pecked her on the cheek and left her dreaming about Malcolm and Elton.

As I ambled home up the High Street, I decided to quickly nip into Boots and buy some anti-wrinkle cream. Big mistake! There was nothing quick about it. Forty-five minutes after being pointed in the right direction by a disinterested sales assistant, I was still studying tiny tubes and minute tubs of the stuff which ranged in price from five to thirty quid. How did you know what was best? A tub with pentapeptides, a pot with coenzyme Q10, or a tube with alpha lipoic active ingredients? Were these weird-sounding things actually real or did the manufacturers have a right old laugh making them up, hoping to fool us? Did they all sit around a boardroom table blurting out the first thing that came to mind – 'I know, let's call it floppynaptids, the public will believe that one!' – or perhaps – 'No, no I think we should call it saggyalphawaddles, that's much more believable!'

I agonized over the decision for an hour. An hour! Can you believe it? Were the more expensive ones necessarily better? Which ingredients were the most effective? And why was Oil of Ulay now called Oil of Olay? Finally, I bought a pot with Q10 because it was cheap and full of promise.

When I came out of Boots, swinging my prized possession, I

caught sight of Kalem about twenty metres in front of me coming out of another shop. With a woman! They were having a good old belly-laugh about something. He tipped his head back, roaring with laughter as she gently rested her hand on his arm in a very familiar way – a bit too familiar for my liking. I froze in horror. Mouth open, eyes wide, heart racing like a jockey in sight of the finish line. It was Zerdali. My nightmare had come true. I stood rooted to the spot, watching them as they carried on up the road ahead. She kept sneaking glances at him as she tossed back her mane of hair. As for Kalem, well, he looked like he was having a very good time indeed. I watched until they disappeared round the corner.

All the energy drained from my veins, and I shuffled back home feeling very sick indeed, my eyes stinging as I choked back the tears.

# Chapter 25

At half past five, I was half-heartedly doing what all girls do before a date. Primping and preening myself in a long leisurely bath. I decided against the Hollywood, or the Las Vegas, or anything else that would involve itchy re-growth. I spent forty-five minutes locked in a fight with my straighteners, and when I finally I checked out the full effect of my efforts, I hardly recognized my new sleekness.

I'd decided to myself that from now on, I would just let fate take its course and let whatever was going to happen just happen around me. Maybe everything did happen for a reason; it had just taken Ayshe's challenge for me to finally learn what the death of my parents should've taught me years ago: That life was too short for worrying and wondering and accepting second best. Life was for living, not wasting, wishing for something that you might never find. Now I'd regained my self-confidence, I knew I could find happiness in myself without a husband and children; I could feel complete without a family of my own. That wasn't half a life after all, just a real one. This challenge had shown me that at any moment, the unexpected could happen if I took a chance on life, and if I wasn't meant to be with Kalem, then I would simply have to move on. It was time to feel good about me for a change.

I tried on three outfits, but they were either too tight, too baggy or too boring. What was the usual attire for a boxing match? I hadn't got a clue. Was it casual gear for a quick punch-up on the side lines? Or was boxing the new ballet where you got all poshed up?

In the midst of my dilemma, the phone rang. I dived over the bed in my black camisole top – with hidden support, of course – and new cheeky knickers from *La Lingerie*.

I snatched the phone from its cradle. 'Hello.'

'Is this Ms Grey?' It was the return of the dreaded telesales monsters. I could tell before she even went any further.

'Yes,' I snapped. Hurry up; don't you know I've got a date to go on?

'I am pleased to tell you that you have won our competition for a free holiday. As long as you and your husband are between the ages of eighteen and sixty-five, you are entitled to a free Mediterranean holiday worth up to eight-hundred pounds,' the saleswoman gushed.

'Oh, what a shame, I'm only seventeen and my husband's sixty-six.' I slammed the receiver down. Bloody people!

Five tops and three pairs of trousers later, I settled on some tan, suede hipsters and levered myself into a figure–hugging, black, V-necked top with three-quarter length sleeves. Back on with the ever-faithful and versatile black high-heeled boots and I was done, all except for the war-paint. After a quick, ten-minute spruce-up, I was out of the door, swinging my brown leather hand bag for good measure.

I wandered leisurely up the High Street, trying to avoid eye contact with the early evening Friday night drunkards who'd probably been in the pub since lunch time, arriving at the rendezvous spot at seven-forty. As I loitered outside the door of the Watermill, a thickset bouncer glanced up and down at me. I decided to do the same to him. He had a shaved head, neck as wide as his shoulders, standard, security-issue, black trousers and white shirt, ear piece, blah, blah, blah – in other words: the usual package. He must have been a close relative of the hefty gym boys.

'Evening,' he said.

'Hello.' I smiled at him as people wandered past me, heading straight to the bar inside to beat the rush.

I looked up and down both sides of the road. No Nick. After ten minutes or so I poked my head inside the door and scanned the room for any sign of him.

'You looking for someone?' the bouncer smiled, revealing a gleaming gold tooth.

I looked at my watch again for the tenth time. 'Mmm,' I replied, distracted. I could have sworn we agreed half-seven. I'd only been ten minutes late, surely he couldn't have gone already.

I hopped from one foot to the other trying to keep warm whilst the wine bar filled up inside. I checked the time again. Eight pm.

'I think you've been stood up,' the bouncer declared so everyone piling into the place could hear.

'Shush,' I whispered. 'No need to shout it out.'

'No, she hasn't.' I heard a voice I recognized coming from the direction behind me. Swinging round, I saw Kalem standing there, looking relaxed in pair of pert-arse hugging jeans and a

195

black leather jacket.

'Kalem! What are you doing here?' I ran my fingers through my long, sleek and super-shiny locks.

'I popped out to get some money from the cashpoint.' He pointed to the bank on the opposite side of the road. 'I thought it was you, so I came over. What time are you meeting your date?'

'I don't think I am. He hasn't turned up. I was just about to go home.'

'Maybe he's been held up somewhere.'

I pulled a face. 'Well, he could have rung me if that was the case. And to be honest...I wasn't really looking forward to it anyway.' I smiled up at him. 'It just goes to prove what they say about plumbers, though.'

'What's that?'

'You can never get a reliable one.'

'Aren't you cold standing out here?' He grinned at me in that casual, sexy way that made me melt.

I grinned back at him, hoping he saw my casual, sexy grin I'd been practising in the mirror. 'Bloody freezing,' I muttered as my teeth started chattering.

'Come on. Let's go for a walk along the canal. The exercise will warm you up a bit.' He slipped off his jacket and placed it around my shoulders.

'A walk! Are you mad? It's the middle of winter.' But actually, I could force myself to take it like a woman, if it meant spending some time with him.

'It'll do you good. You need a bit more exercise.'

'Oi!' I trotted off to keep up with him as he sauntered off up the road with his hands thrust deep into his pockets.

Just off the High Street was a canal which was home to a few barges and house boats – and the odd duck, tramp and plastic bag. Darkness had settled over the water with a soft glow from the street lights cutting into the gloom. We headed along the deserted path, my heels clacking on the pavement.

'How come you're always taking me to remote places?' I joked. Not that I minded in the slightest.

'Can't help myself,' he drawled.

'Did Atila pick the suits up today?'

'Yes, did you give yourself a Hollywood?' He grinned.

'No, I couldn't be bothered.'

'Good job, really. Probably would have involved some sort of

196

trip to Casualty knowing you.'

'Ha-ha.' I rubbed my hands together, trying to get some warmth into the tips of my fingers, which were rapidly turning blue.

As he walked beside me, Kalem took my hand, rubbing it with his. 'God, your hands are like ice.' When he finished, he held on to it tightly.

Molten larva exploded in my stomach.

'I can't believe my little sis is finally tying the knot.'

'I know. They're so well-suited, though. I'm really happy she's found the right one.' I looked over at one of the barges; its dimmed lights twinkled through the tiny windows.

'And what about you?' His dark eyes seemed to see right through me.

'What about me?'

'Do you think you'll find the right one?' He squeezed my hand.

The question floated between us.

I couldn't speak for fear my voice would give me away so I changed the subject, trying to untie the knots in my stomach. 'What happened with Emine, then?'

'We were just too different, really. She was much too high-maintenance for me. We didn't see each other for that long, anyway, so it's nothing major. Actually...' He paused, 'she should have been with Justin. They would probably have made a good pair. Both of them were very shallow and only interested in themselves.' He flashed me a wicked grin.

I giggled.

We walked along in silence, the questions eating me up inside. 'So do you think you'll meet Mrs. Right?' I asked finally. I wanted to find out about Zerdali and demand to know just what qualifications she had for the job.

'Hopefully. I've been thinking about us actually, about how we both always go for the wrong people.'

Ooh, tell me more.

'The thing is, sometimes you can't see what's right in front of your eyes.' I gazed straight ahead, not wanting to look at him in case he could read my expression.

'That's exactly the same conclusion I came to,' he said as we came up to a lock where a barge was waiting for the water level to change so that it could be on its way.

197

'Well, the question is, what can you do about it? You know, to make sure you don't make the same mistake again.' I wondered out loud, my stomach lurching with the magnitude of my feelings.

He shrugged. 'Maybe take some time to get to know the person first, as a friend.'

Mmm, just like Zerdali, I thought with disappointment.

'Have you eaten? I bet you haven't, knowing you,' he said suddenly.

I was feeling a tad peckish and could have managed to eat a small horse. 'I'm starving actually.' My face launched into a massive grin.

We turned back, retracing our steps. 'Come on.' He pulled my hand. 'There's a nice little pub up the road on the banks of the canal that does good food.'

We walked into the quiet, cosy pub and studied the chalk board menu above the bar while we ordered a drink.

'Would you like the usual, to drink?' he asked.

'Mmm.' I nodded, trying to decide between fish and chicken.

He handed me a glass of wine and soda and looked up at the board. 'I think I'm going to have fish pie, how about you?'

'Beer-battered cod and chips, please.' I leaned my elbow on the bar.

'Why don't you go and grab a place over there?' He pointed to a snug little table for two in the corner next to a roaring fire.

I carried our drinks over to the table, shrugged off my coat and draped myself seductively over the chair. Not that there was any possible chance of competing with the perfect Zerdali, of course, but a girl's gotta do what a girl's gotta do, right?

'Food won't be long.' He sat down, putting cutlery and salt and pepper on the table. 'I have to ask...what have you done to your hair?'

I smoothed my hair down. 'Why, does it look rubbish?'

'It looks good both ways.' He leaned forwards, elbows resting on the table, his shirt stretched taut against his muscular shoulders.

I gazed at his chest with hungry eyes and took a sip of wine. As I set the glass back down, I misjudged the height of it and the bottom of the glass clipped the ashtray. The glass toppled over and its contents flew all over the table in Kalem's direction. He shot up, but not before a splatter of red wine had sprayed onto his jeans.

'Oh!' A hot flush crept up my neck as I took my paper napkin and tried to blot some of it off the table.

He walked to the bar to get some more napkins. 'Have you got a licence for that?' He jerked his head towards my wine when he came back. 'You're armed and dangerous. Helen Bond 007, licensed to cause havoc.' He regarded me warily in case I threw something else over him

'Sorry.' I grabbed some of the napkins to give him a hand.

'I'll do it.' He looked at me with a blank expression on his face, and I couldn't tell if he was really angry or not.

'Oops. I feel terrible.' I pulsed with shame, sitting back and surveying the damage.

He smiled at me. 'It's OK. Don't worry, I'm sure it will come out in the wash.'

But I wasn't too hopeful, unless he got the stain remover on it straight away.

I jumped up. 'I've heard that if you pour white wine on top of red wine the stain will come out. I'll go and buy a glass of white,' I squeaked, my throat dry.

He grabbed my hand, pulling me back to the chair. 'What, so you can throw another one over me? No, I don't think so. You've done quite enough for one night.'

'Well, at least it makes us even in the wine-throwing stakes now,' I offered, as he soaked up as much of the red splodge as he could. That probably wasn't quite the right thing to say, so I bit my fingernail and steered the conversation elsewhere. 'How's work?'

'Fine since you left,' he drawled. 'How's yours?'

'After Ayshe's wedding I'm quite quiet for winter. Not many people want to get married in December; it's a bit too cold.' I gave a mock shiver as I unwrapped my knife and fork from the napkin. 'God, I hate winter. In fact, I could do with some sunshine. We haven't even had a summer this year.'

He stretched his legs out in front of him and crossed them at the ankles. 'I know what you mean. I can remember when I was little; we always used to get a summer. These days it's just rain, rain and more rain. It's depressing.'

'Totally.'

'I've been having a nightmare trying to think up my best man's speech,' he groaned. 'I've been thinking about all the

things we used to get up to so I can put some funny stuff in it.'
He sat forwards. 'Do you remember how Dad always used to
have crazes on stuff and drag us out to do all those stupid
things?'

I laughed. 'Yeah, first of all, there was the jogging, and he
used to make you, me and Ayshe go every night at six o'clock,
on the dot.'

'You hated exercise from an early age, didn't you?'

'But I'm going to be good from now on. I've read Gloria
Cox's book, you know. There'll be no stopping me now.'

'And then it was fishing. He used to make us go every Sunday,
and you accidentally caught yourself.' He tilted his head back,
laughing.

'The only thing I caught was a soggy, used condom.' I tutted.
'After that it was flying lessons, but luckily we were too young
for that.'

'Good job. You'd probably have killed yourself if you had
done that. You were bad enough at driving lessons.'

I had a flashback of driving through a country lane with my
instructor. Suddenly, a conservatory attached to a nearby house
had jumped out and hit me. Needless to say, it was a very
expensive lesson, and I couldn't face doing any more after that.

'Do you remember when you were going out with your first
boyfriend, Chris? The time you both jumped on his moped
outside our house but he'd forgotten to undo the steering lock:
you both fell off and the bike landed on top of you.'

'That hurt!' I rubbed my leg. 'I've still got a scar there. And
then your dad gave us a lecture for an hour on the dangers of
motorbikes. I mean, he was right, but none of us listened, of
course.' I smiled, reminiscing.

'And then the next one was that horrible Justin.' He shook his
head as the waitress arrived with the food.

I cut into my crisp batter and took a mouthful of hot fish.

'I saw him in town a few days ago with a woman.' His intense
eyes gazed up at me. 'They had a baby with them too.'

I jerked back in my chair, thoughts screaming at me. I knew
there'd been something a bit odd about his excuse for being at
the hospital, but I couldn't quite put my finger on it at the time.
Hadn't he said he'd been visiting the maternity ward? I knew
he'd been lying when he said it was all over with his boss, but I
hadn't realized quite how self-centred and shallow he was until

that second. I waited a moment, expecting to feel disappointment and regret. Jealousy, or rage, or…anything. And then I felt it.

Nothing.

It should've been the ultimate kick in the teeth that he'd settled down and had a baby, but in actual fact I'd had one hell of a lucky escape. If he was capable of doing this to me now, just think of the wreckage he could've left behind if we'd got married and had kids. And it was weird, but I really didn't feel anything at all. I wasn't upset, devastated, heart broken to hear the news. I was free of Justin. He didn't affect me in the slightest. And it felt pretty damn good.

'What a lying, sneaky pig! I knew there was something fishy going on when I saw him at the hospital,' I said, filling Kalem in on the details. 'Anyway, I don't want to waste my time talking about him anymore. Oh, you'll never guess what happened to Charlie.' I told him about the handcuff incident. 'But don't tell anyone. I promised not to say anything.'

'Strange, huh? We've known him for years, and yet he never ceases to amaze me.' He paused for a moment. 'Actually, neither do you.'

'What do you mean?'

'Well, how can anyone get themselves into so many accidents and predicaments?'

I smirked as I swigged the dregs of wine still left in my glass. 'Well, at least I'm not boring then, am I?'

'Let's just say; there's never a dull moment with you.'

I twirled my hair round my finger, trying to be sexy.

'How's your nan by the way? I popped in to see her a few weeks ago and she said you never visit her.'

I stopped twirling. 'I go every week, she just doesn't remember.'

So, he had been to see her. Had he told her that he wanted to marry me? Had she been lucid when she told me that?

'So, what did you talk about with Nan? Was she…you know…normal when you spoke to her, or was she having one of her cuckoo moments?' I dug my nails into the palm of my hands, waiting for the answer.

'Just the weather and stuff. She wasn't really with it; she kept talking about Elton John and Baywatch.' He paused. 'Why?'

'No reason.' I unclenched my fists. So he hadn't said anything after all. I sank back in the chair, forced a smile and tried to concentrate on what he was saying.

We spent the rest of the evening reminiscing and gossiping, and when the landlord started throwing out the few stragglers – and a very pissed old man who'd fallen asleep in the corner – into the cold night air, I was bitterly disappointed. Kalem dropped me off in the car park outside the flats, and as I went to kiss him goodbye on the cheek, it went hideously wrong. Our lips headed towards the same side of the other's face and we both stopped and went the opposite way, somehow ending up in a full-frontal, lip-smacking lock. He immediately pulled back and looked at me, stunned.

'Helen, I didn't know you liked me so much!'

I let out an almost inaudible squeal in case he thought I'd done it on purpose. Aagh! I had to get out of there. Fast.

I tried to hurl myself out of the door, but I appeared to be stuck to a piece of tape on the leather seat that Kalem had used to patch up a tear. I heard my trousers catching on it as I peeled myself forward and jumped out of the door muttering, 'Iyi yakşamlar,' which is Turkish for 'Good Night'. He shouted after me as I ran across the car park, but I ignored him and, with a quick wave of my hand once I was safely in the communal entrance, I turned my back on him and legged it all the way up to the flat.

# Chapter 26
## Saturday, day 13 – Secrets Are for Wimps

It was no use. I couldn't sleep. Buzzing on raw energy in my lonely bed, I tossed and turned for hours, getting nowhere. My alarm clock ticked like Chinese water torture in the darkness. Even the sheep I'd started trying to count had all got bored and run off down the grassy knoll for some chow.

What was I going to do? Should I tell Kalem how I was feeling? But why would he want a complete disaster freak like me when he could have someone girly and sophisticated like Zerdali? But – oh! What was I thinking? Maybe that was the point: I wasn't thinking clearly at all. Of course I couldn't tell him. His family would hate me and everything would be a complete mess if they found out. I couldn't betray the love and trust they'd wrapped round me like a comfort blanket. The very thought of losing them all would be like losing my parents all over again, leaving a void in my life too huge to even contemplate. I just couldn't do it to them. It would be like a can of worms exploding everywhere. I shuddered.

Shut up, Helen, I told myself.

Pulling the covers up to my nose, I tried to switch my brain off. I started on some deep breathing, but instead of relaxing me, I got really hot and chucked the covers on the floor. Five minutes later, I shivered, gazing into the pitch–black darkness. Sitting up in frustration, I drew up my knees and hugged them tightly as I listened to Charlie banging around next door. Didn't he ever sleep?

I launched myself out of bed and paced around the room – arms folded, clutching my elbows – until I couldn't stand it any more. I was going to have to talk to someone. It was half past two when I tapped on Charlie's door in my dressing-gown.

'Who's there?' he whispered from behind the door.

'It's the noise police. We've had a complaint. Open up, please.'

He pulled the door open an inch, his eye-ball peering through the crack. When he realized it was me, he threw the door open and pulled me inside. 'What are you doing? You'll wake everyone up.' He popped his head out of the door and looked up and down the corridor.

'Ha. You're a fine one to talk. Why are you banging around at this time of night?'

He sashayed into the kitchen and switched the kettle on. 'Can't sleep. I've been trying to do some work, but I'm not in the mood. Do you want a chamomile tea?'

'No thanks. Got any coffee? I know caffeine is supposed to keep you awake but I'm wide-a-bloody-wake anyway.' I headed into the lounge and flopped onto his sofa.

'You too? Why can't you sleep?' he shouted from the kitchen.

'Man trouble.' I folded my legs up beneath me, wrapping my dressing-gown around me for warmth. 'And you can't tell anyone about it.' I knew Charlie had a mouth bigger than a giant abyss, but I had a secret weapon up my sleeve. 'Otherwise I'll tell everyone about your little handcuff mishap.'

'Ooh! I've got to hear this. Wait a minute, dahling, I'll be there in a jiffy.'

After a few minutes of bumbling around in the kitchen he returned, handing me a perfect-looking cappuccino. I rested it on my thigh, then stuck my finger into the foam and licked it.

He sniffed his foul-smelling tea and looked over at me. 'Well?'

'I have to talk to someone, and I can't talk to Ayshe because she might get annoyed.' I bit my lip.

'Well spit it out.'

'I've got a bit of a problem,' I started. How did I begin? 'I think I'm in love with Kalem,' I blurted out, waiting for a reaction.

'Whaat?' He took a sip of tea as he said this and in his surprise, he sucked in too much, burning his lips. 'Ooh, that hurt.' He rubbed his mouth. 'Since when?'

I ran a despairing hand through my hair. 'I don't really know. Definitely in the last few weeks, but maybe even longer. Only…I just didn't know it, I suppose.'

And at that moment, I finally realized that these feelings had been there all along, trapped in my subconscious somewhere. They had been lurking in the dark, waiting to pop out and smack me straight between the eyes, like Frank Bruno punching his opponent's lights out in a world title fight. Hammering away – Pow! Bang! Zap! – have you got the picture? I slapped my palm to my forehead as I recognized this new discovery. How had I

204

not seen it before?

'Have you told him?' He crossed his legs on the coffee table and shot me a surprised look at my sudden head-slapping aerobics.

'That's just it. I'm in the middle of a dilemma of mammoth proportions. What should I do? What would you do?'

He puckered his lips. 'Mmm, tricky.'

'Do you think I should tell him? I had a crazy idea that maybe I could tell him after the wedding. But now he's seeing Zerdali, and I haven't got a hope in hell's chance. He clearly doesn't feel the same about me, and it could ruin everything because I know his family would want him to be with a Turkish Cypriot girl.' I finished off my coffee and set it on the table.

'Is Zerdali that perfectly perfect, lovely, sweet girly, I met at Ayshe's house once?'

I grimaced. 'Yes that's the one.' All right, don't rub it in!

'Well, what are the pros and cons? Let's make a list.' He jumped up, grabbing a pen and paper. 'Right, fire away. Pros of telling him?' He slid his reading glasses onto his nose.

I looked up to the ceiling. 'There might be a slight chance he feels the same, and we can live happily ever after,' I said finally.

He scribbled it down. 'Good one, anything else?'

I hesitated, took a deep breath, then shook my head, trying to rack my brains. 'I think that's it.'

'OK, what about cons?'

'He probably doesn't feel the same – is blissfully in love with Zerdali, and then it will ruin my friendship with him.'

He nodded dynamically. 'I agree. What else?'

'Ayshe might go ballistic and not like the idea, and then it might ruin our friendship.'

'Yes, anything else?'

'His family will hate me.'

Charlie nodded. 'Probably, wasn't there a big family ding-dong years ago when one of Ayshe's cousins married an English bloke?'

'Yes.'

'Hmm, that's not good. What else?'

'He can't take me seriously because he thinks I'm just a disaster magnet.'

'Yes, good point.' He mouthed the word 'freak' and jotted it down on the list. 'Is that about it, then?' He asked, chewing on

205

the end of his pen.

'He thinks I'm a...flasher.'

'Hmm.' Charlie mouthed the words 'freaky flasher' and wrote it down. 'Anything else?'

'I think that's plenty.'

'Right, let's have a re-cap, then. If you tell him, there's an ickle, tiny, slim, almost remote possibility he might feel the same – or at least want a quick shag– '

'Hey!' I stretched my leg out and kicked him gently in the shin. 'Thanks a lot.'

'Or, you might end up with no friends and no boyfriend and his family will want to kill you. Is that about the size of it?' His eyebrow lifted a centimetre.

I let it sink in for a moment and then my face crumpled. 'Suppose so.' I slumped back on the sofa.

His eyebrow shot up towards his hairline as he screwed the paper in a ball and threw it in the bin in the corner of the room. 'Well, that settles it, then. You're scuppered. You – absolutely – definitely – one hundred percent – can't tell him.' He wagged his finger at me.

'What's the surprise, then?' Ayshe asked, linking my arm as we walked into town later that day.

'We're going to get our nails done at Marco's. You need a manicure for the wedding, and I've never had one.'

'OK, only if you insist. I like being pampered, just not when I have to deal with disgusting masseurs.' She shivered. 'Is this your challenge for the day? It doesn't seem like much of a challenge to me.'

'No. I've decided today's challenge is a personal one. I have to tell someone how I really feel about them.'

'Justin? I thought you'd already decided about him.'

'I can't tell you about it yet.'

'Who is it?' She stopped in front of the shop, her oval eyes questioning mine.

'You'll find out later.' I pushed the door open.

We blew in through the door as a sudden gust of wind whipped up behind us. The door bell made a flat ding-dong sound.

'Sooz! Get some new batteries for this door, pronto!' Marco snapped his fingers.

Susie looked over at us with a glum expression as she finished off a shampoo and set on an elderly lady. Today Susie's hair was a weird shade of green.

'Hello girls.' He beamed, putting one hand on his hip as he studied our hair. 'Are you having your hair done? I haven't got you booked in.' He threw a dirty look in Susie's direction in case she had forgotten to put our appointment into the book.

'No, we're having our nails done.' I smiled.

'Freaky.' He nodded. 'Gemma!' He turned round and shouted towards the staff room. 'Nails!' Turning back to us, he asked, 'When are you getting hitched?' He picked up a lock of Ayshe's gleaming hair, checking it for split ends. 'Come here.' He looked at me and then did a repeat performance with mine.

'Tomorrow,' she said.

'Aagh!' he screamed in a voice, high-pitched and sharp enough to crack glass. 'What about your hair?'

'I'm going au naturel.' She smoothed her sleek hair back down, and it fell back into place. She was so lucky. She didn't need to do anything with her hair. It always looked immaculate, whereas mine looked like I'd been dragged through a hedge backwards most of the time, especially now that the wind had frizzed it up into a rather fetching, puffed-up scarecrow impersonation.

He wagged his finger at her. 'You are so super-freaking naughty. Why don't you want the great Marco to do it, hmm?'

'I just want to keep it simple.'

'It'll be fine,' I said as Gemma came through the door munching on the remains of a bacon sandwich.

'Don't let the clients see you eating.' He sat down, flicking through a magazine.

'Right, who wants to go first?' Gemma said in a whiney voice.

'Me.' Ayshe sat down in front of Gemma's table where we could see nail files galore, buffing equipment and nail varnish. I sat next to Marco and tried to read the magazine over his shoulder.

'Charlie's coming in soon. He wants his hair to be colour-coordinated with his outfit for the wedding,' he snorted.

'Oh, God. And what colour is that?' I dreaded to think.

He crossed his legs and leaned over to me. 'Pink, of course,' he whispered, with a dramatic roll of his eyes. 'OK girls.' He clapped his hands. 'As you're getting married tomorrow, the topic of the day should be weddings. Did you know Whoopee

Goldberg has got married to Peter Cushion?'

'No,' Ayshe muttered, concentrating on her nails.

'It's true. She's now called Whoopee Cushion!' he cackled at his own joke.

'God!' I snorted.

'Hello, fabulous people,' Charlie sang as he swayed through the door.

'Hi, Charlie,' everyone said.

He went straight up to Marco, put one hand on his arm and picked up a clump of his own hair with the other one, waving it madly in his face. 'It's got to be pink.'

Marco pulled back, frowning at it for a few seconds. 'What, all of it, or just bits?'

'All.'

'OK. Come with me, you idiotic little man.' Marco dragged him off to a chair nearby.

'I've got an announcement to make.' Charlie surveyed the room to make sure we were all listening.

'What's that?' I asked.

'Me and Marco are now officially off. Aren't we?' He poked Marco in the ribs.

Marco sighed. 'Yes. It's a mutual decision so don't anyone get upset about it.' Marco poked Charlie back.

'And we've both got new boyfriends,' Charlie went on.

'Who?' Ayshe asked.

'I'm seeing my salsa partner. He's got a better body than you.' Marco poked Charlie again.

'I'm seeing the stripper from the hen night, and he's got a better body than you and your new boyfriend,' Charlie said.

'I didn't think the stripper was gay!' I said. 'He seemed quite...macho.'

'Mmm.' Charlie gave me a knowing smile. 'He has to put on an act for the ladies, otherwise he won't get any hen night gigs. Believe me. He is definitely gay.'

I shook my head. 'Wow.' I picked up the magazine Marco had left and scanned the pages.

'Did you also know Whitney Houston has married Gene Pitney?' Marco mixed up some dye for Charlie's hair.

Ayshe moaned. 'No.'

'It's absolutely true. She's now called Whitney Pitney.' He roared with laughter and then poked Charlie hard in the back.

208

'The conversation of the morning has got to be weddings.'

'Ooh, right. What famous person would you most like to marry, then?' Charlie threw the question open to anyone who really cared enough to answer.

'Brad Pitt,' I shouted.

'I would too,' Charlie said. 'I would even settle for his armpit – or his cockpit!'

'George Clooney,' Ayshe said.

'Leonardo da Vinci.' Marco brushed some weird looking concoction onto Charlie's head.

Charlie snorted. 'He's dead. He doesn't count.'

'No he's not, he wrote a book a little while ago.' Marco dug the brush in to Charlie's head.'

'Ow!' Charlie leapt up and Marco pushed him back down in the chair. 'What book?' He looked puzzled.

'The Da Vinci Code,' Marco growled at him.

'Ha! Don't be ridiculous. I wouldn't mind Leonardo DiCaprio instead.' Charlie's eyes glazed over as he clenched his fists in excitement.

I said goodbye to Ayshe at the hairdressers and headed up the High Street. A crisp wind wafted across my face as I weaved in between the busy Saturday morning shoppers. I shivered, wrapping myself tighter inside my coat. It was now or never. I had to tell him my secret, or I was going to burst. Words were hovering around at the edge of my mind as I silently repeated a dozen various sentences. What would I say? How could I tell him? Could I even tell him when I got there? No, this was my own personal challenge. If I didn't let him know now, I would have failed myself. And a life without risk was like no life at all, right?

Be proactive. Be assertive. You can do it.

I stumbled along the pavement, looking, but not really seeing. As I passed the coffee shop, I turned my head and caught my reflection in the mirror. Did I look OK?

I stopped, gazing through the window. And came face to face with Kalem.

The jumble of words disintegrated in my head. My pulse took a Grand Prix race around my body. He hadn't seen me. He was sitting on his own, sipping orange juice and reading...what was he reading? I peered closer through the window. A Land Rover magazine. I felt the corners of my mouth lift.

I pressed my shoulders back and lifted up my chin. This was it. Do it, or die trying.

Come on legs, work. Move forward. One foot in front of the other. That's it. You can do it.

Somehow I floated over to his table, vaguely aware of sounds and people, but they were on the periphery of my conscious. All I could see was him.

He glanced up, sensing a presence as I came closer to him. He put the magazine down and smiled. A real smile that travelled to his eyes.

I slipped onto the chair opposite him. 'I have to tell you something.'

'Are you OK? You look a bit...odd.' He studied me.

'I'm fine. Well...no, actually I'm not fine. But–'

'Are you ill? You look...pale.'

'No, I'm not ill. I just–'

'What's up, then?' He leaned forward, resting his elbows on the table.

I leaned towards him, our posture a perfect mirror image of each other. 'I love you,' I blurted out before I could change my mind.

His jaw fell open as he looked at me in silence. Time stopped but my heart carried on ticking.

He licked his lips. A face devoid of expression looked back at me. He closed his mouth again.

Tick tock. Tick tock.

Nothing. Not a word. He didn't acknowledge what I'd said. Didn't he know the courage it had taken to share my feelings with him? Wasn't it written all over my face?

A lump rose in my throat.

A second passed. Maybe two, but it felt like a hundred. And then...

'Helen.' He drew closer, his voice low, barely a whisper.

I tried to interpret any signals in his eyes. All I could see was my own reflection.

'How can I say this?' he started, locking his gaze with mine.

Barely inches apart, his warm breath laced with orange tickled my skin. My heartbeat chopped through me.

'This is a really bad time,' his eyebrows lifted a fraction.

'It's OK. You don't have to say anything.' A nervous giggle

leapt out from between my lips.

'I'm–'

'Really, this was all a really bad idea. I shouldn't have said anything. I'm sorry.' My mouth twitched as I stood up to leave.

He grabbed my hand and pulled me back down to the chair. 'Let me finish.'

Tick tock. Tick tock.

'I can't talk about this now. I'm seeing Zerdali.'

His words kicked me in the stomach. I put my hand up to stop him as the blood drained from my face and a ton of glass exploded deep within me, sending shards of pain around my body.

As if on cue, a shadow loomed behind me, falling over the table. Kalem sat back and glanced upwards behind me. I knew it was her. Zerdali.

'Hi.' She stood, smiling at Kalem and then at me. 'Are you ready to go?' she said to him.

He looked from her to me, and back again.

'I have to be going now too.' My voice quivered as I shot off the chair and wound my way round the other tables, stumbling out the door before I even realized it. I walked to the end of the road, shoulders heaving.

Tick tock. Tick tock.

I was numb. I couldn't feel anything.

# Chapter 27

A blanket of despair suffocated me as I plodded home on auto pilot, replaying the scene over and over in my head in a constant loop. Backwards, forwards I went, questioning myself. I dragged myself up the stairs to my flat with heavy legs and an even heavier heart. I had no recollection of the journey home. Once inside my safe haven, I leaned my back against the door, pushing it closed with my weight. Slowly, I slid down it, bottom resting on the floor with my knees bent. Wrapping my arms around my knees, my forehead collapsed onto my kneecaps.

I sat, unmoving for an hour, looking deep within myself and mulling over the last two weeks in my head. This was all my fault. I'd opened myself up to this stupid challenge and what had I achieved? I'd mended my heart just to have it shattered again. I knew that I'd changed, but in doing so, I'd also messed everything up. I'd lost Kalem, and when Ayshe and her family found out…well, I'd probably lose them, too.

But…hang on a minute. Something wasn't quite right. I lifted my head, gazing out the window, pulses of information dancing up and down my spine. I narrowed my eyes, deep in thought. What was it? My subconscious was yelling at me but nothing made any sense. Messages flickered in my brain like a dodgy light bulb.

And then it hit me.

Anger.

Toe curling, effervescent anger. How could I have been so foolish? It all added up now. I'd been a complete idiot. The pieces slotted together perfectly. I'd thought that Kalem was the complete opposite of Justin, when in actual fact he wasn't. They were exactly the same. How could I not have seen it before? Kalem hadn't wasted any time in starting a new relationship with Zerdali. I bet he hadn't even waited until Emine was out of the picture. He'd also turned up at the speed-dating. Why was he there if it wasn't to try and meet yet another woman? How many did he want? He probably had a handful of girlfriends all over the place. I didn't believe his excuse about going to a B.O.G meeting. What sort of organization would be called that? Obviously, he'd just been embarrassed to see me there and made

212

up the first thing that came to mind. And why had he been at the singles' night shopping? Was he hoping to pick up a new woman with his orange juice and loaf of organic wholemeal? Yes, I decided. The signs were crystal clear. He was exactly like Justin. He was a serial shagger!

I clambered to my feet, eyes flitting around the room like a cornered animal. I suddenly had so much energy and tension that I had to find a release. I spied the Hoover. That was it. I'd clean all my frustrations out of my system.

I spent the rest of the afternoon tearing round the chaotic lounge, hoovering like my life depended on it. I even got the furniture polish out and that was almost unheard of. When I finished, I collapsed on the sofa, sweat running down my forehead and stinging my eyes.

As I was about to go up to Ayshe's later that evening, the phone rang so loudly it almost frightened me in the silent flat.

'Hello, is that the home-owner?'

'Speaking.'

'I'm calling from Xanadu Windows. If you were to buy new double-glazed windows, how many would you buy? Two, three, four or five?' a well-spoken man launched into a sales pitch.

Now, if this had been an ordinary day, I would have politely told the voice on the other end that this was actually the seventeenth time this month that he'd phoned me, and ask him to stop. If this had been an ordinary day, I would have also pointed out that I'd asked his manager many times to take my number off their list. But it wasn't an ordinary day. It was the day I realized that I was in love with my best friend's brother and things would never be the same again. The same day that I laid my heart on the line and got punched right through it. And I'm embarrassed to admit that at that point something inside me just snapped, and I did something a teensy bit wicked.

'Oh no, much more than that!' I said, my voice dripping with promise.

He carried on with his spiel in a bored voice. 'OK, then, madam, how many would you like to replace?'

'Well, my husband is doing up a seventeenth-century manor house and there are twenty in the east wing alone that need replacing.' I put on my poshest telephone voice, smiling to myself. Take that you annoying little man!

213

He choked in surprise. 'Well, that's excellent news.' I could hear him rummaging around with a bit of paper as if checking to see what he should say next when someone was actually interested in his bloody double-glazing.

'And,' I added, 'about sixty in the rest of the estate.'

'Would you like our sales representative to contact you?' he asked. I could visualize him rubbing his hands together, thinking of a tidy spot of commission.

'Well, this is a restoration project, and we're trying to restore the house to its original features. Do you do them in oak?'

'No, but we do have brown PVC wood-effect windows.'

'Oh, I see, well that's not quite the same, is it?'

'Well…no, but we have supplied a lot of refurbishments for older style properties and our customers are always delighted by how much they look like real wood.'

'Do you think brown PVC windows would look suitable, bearing in mind we are renovating a very old manor house?' I repeated it back to him to see if he realized what an idiot he was being.

'I'm sure when you see our product, you'll be very impressed, madam. If I could just get your address, I'll have our sales representative call on you at a convenient time.' His voice wavered with excitement.

'Yes, but would they look authentic?'

'Of course, they're a very high quality product.' He was almost squealing with delight now.

'Well…I really don't know what my husband would think.'

'I'm sure he would be very pleased. Please give me your address, and I will arrange for a member of our professional team to call on you,' he cried. I could practically hear him frothing at the mouth.

'Well, why don't you give me your home number, and I'll contact you later.'

'But…I'm at work, madam. Why do you want my home number?'

'Because you've phoned me at home when I've had the shittiest day of my life! Give me your number and I can do the same to you when you're having a shitty day!' I shrieked at him, slamming the receiver down.

\*\*\*\*

214

Ayshe practically pulled me in the door the minute I knocked on it.

'Oh, my God! Guess what?' She paused, waiting for me to guess, then carried on almost instantly. 'I'm pregnant! Aagh! Can you believe it?' She jumped up and down clapping her hands together, frothing with delight.

'Wow.' I hugged her. 'When did you find out?'

'Just now, my period was a bit late, and I've just done a test.' She walked over to the mantel-piece, picking up a little white wand and waving it in front of my face. 'See?'

I set down the bottle of bubbly that I'd been carrying and held her shoulders, jumping us both up and down. 'Oh.' I stopped. 'Are you allowed to do this?'

''Course. I'm not an invalid, you know.'

I sat down, beaming at her. 'Guess that means no bubbly for you tonight, then. Oh well, more for me. What did Atila say?'

'He couldn't believe it either. I mean, we were going to start trying on our honeymoon, but we're both thrilled to bits.'

'And I'll be almost like an Aunty, then.' I elbowed her in the arm.

'Of course.' She nodded with enthusiasm. 'And Godmother, and babysitter. You can't tell Mum and Dad until after we're married, though. I know they're a lot more liberal since living here, but I think they'd have a bit of a freak out.'

I scrambled around in the kitchen looking for some glasses for the champagne. 'Here's to the baby.' I held my glass up and chinked it with Ayshe's, which only had the tiniest amount in it.

'Let's think up some baby names.' I put my feet up on the coffee table and sipped my drink.

'Maisie,' Ayshe suggested.

'But you have to put it with the surname to see if it sounds alright.'

'I quite like the name Halle, after Halle Berry.' Ayshe looked at me.

'Yeah, but Halle But sounds too much like Halibut.'

'Hmm, see your point.' She paused. 'What about Daisy?'

'Yeah, that's nice.'

'Or Kelly.'

'Kelly But. No, she'd get called Smelly Butt at school, and it might affect her psychologically for the rest of her life.' I pursed my lips together in thought.

215

The conversation became rapidly more ridiculous as numerous words were inserted in front of her surname-to-be, until we had got just about as much mileage out of it as we possibly could – which included – if I can remember rightly: hairy, big, spotty, flabby and squashy.

'How about Fag But, that's quite a nice one,' I cried with laughter. 'Or Head But.'

'I know. It's an awful surname – OH! The pizza.' She rushed in to the kitchen to turn the oven off. 'Atila's made us a goat's cheese and veg pizza. I might've burnt it to a crisp, though.' She pulled the oven door open. Luckily, it was still edible, just a little worse for wear round the edges.

'Here.' She put half on a plate and handed me a napkin.

I bit into a delicious, steaming-hot slice.

'Let's talk about you for a change.' She stuffed some pizza into her mouth.

'What about me?' I hoped Charlie hadn't been spilling the beans on our secret-squirrel conversation.

'Well tomorrow is Day Fourteen of your life-changing plan. Has your life changed for the better?' She bit into her pizza, waiting for an answer.

'Yes…and no.'

'What do you mean?'

I debated for a complete second whether to tell her, then decided just as quickly not to.

'I'll tell you another time,' I muttered. She wasn't going to drag it out of me. No way.

'OK, little Miss Secretive, don't tell me.' She polished off the remainder of her pizza as Felix jumped onto her lap and had a quick sniff of the empty plate. 'But I think it was worth it. I can see the changes in you, even if you can't. '

'Hmm,' I said, thankful she didn't push it. 'Maybe we should get Felicity to do it.'

Quick! Divert the attention away from me.

'I don't think she needs to. She rang me yesterday and asked if she could bring Frederick to the wedding.'

'Who's Frederick?' I scratched Felix behind the ear, and he burst into a purring attack.

'You know, that bloke who was pierced to death from the bikers' café.'

'Ah, him.' If there was hope for Felicity, there was definitely

216

hope for me. 'It's strange, but I'm sure I've met Frederick somewhere before. I just can't place him.' I shook my head. No, it wasn't coming to me. It couldn't be important.

Ayshe bit her lip, a hesitant look on her face.

'What?'

'Go on. Tell me your little secret.'

'No.' I jumped up to light some candles which were resting on the coffee table.

I picked one up and sniffed it. It was supposed to be cappuccino flavour, but it smelled more like a blend of cheap coffee and used kitty litter. Felix was also of the same opinion, because as soon as he caught a whiff, he started sniffing around wild-eyed, his tail bristling up to Christmas tree size proportions. Then he rolled on his back in ecstasy – severely hyped-up – and tried to bonk Ayshe's shoe, humping away with his little pop-up lipstick on full display.

'Felix!' she hissed at him.

Growl.

'FELIX.'

Bigger growl.

'FELIX!' Ayshe prodded him in the side with her foot.

He threw her a filthy look, as if she'd ruined all his fun, and from then on he had it in for us.

We spent the next two hours watching a girly DVD as Felix tried to gnaw off our toes, scratch our legs and jump on our heads.

'Yoohoo.' Charlie banged on the door as the credits rolled. 'I come bearing gifts.' He carried on banging even louder.

'Hi, Charlie,' we muttered as he strolled in carrying a bunch of wilted flowers which looked like he had just picked them from the park across the road.

'Oh...great, thanks.' Ayshe sniffed them and gawped at his hair.

'No, that's not really the gift.' He produced a bottle of champagne from behind his back. 'Da-nah!'

I held my bottle up. 'Snap. What have you done to your hair? It looks like a piece of candyfloss stuck on the top of your head.'

Even Felix found it a bit scary: he took one look at Charlie's hair, shrieked loudly, and shot off to safety under the sofa.

'Great, isn't it?' He looked serious. 'Oh, goody, the boys are out. We can have a little girly drinky-poo together.'

217

'Charlie, guess what?' Ayshe said.

'You're getting married tomorrow.' Charlie looked a bit confused.

Ayshe rolled her eyes. 'Apart from that.'

'Atila's admitted he's now gay?' he offered.

She shook her head. 'Try again.'

'Um...Helen's fallen in love with Kalem?' he blurted out, then slapped one hand over his mouth.

Ayshe looked between me and Charlie as I gave him my best moody stare.

'What?' she shrieked.

Oh God, I was going to get it now. 'Oops,' was all I could manage, sitting bolt upright, waiting for the onslaught.

'Is that true?' She stood up, hand on her hip, waiting for an answer

'Um.' I glanced around the room nervously and thought about fibbing, but then realized I couldn't lie to her, and actually, what was the point? After Charlie's little revelation, I had to come clean with her. 'Yes,' I caved in, my voice a crushed whisper.

It was her turn of the night to be shocked. 'Since when?' She flopped down with a giant frown on her face.

Charlie shrank behind a cushion. I glared daggers at him through it, hoping I'd suddenly developed X-ray vision.

'Definitely in the last few weeks, but probably forever,' he blabbed from behind his hidey-hole.

'Shut up, Charlie!' we both shouted.

'Why didn't you tell me?' Anger oozed from her voice.

'Because I thought you'd be really, really annoyed.' I poured myself another drink for bravery.

'I am really, really annoyed!' Her voice exploded, filling the room.

I winced, shrinking lower on the sofa.

'So, that would explain why he said you tried to rip his jeans off in the pub and then tried to snog him last night. I thought that didn't sound like you.'

'I did not!' And then I remembered the wine-spilling incident and the good-night kiss. 'Oh, that. It was an accident.' I let out a shaky breath.

She stood up again, narrowing her eyes at me. She meant business. 'I can't believe you didn't tell me this. He's my brother, for God's sake! You've known him since you were a

218

little kid. It's almost like...like incest!' she screeched.

Charlie poked his head up.

'How long have you known about this?' she asked Charlie.

'Well...er–' Charlie's eyes darted between the two of us.

'Why am I the last one to find out?'

I opened my mouth to say something and closed it again, feeling the fire emanating from her. I didn't have a clue what to say.

'I think you'd better leave.' She pointed to the door.

'I...I'm really sorry.' I pulled myself to a standing position.

Any minute now she would laugh and tell me it was all a big joke. I waited. She glared. I waited some more. She glared harder. She actually meant it.

I hurried out the door and flew down the stairs to my flat. Ramming the key in the lock, I jerked the door open and stumbled in, throwing the keys on the sofa and slamming the door behind me.

Shit. Shit. Shit. What was I supposed to do now? I'd ruined everything. Ayshe was getting married tomorrow and probably wouldn't even speak to me. At that moment, I hated myself.

There was only one thing for it. I was going to get blind drunk.

With determined steps, I made my way to the kitchen. I flung open all the cupboard doors until I found a bottle of Cabernet Sauvignon. I forced the corkscrew in, twisting and twisting until I almost broke the cork.

Take that, you stupid little cork!

Pouring half a glass of wine, I threw in a couple of ice cubes and filled the rest of it with soda. Leaning back against the worktop, I took a big swig. And another. And another.

I was on my fourth glug when I heard a soft tapping at the door.

'Helen, open the door. It's Charlie.'

'No, I don't want to talk about it.' I took another gulp.

'Come on, open up.' The tapping turned into a repetitive knocking.

'No! Go away.' I downed the rest of the glass and went through the process again.

Wine. Ice. Soda. The cool, fruity liquid slid down my throat easily.

Charlie carried on knocking for a few minutes until it suddenly went quiet, and I heard the door to his flat open and close.

Half a bottle later he was back again. Bang, bang, bang.

'Charlie, go away!'

'It's Ayshe.'

I swallowed. Had she come to have another go at me?

'Open the door. I need to talk to you.'

Did she still sound angry? The door was muffling her voice. I couldn't tell.

'It's OK, you don't have to say anything. I know you hate me.' I sniffed.

'Look, I'm not going to have this conversation from the hallway. Open up.' She rattled the door.

I hesitated. She was going to kill me.

'Come on, open it!'

I jumped. What should I do?

I opened the door of couple of inches and peered out, waiting for a fist to come flying at me.

'Can I come in?'

I nodded, opening the door wider.

She barged in and swung round, facing me.

I held my breath, ready for the onslaught.

'I'm really sorry.' Her face softened. 'I think I've just been under so much stress with the wedding, and I'm feeling very hormonal at the moment.'

Relief washed over me as I exhaled.

'I was just so...well, shocked. You've never said anything to me before.'

I hung my head and stared at my feet. 'I'm sorry too, but I just couldn't tell you. Don't you remember all the trouble when your cousin married that English guy? Your family was so angry. I didn't want to lose you all, and I knew if I told you, you'd go mad.'

She reached her fingertips out and lifted my chin up. My eyes glistened as they met hers.

'I know, I know. It's a really bad idea,' I said.

'I thought we told each other everything. I was really angry that you didn't talk to me about it and–'

'But I was so worried that you wouldn't approve. I couldn't tell you, and I can't believe Charlie blurted it out.'

She let out a soft laugh. 'Charlie's the worst at keeping a secret.'

The beginning of a grin snaked up the corners of my lips. 'I know.'

'I've been thinking about it and…once I got over the initial surprise…I actually think that you and Kalem are made for each other.'

'Huh?' I took a step back 'You do? But I'm just a complete disaster. I always mess everything up.'

'No you don't, you just think you do. Your heart's in the right place, and that's all that counts. I think you two would be great together.'

'Really?'

She smiled. 'I really do. You're my two favourite people in the world and I want you both to be happy. I honestly don't think my parents will mind, they've been in the UK for so long now, their attitudes have changed a lot.'

'Really?'

'Yes, they're much more liberal than they were when they first came here. In fact, I think they'd be really happy about it. You are like a second daughter to them after all.'

'But it's too late now anyway, he's already got a new girlfriend.' My shoulders drooped.

'What do you mean?'

I told her about Zerdali.

'Well, I don't know about that, but I do know one thing for sure.'

'What?'

'Kalem has been acting pretty secretive about his love-life lately, but there might be a perfectly reasonable explanation for it. Maybe he's not with Zerdali at all, and you're just reading too much into it.' She stepped towards me and wound her arms round my shoulders. 'I'm sure it'll work out OK in the end. If it's not OK, then it's not the end.' She patted my back, our heads resting against each other. 'Now come on. Come back upstairs and we can enjoy the rest of my last night as a single woman.' She released me. 'There's still lots of champagne to drink.' She reached out her hand.

I hesitated for a few moments. 'Why is it that whenever you want something to happen so badly, it never does; and yet when you don't really care about something, it always seems to come really easily?' A single tear snaked its way down my cheek.

'Maybe it's just an accident; a quirk of fate.'

'I know all about quirks and accidents.' I sniffed. 'I'm Miss

221

Quirkarama, the Queen of Accidents.'

'Well, then surely you must fit right in.'

# Chapter 28
## Sunday, day 14 – Here Comes the Sun

As it turned out, Ayshe's famous planning went to pot very early on. We didn't get up at 07.45 as predicted because the alarm I had set so carefully didn't go off, and Felix actually woke us up at nine, vomiting all over the bedroom floor. This was after a battle between Ayshe and me – which had gone on for most of the night – over who had most rights to the duvet. We both slept in Atila and Ayshe's king-size bed as she didn't have a spare one. She also didn't get her smoked salmon and scrambled eggs because Ayshe had forgotten to buy the eggs, and after drinking too much champagne the night before, I'd accidentally forgotten to close the fridge door properly and Felix had eaten all the salmon, which had obviously prompted the vomiting spree. He must have been very sorry now about his piggish behaviour.

'You still snore like a donkey,' I moaned.

'And you still wrap yourself up in the duvet like a Swiss roll. I was freezing last night! I only had the label to keep me warm.'

'Urgh, that stinks.' I held my nose between my forefinger and thumb.

'Aagh!' Ayshe screamed, looking at her long wedding dress, which hung up on the handle of the wardrobe. The bottom of the dress was covered in bright orange vomit where it had been trailing on the carpet. 'Oh no, how am I going to get the stain out?' She leapt out of bed, picked up the hem of the dress and studied it as I jumped out too, and trod straight in a pile of mushy cat-puke.

'Shit!' I muttered, hopping off to the bathroom to wash it off.

When I came back, Ayshe stood transfixed, staring at the stain. 'Don't worry.' I put my hand on her shoulder. 'I'm sure it will come off. Let me try and rinse it.'

'I don't think it's a good idea to let you loose on it.' She sank on the bed and flopped her head in her hands. 'Have you got any stain remover at home?'

During my many years of spillage magnetism I'd amassed a modest collection – big enough to supply a large chain of supermarkets, actually.

'I'll go and get some.' I threw on last night's clothes and hot-tailed it out of there.

On my return, I pushed open the door to Ayshe's, laden with some Carpet Rejuvenator, Dirtbuster, and some weird little concoction called Blot Blaster, which had decided to erupt out of its canister at some point during the last five years, turning the outside of it rusty. I banged the door closed with my hip, resting against it, breathing hard.

'Did you get any?' Ayshe hurried out of the bedroom towards me.

I carried my selection to the bedroom, putting them all down on the floor next to the dress. 'Don't get stressed, it's not good for the baby.'

'I'm not bloody stressed!' She picked up the tins and read the instructions. 'This is an omen. Everything bad is happening today. Oh, my God, oh, my God…what are we going to do?'

I grabbed her hand and rubbed it. 'Don't panic. It's not an omen, it's just…' I searched for the right words to describe recycled smoked salmon on the wedding dress, 'unfortunate.'

Someone knocked on the door, making us both jump. Ayshe dropped the Blot Blaster which made the lid fly off, and squirt a rusty residue on the bottom of the dress. The good news was that the disgusting feline deposit was now covered up; the bad news was that the stain now looked even worse.

'Damn.' Ayshe stamped her foot.

'I'll get it.' I rushed off.

'Merhaba canim.' Yasmin and Deniz kissed me as they wandered through the door.

I looked between the two of them. 'There's been a problem with Ayshe's dress.' I said, staring at Deniz's face. He had what appeared to be a massive carpet burn down one side of his face. Red raw and blistery, like the surface of Mars – that wouldn't look too impressive in the wedding photos, I thought. 'What have you done to your face?' I tried to stop staring, I really didn't want to be rude, but it was just too difficult.

Yasmin rolled her eyes in a for-God's-sake-I-can't-believe-I-married-him kind of a way. 'I'll tell her, shall I?' She threw him an irritated look. 'After the stag night he was very drunk – just for a change – and he attempted to pull his trousers off. So there he was, in the middle of pulling off his trousers – they were around his ankles by this time – when he goes and loses his balance,' she sighed. 'Then he pogo-sticks haphazardly at speed around the room and launches himself violently towards the TV – knocks that flying and smashes it to smithereens. He ended up with his head buried in the carpet. That's how he did it. Honestly! He's been taking his trousers off all by himself for sixty-five years – he should know how to do it properly by now!'

Deniz looked very subdued.

'MUM!' Ayshe shouted out.

'I'm coming. Do you want me to read your coffee cup?' Yasmin followed the sound of Ayshe's voice as we followed in quick succession. 'Agh!' Yasmin flung her hands to her cheeks and stared at the bottom of the dress.

'Bloody hell! Who's chucked up in here? It reeks.' Deniz pinched his nose.

'Felix,' Ayshe said. 'Do you think you can get it out, Mum? – Oh God, Dad, whatever's happened to you?'

Ayshe's mum, calm as always in a crisis, reassured her. 'Your Father has been an idiot again, that's all. Anyway, don't worry about it; I'm sure I can get the stain out. When you've known Helen for as long as I have you get used to clearing up this kind of thing.'

Ayshe wandered over to inspect her dad's face. 'That is going to look terrible in the wedding pictures! Come here, I have to put some concealer on it.' She rummaged around in her drawer and pulled out a small stick of beige make-up.

'Argh! You're not putting make-up on me. It's poofy.' Deniz wrinkled up his nose.

Ayshe rested her hand on her hip, giving him a look which meant business. A silent angry stare was all it took to make him relent.

'Oh, OK, then, but only a tiny bit.' Deniz succumbed as Ayshe rubbed the stuff over his shrieking, blistery face. The only problem was that the concealer was a bit too dark for him and didn't match his skin tone at all, which made it look about ten times worse, but I didn't like to say anything.

By twelve o'clock all traces of the stain on the dress had vanished – unless you looked really hard, but even then you could only see a faint, yellow tinge. I doubted anyone would be in possession of a magnifying glass, so it was pretty safe to say that no one would notice.

'Thanks, Mum.' Ayshe hugged her.

'I can't stand that pong.' Deniz held his nose. 'Smells like an old people's cat's home.'

Yasmin glared at him. 'You're not helping.'

'Maybe if I had a little tipple, I would be able to stand it. Have you got any whisky?'

'You promised you wouldn't have any until after the ceremony.' Yasmin slapped him on the head.

'No, I didn't!' he replied, clearly piqued, as if she'd just suggested that he wasn't allowed any food for the next four years. 'You were the one that said it, not me.' He sat down in the lounge and crossed his legs.

'I can't smell it any more, I've got used to it now.' I busied myself in search of a much needed caffeine rush.

'You can't make coffee; we have to start getting ready.' Ayshe dragged me out of the kitchen as the kettle boiled. 'Where's Leila? She should be here by now. Oh, everything's going wrong.' She stomped into the bedroom and turned her straighteners on, to heat up. 'Right, you get dressed first and do your make-up while I sort my hair out.'

I quickly tousled my hair with some wax and applied some eye make-up. I was going to leave the lipstick until I was firmly ensconced in my dress, just in case I smudged it all over the front when I pulled it over my head.

'Here, let me help you.' Yasmin helped me into the long, simple, Grecian-style lilac dress, which had ruched straps falling into a V-line at the front, and a high-waisted fitted bodice. I looked over at Ayshe for approval as she ran the ceramics through her hair. 'What do you think?'

'You look lovely,' she assured me, smiling. Luckily, she'd calmed down a bit now, thank God.

I surveyed myself in the mirror. 'This dress is gorgeous.' I twisted round to see if my bum looked liked the rear end of a hippo in it. 'Have I got VPL?'

'Huh?' Ayshe muttered, banging her straighteners on the dressing-table. If they didn't work there was going to be a full-scale, tsunami-style panic attack.

'Visible Panty Line. Can you see my knickers?'

Yasmin studied my bum. 'No.'

'I've got VPL – Very Pissed Liver.' Deniz chuckled from the kitchen as someone banged on the door. 'I'll get it.'

Kalem entered the flat, shaking his head at his dad. 'What have you done to your face?'

Deniz shrugged and wandered off once more on his quest to find a glass of falling-down-water.

'Don't ask,' Yasmin yelled from the bedroom.

'Ooh, can you get the flowers for me?' Ayshe asked me as she concentrated on her already perfect hair.

I padded into the lounge to see Kalem standing there looking amazing in a black and grey pin-striped suit, with a crisp white shirt and a black bow tie. His hair was freshly cut, and he smelled of aftershave and shampoo. When he saw me, he almost dropped the cardboard trays of bouquets and buttonhole flowers in his hands.

'Wow!' He fixed his huge dark eyes on me. 'You look absolutely stunning.'

I flushed with pleasure beneath his unwavering gaze. 'Thanks, you look really nice too.' I held my hands out to take the trays.

He looked down slowly at what he was carrying. 'What? Oh, yes, here you go.' Placing the flowers on the diningroom table, he wrapped his arms around me. His lips brushed against my face as he kissed me, in the Turkish style, on both cheeks. I breathed in sharply, feeling the warmth of his touch through the thin fabric of my dress and a white water ride of adrenaline cascaded through my body. He pulled back. Clasping my hands, he gazed at me intently in complete silence. I couldn't tell you how long it lasted. Time seemed to stop and so did my heart.

Deniz had found Atila's stash of cooking spirits and held a hefty glass of brandy. He gave us an odd look from the doorway of the kitchen, sipping his drink slowly. 'What's wrong with you two?'

'Are you on the brandy already?' Kalem tutted at Deniz, letting go of my hands and looking embarrassed.

Deniz shrugged, mouthing the words, 'Don't tell your mother.' Then he studied what I was wearing. 'You look stupendous. Exactly like a meringue.' He obviously thought that was a compliment.

'Where's Ayshe?' Kalem asked me.

'Bed...room.' I flustered, looking down at the flowers, which looked suspiciously like the wrong ones.

'Are you decent?' Kalem called out to Ayshe.

'Yes, I'm just finishing my make-up,' Ayshe yelled back.

When I went back into the bedroom, Ayshe and Kalem's dark heads were locked together in deep discussion.

'Hi, guys,' I interrupted, as I wandered in carrying the flowers.

Ayshe's eyes flew to the bouquets, looking worried. 'No! They've made up the wrong ones.' She came over and inspected them. 'The bouquets are supposed to be lavender in the centre and cream lilies around the outside.' She picked one up. 'These haven't got lavender at all, and they've put red roses in the centre.' She held it next to my dress examining the lack of colour co-ordination. 'Red won't go with the lilac theme, will it?'

It was a bit yucky, but I didn't want to agitate her. 'Well, it's too late to change them now,' I said, trying to be practical. 'No one will notice.'

''Ello everyone.' Leila waltzed in and kissed us all. She had already sorted out her hair and make-up at home and just needed to get gowned-up.

Ayshe waved the flowers under her nose. 'Do these look awful with the lilac dress?' She rested one hand on her hip.

'A little bit.' Leila shifted on her feet. ''Av they messed them up? Stupid people.'

'Don't worry.' Yasmin came up behind her, taking one out of the tray. 'I can fix it. I'll just undo the ribbons and take the roses out. Here, give it to me.' She took the tray and quickly got to work on the diningroom table.

'How's Atila?' Ayshe looked up at Kalem and pulled her shoes out of a box.

'He's quite calm actually, not like you bunch of crazy women.' Kalem grinned and left us to finish getting ready.

'OW!' Deniz bellowed from the kitchen. 'Stop slapping me, woman!'

'Get off that brandy!' Yasmin tried to confiscate it, but it was like trying to prise a baby seal away from a great white shark.

'Dad, stop drinking! Mum, get on with the flowers!' Ayshe ordered.

'Atila's probably shitting potatoes, I should think,' Ayshe's dad bellowed. Then there was silence, followed by a loud slapping noise as Ayshe's mum chastised him again.

'Go and do something useful Dad, like empty the dishwasher for me,' Ayshe yelled out.

'He's not been allowed near a dishwasher since he put ant powder in it instead of salt,' Yasmin said.

'Cleared the ant problem up, though, didn't it? We never had any ants near the dishwasher after that.'

'God!' Ayshe rolled her eyes. 'Oh...by the way,' she looked at me, 'Kalem says he's thought of a grand finale for the last challenge for you.'

With all that had been going on, I'd completely forgotten it was the last day of the whole crazy experience.

'What is it?' I asked, setting up my camera.

'Don't know, he wouldn't tell me.' Ayshe pulled her shoes on, rubbing at a dirty mark.

How peculiar, I thought. Why would Kalem think up a challenge for me? 'But I won't have time to do any challenges. I've got my hands full with the pictures.' I waved my camera around. 'Anyway, it doesn't matter any more. I think I've got my Hong Kong Fuey back.'

'Eh?' Leila didn't have a clue what I was on about.

'Oh. My. God.' I blurted out, suddenly realizing why Frederick the Pierced seemed so familiar. 'It's him!' I froze, camera in hand, my stomach tight as a sailors knot.

'Who? What are you talking about?' Ayshe stared at me.

'Can someone help me out of the toilet, please? The lock's stuck,' Deniz shouted from the bathroom.

Ayshe glanced between me and the doorway. 'Argh! Mum, can you try and get him out.' She looked back to me again. 'Helen, what are you going on about?'

'Bloody man, he's got a phobia about toilets now. He's been double-locking the loos since that stupid conversation the other night,' Yasmin moaned in the distance.

'I...I...Frederick, Felicity's biker guy. I thought I recognized him, now I've worked out who he is.' I grabbed Ayshe's phone resting on the dressing table and punched in Felicity's number.

Ring, ring, ring. 'Come on, come on.' I wailed, bouncing up and down on the spot, willing her to pick up. My head was spinning.

'I'm never going to get to my wedding at this rate!' Ayshe stamped her foot.

'Agh! No answer. Damn, Damn, Damn.' I stuffed my camera in its case. 'I'll meet you at the Priory. I have to warn Felicity.' I dashed out the door and sailed down the stairs, my dress billowing out behind me.

I ran all the way to Felicity's house, wobbling and clattering up the road in my high heels, which was an amazing achievement in itself. The possibility of a sprained ankle didn't

229

even enter my head. Even if I learned nothing else in the last two weeks, I now knew how to run a marathon in two inch wedges.

Bile rose in my throat as I neared her house. I swallowed, forcing it back down.

I ran up her path, taking a final leap up the steps. 'F...city!' I banged on the door. 'F...city! Open...the...door!' I carried on banging, trying to catch my breath.

I waited one minute. Nothing.

I banged again. 'Open...the door,' I wailed.

Nothing.

'Come on, come on.' I rang the doorbell five times in quick succession, beads of sweat pricking at my forehead.

The door swung open. Finally.

'Helen! What's the matter?' Felicity gasped when she saw the state of me.

'Uh.' I pressed my hand to my chest and tried to breathe.

'Are you OK?'

I rested my hands on my hips, chest pumping hard. 'Fre..dick...sa...ga...ster.'

Tiny creases appeared on Felicity's forehead as she crinkled up her nose. 'Huh? Dick's against the stairs?'

I shook my head and doubled over, wrapping my arms round my stomach. Breathe. For God's sake, breathe.

'I don't understand,' Felicity said.

I raised my chin a fraction, my eyes travelled to her face. 'One...minute,' I managed to gasp, raising my hand in the air.

'Whose dick is against the stairs? Are you alright dear?'

'No,' I spluttered.

'Let me get you a glass of water.' She dashed off into the house.

My chest heaved up and down as my breathing slowed enough for me to speak. Maybe the marathon running wasn't such a good idea after all.

I sank down on the steps as she returned; glass of cloudy, tepid liquid in hand. She held it out to me, and I grabbed it, downing it in one quick gulp. 'That's better.'

'Whatever has happened?'

'Felicity, I have to warn you about Frederick.'

'What about Frederick?' Her glasses slid down her nose.

I yanked her hand, dragging her down onto the step next to me. One final exhalation and I was ready to spit it out. 'He's the crazy Vincent Price Sound-a-like. He's the whacko who's been phoning me up demanding money from me. He's a gangster. You have to be careful.' My shoulders heaved up and down.

'Oh, that.' She let go of my grasp and pushed her glasses further up her nose.

'Huh?'

'I know about that.'

What was she talking about? How could sweet, Bible loving Felicity know about it?

'What do you mean, you already know? Aren't you scared? He could chop you up; steal all your money; rape and pillage you!' I reached out for her hand again. Was she feeling alright?

She patted the back of my hand. 'He used to collect debt money for the Bikers, but since he met me, he's discovered the Bible and turned over a new leaf. He's repented for the wrong path he chose.'

'What?' My pupils dilated.

She paused. 'He's found God.' She let out a soft, approving sigh.

'Huh?' I couldn't believe it. 'But he said he was going to send the Meat Packer round to chop me up. How do you know he's changed? He must've done some really crazy and…not very nice things to people.' The knot in my stomach started to unfold. Could this be true? Had Felicity tamed the whacko?

'He just needed some guidance to take the right path.' She gazed down at her shoes. 'He's found enlightenment and the path to goodness.'

I stepped back, frowning. 'Really?'

She nodded. 'He's admitted it to the Lord. If he's not telling the truth, there'll be hell to pay.' She blinked at me. 'The Mighty One will strike Frederick down and gouge his eyes out.'

I didn't really want to be around if there was going to be any gouging or striking. 'So, you know all about it, and you're not in any danger?'

'Yes.' A smile reached her eyes, lighting up her whole face.

I peered at her. 'You're sure?'

'Absolutely, he's a changed man. We've been having constant Bible study sessions since I met him. He's become a Born Again Christian.'

'You're positive?'

'Yes. Now don't worry about us. You get off to the Priory

231

now, and we'll see you there later and you can ask him yourself.'

I scratched my head. 'Well...if you're sure...' I gave her a shaky smile.

'I am. Off you go. Everything's all going to turn out for the best.' She picked up a Bible resting on a small table in the porch and pressed it to her stomach. If I didn't know better, I could have sworn a halo of light shone above her head for a second before disappearing. If anyone could tame the psycho Frederick, I was sure it was Felicity.

'Er...OK. I'll see you there, then.' I shuffled down the path, thinking that was the most surreal conversation I'd ever had in my life.

# Chapter 29

Ayshe, Leila and Deniz and I managed to get to The Priory without any further mishaps. The wedding car arrived on time, and as they rolled up in the white Bentley most of the guests were already inside the cosy room which was reserved for ceremonies. A few people loitered outside to get a shot of Ayshe as she stepped out into the brilliant sunshine. Deniz – quite merry by this time – swaggered around on unsteady feet.

Ayshe rushed up to me, her eyes huge. 'What happened? Who is Frederick?'

I filled her in on the crazy details.

'So she's really OK and not in any danger?'

'No.' I shrugged. 'He's discovered God and become a new person apparently.'

'You look as gorgeous as the baklava my Mother used to make,' Deniz said to his daughter, changing the subject. 'Let's get these photos taken. The quicker we have the ceremony, the quicker we can start the celebrations.'

I positioned Leila, Ayshe and Deniz against the backdrop of the wedding car to take some photos before we went inside.

The Priory was an olde worlde building with stone floors and a red-brick interior. Winter jasmine covered the archway entrance, and we ducked under the trailing flowers and stepped inside. In the entrance hall, light was streaming through the sash windows giving a slightly ethereal ambience. I could see the door to the ceremony room was open and Kalem waited outside it to direct guests and give out the buttonhole flowers. He looked drop-dead-gorgeous.

The wedding coordinator rushed up to us, in a real fluster. 'I'm sorry, but the registrar has contacted us to say she is ill and has sent a replacement, but he hasn't turned up yet.'

'What else is going to go wrong today?' Ayshe muttered under her breath.

'Ah, this must be him now.' The coordinator went outside to meet a midget of a man with very greasy hair which he wore in a horrendous slapover style. It looked as if he had wound one thick strand of hair over his obviously-bald head about a hundred times, but you could still see a giant, bare patch in the middle.

He came forward and introduced himself nervously. 'Hello...
I'm Peter.' He uttered the words so quietly we almost couldn't
hear him and then gave us all a sweaty handshake.

'Pardon?' Deniz shouted in his ear.

He jumped. 'My name is Peter,' he replied, a little louder. As
his head moved, his slapover developed a mind of its own and
fell into his eyes. He patted it back into place again and started
sweating. 'I apologize in advance, but I'm quite new to this. Are
all your guests here?'

Kalem stepped forward and grinned at all of us. 'I think so.'

'Right, I will just go in and sort myself out. When the music
starts, we will begin. OK?' Mr. Slapover looked round at all of
us for confirmation.

'What? You need to speak up a bit?' Deniz frowned, poking
his finger in his ear to clear it.

Ayshe shot her dad a warning look as she strained to listen to
Mr. Slapover.

'What?' Deniz rummaged around in his other ear. 'I can't hear
him.'

The registrar and Kalem disappeared. I followed after them so
that I could get a bird's eye view to capture the event during the
service.

My eyes danced around the room, taking in the surroundings.
The room was packed full of Atila and Ayshe's relatives. Atila
looked very calm as he chatted with them at the front of the aisle.
Kalem kept catching my gaze, looking at me with an expression
that I just couldn't work out.

If Charlie hadn't stood up and waved at me, I would have
almost missed him. He was very inconspicuous with his
candyfloss hair and shrieking, pink, satin suit with a clashing
ruffled red shirt. Next to him sat Paul-the-Well-Endowed.
Felicity gazed adoringly at Frederick, who was virtually
unrecognizable wearing a white suit and a badge pinned to the
lapel with the words, *I Love God* on it, neatly trimmed hair and
not a piercing in sight. Angie was thrusting her boobs in the face
of an elderly gent who sat next to her, hyperventilating and
trying hard not to have a stroke.

When the music began, the faint murmur of conversation drew
to a close and everyone looked behind them, waiting expectantly
for the bride.

Ayshe glided into the room on her dad's arm. She looked

beautiful in an understated cream, floor-length dress, cut on the bias so it accentuated her slim figure. A subtle bejewelled tiara rested on top of her ebony locks. Atila looked close to tears as Deniz positioned her next to him in front of the registrar.

'Welcome, everybody, to the marriage of Atila and Ailsa.' The registrar had now found his voice was over-compensating by talking in an extra loud voice.

'Ayshe,' Ayshe corrected him.

'Pardon me.' His slapover slid down over his eyes again. 'Atila and Ayshe.' He adjusted his hair. 'What is marriage?' His eyes darted round the room manically, giving him a crazy I've-been-let-out-of-a-mental-home-for-the-day look. I didn't know if he had forgotten his lines or this was actually a question thrown open to the audience because he paused a little too long, and everyone began to shuffle in their seats. 'It is the joining of two people to love, honour and protect each other,' he carried on finally. 'And how do they do that?' He looked around again for another few minutes, then pulled some notes out of his pocket, glancing down now and then to read them. 'They have to grow together like a mixture of plants in the garden.'

I scanned the room and it was obvious that people were either quite baffled or were trying hard not to laugh.

'Once...I planted a rose bush, and it didn't grow. Do you know why?' No one did, and neither did he, as he dropped his notes on the floor. When he bent down to retrieve them, his slapover slid over his eyes, again. 'Hmm.' He coughed, rearranged himself again and studied his notes to see where he'd got to. 'The reason was because I hadn't planted it in the correct soil. And do you know what that meant?' He surveyed the room. A couple of the elderly guests had started to fall asleep and others looked at each other quizzically.

'What?' Deniz boomed at him.

He looked at his notes again. 'Incorrect soil. If you plant a tree or a bush or a shrub, or even a rose, you must give it a good mix of soil, water and love in order to make it grow well. You have to nurture and look after it.' A bead of sweat dribbled down his forehead and, taking a handkerchief out of his pocket, he dabbed at it, which completely messed up his hair again. Having decided there was probably not much point in trying to smooth it down again, he left the dreadful slapover trailing over the side of his face, dangling down by his ear.

Deniz tried to suppress a laugh, but it was no use. It slipped out and the congregation tittered behind him.

'A marriage is exactly the same. It is a mixture of two people, and you have to nurture it to make it grow. If you don't....' He brought his finger up in the air for emphasis. 'It will wither away and die!' He barked out the last cheery word, which woke up a few of the snoozers at the back. Atila giggled.

I caught Kalem's eye. He raised an eyebrow at me, and I had to avert my eyes as the urge to giggle fell upon me too.

'Now, before we carry on, someone is going to read a poem.' He peered at his notes again. 'Kaleb is going to read a poem he has written especially for the occasion entitled: What is love? Where is Kaleb, please?'

'Kalem,' Kalem corrected him. He unfolded a piece of paper from his pocket and stood next to Mr. Slapover.

Kalem concentrated all his attention on me alone and began to read.

'What is love? Is it a midnight breath upon my cheek, when I know she's still asleep?' He gazed at me with sincerity in his eyes, and I felt myself flushing. 'Is it a smile, a touch, or holding hands? Or when I know she understands?' He shifted his feet slightly. 'Is it because it's for me that she only has eyes? Or because I know that forever we're tied? Is Love the thing that we seek the most? If we find it, that's when we can really boast.' He smiled at me and took up his position next to Atila again.

It was short and sweet, but it made my legs turn to marshmallows as his eyes held mine like a magnet from across the room.

After Atila and Ayshe had said their vows Mr. Slapover turned to them, tucking his dangling hair behind his ear. 'I now pronounce Atila and Ailsa – I mean Atila and Ayshe – man and wife. You may kiss the bridge – I mean bride.' He flushed.

Atila and Ayshe grinned and kissed each other on the lips as everyone clapped. I started snapping away, frantically recording the happy moment. After they had signed the wedding books, I took up a position at the beginning of the aisle to photograph them as they wandered out into the gardens.

'Bloody strangest ceremony I've ever been to. I don't know why they didn't want a traditional Turkish wedding. Is it whisky-o'-clock yet?' Deniz muttered to me as he shuffled past.

I spent an hour in the picturesque gardens, arranging and

236

rearranging the guests for the photographs. When everyone had departed to the bar in search of a much needed drink, I kissed Atila and Ayshe, who were both discussing the shortest ceremony in history. Kalem appeared behind me and handed me a glass of Buck's Fizz.

'Are you all done now?' he asked.

'Do you want me to take any more?' I looked at Atila and Ayshe.

Ayshe shook her head, picking up the hem of her dress. 'No, I've had enough now. My face feels like it's going to fall off from too much smiling. Let's go inside and get some food before all the relatives start to pin money on us.' She glanced at Atila, who was clearly ecstatic that they were now finally married as they ambled off into the building again, leaving me and Kalem standing outside in the glorious winter sunshine.

'I loved your poem. I didn't even know you had written one.' I squinted up at him through the low sunlight.

He looked embarrassed as he took a sip of his drink. 'I wrote it for you, actually.'

I almost choked on my drink. 'What do you mean?'

'Come with me.' He took my hand and marched me off to a nearby bench overlooking the river which meandered through the grounds. It was overhung by ancient, low-hanging weeping willows, devoid of any leaves.

He took my glass, placing it on the ground. Shifting in his seat, he looked at the floor. 'I've been offered another teaching job.'

'That's great.'

'The only thing is it's at a university in North Cyprus. My mum's still got the house that she was born in over there, so I'd have somewhere to stay. It needs a bit of renovating, but you should see it,' his eyes sparkled as he spoke, 'views of the sea and mountains, goats and sheep wandering around the hills. It's spectacular.' He paused. 'I just want to get back to basics, you know, get away from the rat-race. Have a better quality of life and wake up to the sun shining three-hundred and sixty days a year.'

As his words sunk in, I felt the weight of them crushing me. I slumped down on the bench, deflated. Only one thought spun round in my brain. He was leaving.

'Oh! Well, that's a...surprise. Well done.' Shocked, I tried to compose myself. I tried desperately to sound pleased for him, but

237

even to my ears, the words sounded forced. 'What did Ayshe say?'

'I haven't told her yet. I wanted to wait until after the wedding. This is her day and I didn't want to spoil it by upsetting her.' He hesitated. 'I'm only going to take it on a couple of conditions, though.'

'What conditions?'

He glanced up at me slowly. 'That you come with me. I've done some research and you could do your photography out there with no problems.'

'What? But why?'

He faltered, as if looking for the right words. 'Because I'm in love with you, too, Helen. There, I've said it now. I've wanted to say it for so long. You're completely crazy and a total disaster magnet, but it makes you unique, and you are so funny – even when you're not trying to be. I can't think of anything else except you.'

His words hung, suspended in air. I gaped at him in speechless amazement for what felt like an eternity. Then I trembled with emotion as my heartbeat increased in tempo.

'Me? Why me? You think I'm a complete nightmare.'

'I know.' He shrugged. 'I love the way you throw wine over people and throw up at snobby dinner parties. I love how you always do ridiculous things, like getting caught shoplifting when you haven't even done anything. I love the way you can't even go food shopping without something completely bizarre happening to you – I'm still not keen on the streaking part, but I know that was an accident, and I kind of over-reacted a bit because I was feeling protective of you.' He paused. 'You're just…just special. You're perfect just the way you are.'

I wrapped my arms around his neck and kissed him on the mouth until my lips hurt. He tasted of champagne and I could smell his sexy Kalem aroma. His arms encircled me, and I could sense his hunger. I fitted into him perfectly. When we both pulled back, he was grinning from ear to ear.

'I feel the same.' I took a deep breath.

'Thank God for that. I've been going crazy trying to work out how to tell you. I didn't want to ruin everything between us if you didn't feel the same way, but then yesterday in the coffee shop–'

'But what about your family? They aren't going to approve,

238

and they'll hate me.' I pulled back, gazing at him with anxious eyes.

'I've already had a chat with them. They love you, too, Helen, they couldn't be happier.'

'Wow!' I let this sink in for a moment. 'But you're seeing Zerdali, aren't you?'

'What?' It was his turn to look shocked.

'You know...Zerdali.' I bit my lip, waiting for his answer.

'I don't know what you're talking about.' A slight frown quivered on his forehead.

'You were going on a date with her.'

He threw his head back, roaring with laughter. 'Yesterday she was giving me some advice about the job offer. She used to work at a university in North Cyprus before she moved here and wanted to show me some curriculums they used.'

'Well what about the other day when I saw you in town together.'

'Helen, I was in town with her because I was helping her choose a birthday present for her nephew.' He paused. 'Don't you know?'

'Know what?'

'She's a lesbian who's been with her girlfriend for about ten years, so she's got no interest in men, other than friendship.'

'Is she? Wow!' I considered that for a moment, head on one side. 'What about the speed-dating, though? Why were you there?'

'Helen, you must know me better than that by now. I really was at the speed-dating for a B.O.G meeting. I just got the dates mixed up and went on the wrong night.'

'But I saw you at the singles' night shopping too.' My eyes flickered up at him.

He raised his head a fraction, a grin spreading over his face. 'The night I saw you at Tesco, I'd been to see my old wood carving tutor. I wanted to get his input about this new career opportunity, and I got back a bit late so I just wanted to get something quick to eat for dinner. I didn't even know they had "singles' night shopping."'

Relief flooded through my veins as I digested the jumble of information.

He took my hand. 'There's something else, as well.'

My eyes searched his for signs of what he was about to say,

wondering what other bombshell he was going to drop on me.

'I've got a confession to make,' he inhaled. 'I knew you were meeting Nick outside the pub, so I got there early and told him you couldn't make it because you'd been called to a family emergency,' he said, exhaling deeply.

I smiled. 'Ah, so that explains why he didn't show up.'

'I just couldn't risk losing you forever.'

'So how long have you felt like this?' I concentrated on his face, explosive bubbles of happiness bursting inside.

'Probably since I was about four.'

I let out an excited giggle. 'So, what's the other condition?'

'Well, the other condition is your final challenge. I just need a yes or no answer.' He bent down on one knee in front of me, without lifting his eyes from mine. He grasped onto my hand for dear life. 'Will you come with me?' He hesitated. 'As my wife?'

'Well, I'm afraid I've only got one thing to say on the matter.' I grinned.

'What's that?'

'I think I need to buy some new bikinis!'


# The End

CPSIA information can be obtained at www.ICGtesting.com
Printed in the USA
LVOW091519301111

257209LV00001B/197/P